Frommer's

irreverent

guide to

Los Angeles

other titles in the

irreverent guide

series

Frommer's®

irreverent guide to Los Angeles

1st Edition

By
Jeff Spurrier

A BALLIETT & FITZGERALD BOOK
IDG BOOKS WORLDWIDE, INC.

a disclaimer

Prices fluctuate in the course of time, and travel information changes under the impact of the varied and volatile factors that influence the travel industry. Neither the author nor the publisher can be held responsible for the experiences of readers while traveling. Readers are invited to write to the publisher with ideas, comments, and suggestions for future editions.

about the author

Jeff Spurrier is a writer, based in L.A., who lives part of the year in Mexico. He writes for *Details*, *Outside*, and the *L.A. Times*. He is a carnivore, a reluctant smoker, and knows the quickest way to get from the West Side to Downtown during rush hour.

Balliett & Fitzgerald, Inc.

Editorial director: Will Balliett / Line editor: Royce Flippin / Executive editor: Tom Dyja / Managing editor: Alexis Lipsitz / Production editor: Michael Walters / Associate editor: Carol Petino

IDG Books Worldwide, Inc.

An International Data Group Company
919 E. Hillsdale Blvd., Suite 400
Foster City, CA 94404

Find us online at www.frommers.com

ISBN 0-02-863356-3
ISSN 1523-0678

Macmillan Travel Art director: Michele Laseau
Interior design contributed to by Tsang Seymour Design Studio

special sales

For general information on IDG Books Worldwide's books in the U.S., please call our Consumer Customer Service department at 1-800-762-2974. For reseller information, including discounts, bulk sales, customized editions, and premium sales, please call our Reseller Customer Service department at 1-800-434-3422.

Manufactured in the United States of America

what's so irreverent?

It's up to you.

You can buy a traditional guidebook with its fluff, its promotional hype, its let's-find-something-nice-to-say-about-everything point of view. Or you can buy an Irreverent guide.

What the Irreverents give you is the lowdown, the inside story. They have nothing to sell but the truth, which includes a balance of good and bad. They praise, they trash, they weigh, and leave the final decisions up to you. No tourist board, no chamber of commerce will ever recommend them.

Our writers are insiders, who feel passionate about the cities they live in, and have strong opinions they want to share with you. They take a special pleasure leading you where other guides fear to tread.

How irreverent are they? One of our authors insisted on writing under a pseudonym. "I couldn't show my face in town again if I used my own name," she told me. "My friends would never speak to me." Such is the price of honesty. She, like you, should know she'll always have a friend at Frommer's.

Warm regards,

Michael Spring

Michael Spring
Publisher

contents

introduction

Los Angeles. Rhymes with scandalous, unscramble us, helluva mess. (Sort of.)

More complex is the image that social critic Mike Davis coined: "The car-sex-death-fascism continuum"—and that's a notion that's hard to argue with, bringing together the light and the dark, riots and beach parties, *Blade Runner* and "Father Knows Best," palm trees trembling as the ground heaves. That's the latest mask, but there are others. Los Angeles has been called Cleveland with Palm Trees, Circus Without a Tent, La-La Land, City of Lost Angels, Iowa By the Sea, Digital Coast. I prefer the Japanese term "Los," so coined because "Angeles" is too full of unfamiliar sounds. And "Los" in Spanish is simply the definite plural article, "the" without any adjoining noun. That's what this place is. "The..." *You* fill in the blank.

As the mystery writer Ross McDonald noted, "There's nothing wrong with Southern California that a rise in the ocean wouldn't cure."

Quite possibly we won't have to wait that long. Anyone living in L.A. who says they don't think about earthquakes is either lying or a newcomer. Angelenos keep unopened water jugs in the garage or in a shed (plus money for when all the ATMs stop functioning) and plan escape routes from work to home and rendezvous points for family. They know it could all come tumbling down tomorrow. Cancelled in midseason, so to speak. They pretend not to worry but never forget that feeling of coming out of a dead sleep, full-on REM, to hear the earth moving, giant claws scratching against a sky-wide blackboard, and the sound of dishes, books, and appliances tumbling off of tables and dressers and chairs and mixing into a jumble on the floor, all broken glass and bits of wood and the darkness over everything. Then the car alarms start going off, seguing into the howls of every dog in the city. It's like when time slows down in the middle of an accident. Everything becomes sharp and clear. Then there's earthquake weather. Depending on your point of reference, that either means unusually muggy (the Long Beach quake of 1925), or dry with Santa Ana gusts (the Slymar quake of '72). There are other warning signs, too. The cat vanishes. Dogs hide in closets. Birds stop singing.

There is a myth that L.A. has no neighborhoods, but in fact the city is nothing *but* neighborhoods—they're just not constructed in the style of jammed European inner urban centers. They're closer in form to the neighborhoods of the people whose lands they come from, Central America and Asia. In the last decade the number of Latino kids in Los Angeles public schools has jumped 25 percent, rising to 41 percent of the total. Whites, meanwhile, have sunk into second place with 38 percent—a 19 percent decrease. Asians, Filipinos, and Pacific Islanders have all registered increases over the same period. The signs are pretty obvious—as they have been for years. The white-bread image of California is gone forever. We have become a microcosm of the Pacific Rim.

There are known borders: Watts, Beverly Hills, Hollywood, West Hollywood, West L.A., Downtown, East L.A., Pasadena, South Bay, South Central. Just north of town looms the Valley, huge and amorphous, the backdrop for "The Rockford Files," the first TV series to show the seamy side of the suburbs, a land populated by con men and cheap hustlers. And in the last 20 years the East Side-West Side dichotomy has become more pronounced—not as a Balkanized division, but rather closer to the Lower Manhattan-Upper Manhattan contrast.

What can I say? L.A. is a city of neighborhoods, and if you don't see the demarcations, it's because you're not from here.

Crime Blotter, *Los Angeles Independent*, a weekly throwaway: "9:15 p.m. 2100 block of North Vermont Avenue. A closely shaved young Latino drove his 1999 gray Nissan

Altima parallel to another driver and asked 'F.
The suspect then chased the victim to Los Feliz
shots at him...."

The Rebellion, the Uprising, the Riots of '\,
lowed the innocent verdict for the cops who be.
King—no matter what name you use, they're still ali\
ple's memories, those warm spring evenings when
plain from Downtown to the sea was marked by tc
columns of smoke—black, not gray—and no hint (
engine sirens anywhere. You heard lots of gunfire—shot\
pistols, semi-automatics. And the very occasional cop s.
Down on Temple, near the Ramparts Division station, the s
streets were blocked off and police in full riot gear sto\
behind patrol cars in tight formation. Everywhere else th
party just went on and on: windows smashed, appliance-store
doors crashed open by mini trucks, all-you-can-carry-away
specials at liquor stores.

Police Chief Daryl Gates deadpanned Calvinistic disap-
proval over the airwaves in his best imitation of Joe Friday, pretending his troops hadn't been hiding, that they hadn't lost
control. Today he's a right-wing radio talk-show host, the city
has community policing, and it's common to see teams riding
mountain bikes in spandex shorts and helmets. The image is
better, but something is still not quite right. Recently a pair of
bike cops shot a homeless crazy woman who "lunged" at them
with a rusty screwdriver. The noir L.A. of mystery writers
MacDonald, Raymond Chandler, and James M. Cain seems
almost innocent by comparison. Only the speed-addled sci-fi
of Philip K. Dick comes close.

This is the end of the continent, where the concept of
reinvention was perfected, a natural development of the studio
system. From breast and penile implants to personal histories
created out of whole cloth, reality is a commodity here, something to speculate on, manipulate when possible, shoot against
a blue screen if necessary and digitize to whatever parameters
the producers are willing to pay for. *Of course* '50s and '60s gas-
guzzling clunkers are hip accessories for the Silver Lake set; *of
course* the tired lounge ambience of *Swingers*-style dives is
hugely popular among 20-something actors and screenwriters;
of course roaming the cemeteries to locate the graves of dead
idols is a major goth E-ticket. These things are *real*: old steel,
roll-n-tuck leather booths, the crumbling bones of celluloid
fantasy.

And isn't it a beautiful day? Again? You can almost see the

San Gabriel Mountains. And once they pick up all those hypodermics someone dumped off the beach in the South Bay, you'll be able to walk on the sand, and maybe even go in the water if the E.coli count isn't too high. This is a great place to live, which is why our home values are appreciating between 8 and 10 percent annually. Thank heavens for the *L.A. Times* Feng Shui column in the Sunday Real Estate section, where one learns to avoid using blues and yellows in a stained-glass pattern for a south-facing front door (not good for the fire of south-based energy).

How much in the American Landscape is Los Angeles guilty for? Think about the drive-in, the supermarket, the strip mall. L.A. is flat, L.A. is horizontal. We are locked into our cars with symbiotic intensity. In the words of art critic Ralph Rugoff, "the city unspools like a film strip." The architecture is jumbled, Craftsman bungalow next to faux-Colonial next to Neutra modern. Los Angeles, said Carey MacWilliams in his classic *Southern California Country*, is "a tribal burial ground for antique customs and incongruous styles." The California bungalow was a perfect fit for L.A., a cheap single-family home made for lateral spread and a mild climate. More than anything, the city's topographical character was defined by the Big Red Car, the best inter-urban public transportation system of its time in the country, maybe in the world. Over four decades, starting less than a decade after the Civil War, this rail line grew, merging public and private lines, linking 42 cities and towns in Southern California. Its tracks covered more than a thousand miles, radiating from Downtown to San Fernando, Riverside, Santa Monica, and Newport Beach. Six hundred cars carried a quarter-million people every day along their routes for under a cent a mile. More than anything else, this system shaped the city as we know it today, with the ability to have far-flung residential/commercial centers removed from the main hub of Downtown. It worked well, so by the '30s automobile manufacturers and petroleum refiners were pushing the notion of an Autopia, an auxiliary automotive mass-transit system. By the '60s, Autopia ruled—and the red car and its assorted peers were summarily ripped up, paved over, buried in asphalt. People want cars, the politicos financed by the corporations proclaimed, and that silly mass transit was just clogging up the roads. Now Los Angeles has the Metro and is belatedly trying to change 50 years of car conditioning. Maybe it'll work. Check back with us in 50 years.

One thing is certain: The city will never stop growing—as long as there's water. And that's what it all comes down to in the end. Until you've lived through a drought here, you can easily forget that in its natural state this is a semi-arid subtropical region. By rights, the San Fernando Valley should be closer to the Mojave Desert in character. It took a cabal of businessmen, big land owners, realtors, and bankers to dream up the Owens Valley project, funneling runoff from the Sierra Nevada mountains to the cow metropolis 250 miles south. The City of L.A., aided by the efforts of the federal government, essentially stole the land of Owens Valley farmers, sealing up water rights for decades. It wasn't as simplistic as Polanski's *Chinatown* implied—after all, that was only a movie, a morality play wrapped up as a mystery. The reality was way more proto-corporate, a reflection of the can-do arrogance of the era, when nature was to be contained, rearranged, or razed, all in the name of progress. The California Aqueduct was completed in 1913 and is considered a modern engineering feat second only to the Panama Canal. When the spigot was finally opened by chief engineer Mulholland, he laconically told the mayor: "There it is. Take it."

L.A. Here it is. Take it.

Los Angeles Neighborhoods

Pacific
Ocean

you
probably
didn't know

The best views of the city... It depends on what you consider "the city," naturally, but for most of the population this means the high-rises of Downtown, as seen in so many establishing shots of TV programs and movies. As an L.A. landmark, that oasis of skyscrapers is as instantly recognizable as Paris's Eiffel Tower. If you're right in the heart of Downtown and want to see what it looks like from close-up, the Bonaventure Hotel bar, on the hotel's top floor, offers the most intimate look at the biggest buildings. Another classic vista is from the seventh-floor Sky Bridge that links the Bonaventure to the Ketcham YWCA. If you want a good overview of the L.A. basin, especially on a clear winter day, head up to the Griffith Observatory's parking lot. From here you can see all the way from the southern Valley to Palos Verdes, Catalina, Hollywood, and Santa Monica. For a midrange perspective, go to Lot 2 of Dodger Stadium on a nongame day, and you'll get a view of the full Downtown skyline, framed by palm trees and some of the huge baseballs that mark the lots, providing for a nice campy touch. To get that typical freeway traffic blur, the overpass on Broadway, between Downtown and Chinatown, is perfect. On this stretch of the downtown four-level interchange you'll see Olympics-themed murals, part of the city's face-lift for the '84 Games. The most delightful, done by the late Carlos Almarez, mirrors the cars passing in endless lanes. His version includes floating icons of L.A. culture drifting in the air above the exhaust. Unfortunately, it was graffitied a while back, and now half of the image is covered in Cal Trans paint.

How to drive the drive... First of all, if you're planning on being here for any length of time or doing more than a minimal amount of driving, buy a "Thomas Guide of Los Angeles." In it, the streets are all indexed, and the front map shows the grids clearly and accurately. The freeways have both numeric and destination names, and people use either interchangeably. When getting directions, always ask for the nearest major cross streets. Rush hours are from 6 to 9 in the morning and 3 to 7 in the evening. If you can travel at any other time, you should. Depending on the freeway, two or three people constitute a car pool and can travel in the Diamond lanes, which are faster and less crowded. A yellow light means step on it. Pedestrians in crosswalks at lights always get (and expect) the right-of-way. Always assume that the other driver is drunk, talking on a cell phone, or incompetent. Defensive driving is absolutely essential. And above all, don't get mad. Rage is for losers.

How to park in restricted areas... If there is a valet parking service anywhere nearby (usually in front of a restaurant), drop your car there, regardless of where you're actually going: You'll save yourself a major headache looking for a safe place to park. This strategy is especially useful around Melrose and West Hollywood. In Beverly Hills, Glendale, and Santa Monica, look for the city-run parking garages. These are metered and require coins, but there are change machines inside the facilities, usually on the first floor. Downtown you'll have to park in a private lot since street parking is limited. When parking on the street, always check the signs for time restrictions—most reflect rush-hour use of parking lanes. Trucks, even mini trucks with normal licenses, can park in yellow zones.

Where to smoke... Outside. That's it. L.A. has some of the most restrictive laws against indoor smoking in the nation. There's no smoking allowed in bars, restaurants, or offices. Many restaurants have now added patios or sidewalk areas for their smoking customers. Even then, you'll still get dirty looks if you light up.

How to stay out of trouble... Don't pick up any hookers on Sunset, don't try to buy dope in MacArthur Park, don't flip anybody off on the freeway, don't use your horn except as a warning, and don't ever tailgate, especially after a rain. If you get stopped by the police, stay in your car, have your license ready, assume the position. MAKE NO SUDDEN MOVES. Offer no bribes, make no jokes or excuses. Finally, don't jaywalk. You will be ticketed if there's a cop anywhere close by. Have a nice day.

Female Trouble... Forget the bimbo image of California blondes: That's strictly media hype. L.A. has more women-owned businesses than any other metro area in the country, employing more than one million people. And our racial intermarriage rate is five times the national average. This isn't New York, so you won't encounter construction workers making grotesque sucking sounds, but at the same time this isn't Tokyo, either. If you're female and out late at night in your car, always drive with the passenger-side door locked and the window up. If you break down on the freeway and can get to a call box, do so. After you report your problem, get back into your car and wait. Do not get out until a tow truck or the Highway Patrol pulls over.

How to see a whole bunch of union guys standing around shooting the s--t with the rent-a-cops while a movie/TV program/commercial isn't being made... Log onto the web site http://www.eidc.com, the home page of the Entertainment Industry Development Corporation. Here you can find out who's to blame for the invasion of big trucks loaded with arc lights and speakers that has taken over your neighborhood and set up a self-contained base camp for the night. They also list road closures, hotline numbers (Los Angeles Film Office, 323/957-1000 during office hours, 8 a.m. to 6 p.m.; after hours, call 800/201-5982), as well as "the honest-to-god official 'Code of Conduct' attached to each permit," in which production companies are reminded "It should not be expected that everyone in the surrounding environment will alter their lives to accommodate the needs of film production." What? Who do you work for? Let me speak to your supervisor!

Why we give our cars names... If you've never lived here, you can't begin to appreciate the significance of our auto-submissive neurosis—a sick relationship if ever there was one. Like, did you know that a '63 Bonneville convertible is considered a steal at $15,000, and that it'll probably go up 15 percent in value in the next year? It's guaranteed. There was an urban legend back in the '80s, during the time of the strong yen, that Japanese investors were buying up all the classic cars of the '50s and early '60s—Ramblers, Dodge Dart convertibles, Valiants, and so on—and crating them up for shipment to Japan. Cars *matter* here—that's all there is to it. Owning one is like having a dogsled in the Yukon during the gold rush. So rent yourself a *nice* car: You'll be spending a lot of time in it. The two most essential drives you should take are along Western and Sunset, starting from Griffith Park and Downtown, respectively, and driving each to its terminus in the sea. This approach essentially bifurcates the city, cutting it into slices of suburbia, strip-mall city, Hollywood, Bel-Air, hookers, Griffith Park, cool sea-refinery breezes, newly cut grass on the lawns of mansions, Olvera Street, the Miracle Mile, the Sunset Strip, Koreatown, O.J.'s Brentwood, the Crip's South-Central, Volvos backed up to turn down the tree-lined streets of Westwood, Cambodian housewives with shopping carts full of laundry waiting for the light in Echo Park, cops directing traffic into Dodger Stadium, burger joints, taco stands, gas stations, liquor stores, and the ocean.

When to plan your vacation... Of course this depends on which movie you want to believe. According to *Escape from L.A.,* in 2013 a 9.6 quake and tidal wave will create an island where West L.A. used to be. Then in *Demolition Man,* it's 2032, and Los Angeles has been reborn as San Angeles, a place where touching is forbidden. It stars Arnold as The Body. The most enduring and true-to-our-nightmares filmscape is the oh-so-stylish *Blade Runner* skyscape of 2019, when the air breathes fire and clouds of acid rain drift over a babble of almost understandable Millennial Spanglish. The best Cold War nightmare of L.A.? *Miracle Mile,* which portrays the city's final hour before nuclear obliteration.

accomm

1

odations

A hotel can be
simply a place to
sleep when you
need a bed, or it
can become a stag-
ing area for whole
subterranean

parts of your personality that need to be visited occasionally in order to keep the rest of you alive. Or dead, it's up to you. But I will declare it a given that you get what you pay for at four-star hotels. It may not always be what you *want*, but that's another story…. Conversely, those fleabag no-tell motels may not have a fridge and mini bar in the room, but you sure can't complain about the price. (And really, that's not blood on the sheets—more like an ironing burn.)

P.S.: Don't worry about cockroaches. This isn't New York.

Of course you have a car. Don't you? Not to worry—it *is* possible to stay in a hotel in Los Angeles and actually commute by some form of public transportation without getting a) shot, b) puked on, or c) bored to death. Anyway, it's always a good idea to pick a hotel close to where you plan to be doing most of your working/shopping/cruising. I mean, why get in the car if you don't have to? And as L.A. continues to mature, more and more areas are emerging as true neighborhoods, where walking is not only possible but actually promoted. In locales like Downtown, Melrose/Beverly, WeHo, Hollywood, Santa Monica, Pasadena, Catalina, and Malibu, you can settle in with no wheels and be absolutely pig-in-s--t happy, going out to great bars, eating in wildly eccentric ethnic restaurants, maxing out your credit card on unnecessary disposables, perfecting that screenplay pitch, and maybe, just maybe, not catching any STDs.

So go where the action is. Or where you've been told it is. And by the way, you *do* have a car. (Don't you?)

Winning the Reservations Game

It's not really a game, especially if you're trying to stay Downtown during a convention. Your best bet is to be flexible. That's why a great rental car can be way more important than a good hotel room. If you're having a hard time getting a room, drop some names, inquire about the distance to the Getty Center for your breakfast meeting, or express skepticism about their security. "There are some very recognizable clients I have to meet with, and I just need to be assured that they won't be harassed.…"

In fact, you don't even need to name names…just a *hint* will do. While Downtown hotels can be jammed, Hollywood is always for sale. Your best bet is to stay in Santa Monica, indicating to everyone that you truly know L.A. and have good taste to boot.

Is There a Right Address?

Is there a right address in L.A.? It all depends on you. The Biltmore, the Inter-Continental, Wyndham Checkers, and the Athletic Club are all classy digs for the Downtowner. The Bonaventure, on the other hand, is strictly middle-class-conventioneer style, totally functional and adequate for someone who's spending a *lot* of time not in the room. In Hollywood, the Standard, Chateau Marmont, the Sunset Marquis, and the Mondrian all have high hipster cachet. The Avalon and the Argyle have loads of character-building back-story as well, especially for those who consider the Sunset Strip accommodations to be last month's flavor.

The Lowdown

Wrong side of the freeway, right side of the wallet...

If you need to be near Downtown, but don't want to drop a bundle, consider staying in Chinatown. Sure, it's on the wrong side of the 101 Freeway and it's something of a hike from there to Downtown proper, but that's what the bus system is for. At the bottom of the budget list—but still totally acceptable—is the **Royal Pagoda Motel**. At $38 a night (10 percent less for weekly), this utilitarian little relic is more-or-less clean, safe, and quiet (at least at night). There's not too much to do in the neighborhood once you've exhausted Chinatown's attractions, but at least the rooms have AC. They're about what you'd expect for the price—drab and dull, but not as depressing as you might think (though this may depend on your medication). They get bonus points for the lack of Lysol aura.... Nearby is the **Metro Plaza** , which is also pretty cheap—under $70—with a cheesy facade that can't help but remind you that you're not here for anything other than doing business on a budget. You get AC, a room safe, maid service, and, if you're lucky, a view of Downtown. But who cares about views? Show me the money! The rooms are cramped but serviceable, the ambience is anonymous, plus it's just a few blocks from Union Station, for you fear-of-flying folk. And Chinatown is right outside the door. On North Hill Street you'll find the **Best Western Dragon Gate Inn**. They call it simply the Dragon Gate Inn, but come on, it's a Best Western—located here mainly because it is in Chinatown, not far from Downtown and Dodger Stadium, and it's close to the cheapest eats this side of Skid Row. To give the Dragon his due, this is one of the nicer places to stay in the neighborhood and is almost completely self-contained, with a beauty salon and the Hill Street Cafe and Cigar Bar (basically a snack shop), as well as a traditional Chinese herbalist and acupressure salon. The rooms are square, the views uninspiring, the "artful Chinese accents" unobtrusive and almost charming in a naive sort of way. And when the Dodgers are in town, you can enjoy the stadium fireworks show for nothing.

Strip joints for the hipeoisie... Hear Belushi giggling in the corner? Welcome to Hollywood's haunted palace, the **Chateau Marmont,** where the ghosts of generations of dead scriptwriters roam angrily in a badly edited purgatory, trying vainly to finish that last rewrite. The Chateau is a cliché, certainly, but it also represents a bit of Hollywood history that every Angeleno visits at least once. For tourists, it's just the right distance from the Sunset Strip, close enough for walking, but far enough away that you won't step in teenagers' vomit on the way to your room. It's also been here for 70 years, which in L.A. terms makes it practically prehistoric. The Chateau is a very private though slightly seedy hidey-hole, perfect to retreat to when you're sweating out a detox. It's like staying in your own apartment, only with a daily maid service that won't tell The Enquirer about the vodka bottles in your trash. On the Strip you'll find the **Mondrian,** one of the Hollywood legends that has managed to reinvent itself for the new century. Thanks to French designer Philippe Starck's severe yet dramatic decorating sensibilities— check out the towering mahogany entrance portal—this 12-story monument to the Dutch painter is still on the A-list. It reeks of starfucker mentality, mainly because the Skybar lounge-patio area is the tippy-top of the current dung heap of places to be seen with your agent, your client, your producer—anyone but your spouse. The rooms are as wonderful as the view, spacious and minimalist, with comfortable furniture and floor-to-ceiling windows—well worth the arm and leg you'll pay to sleep here. On the more reasonable side, there's the **Hollywood Metropolitan Hotel & Plaza** on Sunset. No Starck pretense here, just clean rooms and a good location. Down from Sunset, on a tree-lined street, is the **Sunset Marquis Hotel and Villas,** popular with celebrities, rock stars, and New York magazine editors vacationing on the corporate tit. Remarkably, it's weathered every change that's swept through Hollywood without ever losing its appeal. There are gardens with wonderfully overgrown birds-of-paradise, fish ponds, two very pleasant pools, and best of all, a sense of being miles away from the frenzy of the Sunset Strip (which in reality is just a few hundred feet to the north). The place also has excellent security, since people like Marilyn Manson and Aerosmith are regulars. From here you can hit the original Spago, shop at Tower Records, go to the Rainbow, and still make it to the airport in 20 minutes. If you've got the time and inspiration, there's also a state-of-the-art recording studio on-site. Finally, don't forget the famous **West Hollywood Hyatt,** known for years as the Riot House (or sometimes the Riot Hyatt), back in the days when touring rock 'n' roll superstars would routinely trash their rooms, toss TVs out the window, and drive their motorcycles through the hallways. The hotel's honchos eventually learned their lesson, though, and today it's not likely anyone above the threat level of Hanson would be welcome here. The Hyatt draws the music industry executive crowd, who appreciate its proximity to the House of Blues, its corporate cookie-cutter ambience (despite the Art Deco–esque lobby), and that bland familiarity of a big hotel chain. True, it is on the Sunset Strip in Hollywood, but it's still just a Hyatt—no more, no less. The ghosts of former hipsters—crazy cats like Montgomery Clift and Errol Flynn—are said to roam their old Hollywood haunt, the Roosevelt. Hollywood may have lost its glamour, but the old spots still hold a lot of appeal, and so does the **Hollywood Roosevelt Hotel,** a well-maintained, spacious compound right across from Graumann's Chinese Theater. If you don't know a thing about Hollywood, not even where to park, come here. It's the easiest and best choice in the neighborhood

Conventional choices with unconventional style... When there's a convention in town, the Downtown hotels always book up quickly, even gargantuan ones like the **Westin Bonaventure Hotel & Suites,** with its nearly 1,400 rooms. Once considered an eyesore, the Westin has become something of a classy

ACCOMMODATIONS | THE LOWDOWN

architectural statement of the '70s (oxymoron?). It's served as a location and/or backdrop for too many movies to mention; there are plaques scattered around the place to remind you of its more notable screen appearances. The rooms are on the small side, but the Bonaventure was built with an eye to conventioneers, who are almost never in their rooms anyway. The 35th-floor restaurant, Top of Five, has a spectacular 360-degree view of downtown, while one floor below it the Bonavista Bar slowly rotates, adding a nice disorientation to the evening. Even if you don't stay here, it's worth taking a ride in the exterior elevators. Ever wanted to have sex in an elevator? This is the place to come, especially if you have an exhibitionist streak. Just a few blocks away stands the **Regal Biltmore Hotel**. It simply doesn't get much grander than this: The decor mixes European elegance and Italian Renaissance, with some Spanish and Moorish folderol thrown in for spice. The result is a visual gumbo of carved inlay and rococo flourishes that can be a little hard to digest at first. The place feels more like a church than a hotel, and it can be a humbling experience just walking through the lobby. The hotel recently had a 75th birthday, but you'd never know it, thanks to the multimillion-dollar renovation done back in the '80s. The rooms are also constantly getting overhauled. Right across the street from the Biltmore is the **Wyndham Checkers Hotel**. Compared with the massive blocks of steel and glass all around it, the Wyndham Checkers seems like a transplant from some other, much smaller and more genteel city. It's been designed on a human scale, both in tone and mood. The result is a place that's deliciously civilized and chock-full of very pricey and tasteful art and antiques (although I did find the recent Van Gogh imitations, commissioned by the hotel in celebration of the local artists' show at LACMA, to be kind of cheesy). Bonus points for the in-house Checkers Restaurant on the ground floor. It's that rarity of hotel restaurants, one that's even more popular with locals than with the people staying there. The rooms cost plenty, but this is one instance where you get what you pay for and more.

And for manly men... Before there were such things as freeways and drive-bys, in the days when there weren't crack whores on every Hollywood Corner, Clark Gable once sat by the "lake" at the **Sportsmen's Lodge** and fished for trout. For the better part of a century, this eight-acre compound on the edge of the Valley has existed as a tribute to the masculine side in all of us. There's an Olympic-sized swimming pool, a restaurant where you can binge on huge slabs o' beef, and a sports bar that is a major testosterone hangout. It's practically in Hollywood, but with the waterfalls and the swans and ducks milling about, you'd swear you were somewhere that's wild in a different way. The place gets bonus points for being a short shuttle ride from the Burbank Airport, a much more humane way to fly into the City of the Angels than landing at LAX. Staying here is like visiting some very civilized English estate in the Lake District. The rooms are large, and if you really want to splurge you can get one with a private patio and pool. And if you *really* want to scratch that jock itch, there's always the **Los Angeles Athletic Club**, in the heart of the Financial District and the oldest private club in the city, established in 1880. Charlie Chaplin was a member, as was Rudolph Valentino. Since 1912 (when the current structure was built), club members have won more than 100 Olympic medals. The building was renovated in 1992; as you'd expect, it's the favorite gathering place for the circle-jerk-du-jour of local politicos, CEOs, zillionaire jocks, and attendant flacks 'n' hacks. Living up to its name, the club boasts a superb fitness center, a five-lane lap pool (used by Olympic swimmers), tournament-quality squash and racquetball courts, a full-sized basketball court, every high-tech aerobic/strength machine imaginable, spas, saunas, massage facilities, an indoor running track, and classes in everything from spinning to yoga. Basketball freaks take note: This is also the place that gives out the John Wooden Award each year to the top collegiate basketball player in the country. (Past recipients include Michael Jordan and Larry Bird.) Best of all, it's only a few minutes' walk to MOCA or the Music Center. Plus, there are only 72 rooms, so you won't get lost in the hallways. It's not as stately as the Biltmore or as classically déclassé as the Bonaventure, but it *is* a legend.

Bunking on Bunker Hill... Twenty years ago Bunker Hill was a kind of no-man's land of anonymous office high-rises, totally devoid of life in the evenings and on the weekends. Then MOCA moved here, the teeny funicular railway Angel's Flight was resurrected, and the Water Court began hosting free public concerts all summer long. Now there are plenty of reasons other than business to hang out here. The area's star is the **Hotel Inter-Continental**, a $100-million landmark that is one of L.A.'s most notable and prestigious hotels. With nearly 450 rooms and a location that can't be beat—right next to MOCA, in walking distance of the Dorothy Chandler Pavilion and the Financial District, and a five-minute drive from the convention center—this cousin to San Francisco's Mark Hopkins Hotel (also owned by Inter-Continental) is where top CEOs and visiting dignitaries stay when they're in town to visit the company headquarters in Library Tower or to hold talks with City Hall. Had a good year in the market? Stay in the Executive rooms, each with marble floor and guest bedroom. If you've really got juice, try checking into the Presidential Suite, which comes complete with its own baby grand piano. (Speaking of juice, by the way, the jurors from the O.J. trial were sequestered here.) Major local attractions during the summer include the free noontime and evening outdoor concerts held in the Water Court, right next door.

Boardwalk daze... Who can explain the appeal of Venice? It's got the weirdos on the boardwalk, the bums on the sand, the scummy cream that covers the water of the canals, and the ducks and gulls defecating and fornicating in wild abandon. And we watch it all, hypnotized and passive, like toilet paper going down the bowl in a swirl of water, headed for the sewer but loving every minute of it. My advice? Don't fight it—some people are just meant to be in Venice. So where do they stay? First on the list is the **Inn at Venice Beach**. Don't be fooled by the name, though: This is an inn only in the most general sense. It's really more of a newly remodeled generic motel, all plastic and stucco and sterile. The rooms are small but serviceable, and they have a few "family" suites with raised loft beds that might do for kids in a pinch. Hey, if it's personality you want, there's plenty out on the boardwalk, just a few hundred feet away. A much better choice (if you can get a reservation) is the **Venice Beach House Historic Inn**. This has to be one of the few places that *any* Angeleno would be honored to stay in, if only to get away from the 'hood for a day or two. The house was originally owned by Abbot Kinney, the crackpot who dreamed up the canals and brought gondolas to Venice. It's a classic Craftsman two-story house with a cozy, homey feel, full of period furniture, antiques, and Oriental carpets. Not surprisingly, Europeans love the place. Every one of the nine rooms is unique, and you wouldn't want to be any closer to the boardwalk. Best advice: Book way in advance, sight unseen. You won't be sorry.

Homes for the homeless... You have to give a nod to local comedian Harry Shearer, voice of Principal Skinner (among others) on "The Simpsons," one-third of *Spinal Tap* (one-fourth, if you count the evaporating drummer), and host of NPR's "Le Show," for christening Santa Monica, "The Home of the Homeless." There are indeed mobs of the unwanted, unloved, and unwashed pushing shopping carts around the oh-so-pleasant byways of this West Side beach community. They line up in the Palisades for free food, troll the 3rd Street Promenade for spare change, and never, ever book rooms in any of the toney Santa Monica hotels you might consider staying in...such as the **Georgian Hotel**. Perched right on Ocean Avenue and overlooking the pier and Santa Monica Beach, this is one of the last grand dames of European-style beach hotels in Santa Monica. The suites are all unique, the views are spectacular, and the location is perfect. Toss in the classic 1933 Art Deco design and the 1993 renovation, and you've got just the right place to meet your grandmother for high tea, served every afternoon. Right up the street is the **Oceana Suites Hotel**, which was an old apartment building before being remodeled into a quasi-boutique hotel. Don't let the trendoid associations of that phrase scare you away: This is definitely a home-away-from-home type of hotel. All the rooms are suites, and they all have kitchens any home chef would love. In the garden are lemon trees and geraniums. If the rooms came with a pet cat, I'd move in today. In keeping with this mood, there's no room service. Instead, guests order takeout from Wolfgang Puck's Cafe next door. The Oceana also has great views of the pier, the beach, and the fires in Malibu. You say you want to be right on the sand? You can't get much closer to the beach than the **Loews Santa Monica Beach Hotel**. There's

THE LOWDOWN | ACCOMMODATIONS

nothing between you and the baking flesh of Santa Monicans but the Pacific Coast Highway (PCH) and those pesky homeless. The cavernous atrium in the lobby is the highlight of the place, although luxuriating by the pool while staring at the Pacific runs a close second. There are truly fab ocean views in the higher-priced rooms, but even the "partial views" will give you the full effect. If you're really serious about the Loews experience, you must stop in to sample some foie gras with cranberries or the crisped salmon or venison at Lavande, the hoity-toity Provençal restaurant downstairs. And ordering the lavender-flavored ice cream is absolutely required. The **Hotel Carmel** is another '20s-era Santa Monica facility, one block from the beach with a back entrance that leads right onto the 3rd Street Promenade. That location makes it a big hit with foreign tourists and entertainment industry types who like the convenience of being able to shop and dine with a minimum amount of effort. The Art Deco lobby, completely restored last year, boasts some wonderful carved columns along with a cozy fireplace area. It's one of the better deals in the area, and is considered a "Santa Monica secret" by local rags. Bonus points for their amazingly comfy mattresses.

Slums of Beverly Hills... Local realtors have a term for it: Beverly Hills Adjacent. It means that you're not quite in the slipstream of wealth that swirls around Rodeo Drive and neighboring streets, but you're still close enough to imagine that you're a player. That's why you're staying at the **Carlyle Inn**, a small, 32-room boutique hotel used by Fox and Sony to put up visiting directors and actors—so you know it's, okay, not *real* expensive, and almost prestigious. Best part of it all: The intimate surroundings place you close to the arterial flush of money in Beverly Hills and Century City without forcing you to deplete your own precious fluids. You get a full breakfast to go with the open-air spa, sundeck, and free wine in the afternoon. Whoopee!...

Mid-century marvel... For you cool cats who are addicted to the TV Land channel, check out the **Avalon**, a retro reminder of swinging motels from some imaginary L.A. past, when Cricket lounged by the pool while Kookie played hep-cat beats on the bongos. Formerly the Beverly

Carlton, the Avalon was redone in 1998, adding all the nice modern touches you'd expect, but with a suitably ironic tone. Amenities include a pool, a gym, faxes in every one of the 88 rooms, and completely delightful '50s-style furnishings. The crowd here is generally young, mainly fashion-music-advertising-media types who get their clothes at Swell and look perfect lounging in the Eames-style molded chairs. Bonus historical points for "I Love Lucy" fans: All the "Lucy in Hollywood" episodes were shot here.

For the relocated, recently divorced, or renovating… So you got your ass thrown out? Or maybe you were just transferred to the regional headquarters, or you're in between escrows…. Whatever the reasons, the **Santa Monica Suites** are where you need to head now. It's the only hotel in the Pacific Palisades that does short-term rentals. This is the ideal place for people who are rehabbing their $2-million homes or dads who are getting divorced and don't want to stray too far from the kids. People come for a month and end up staying ten. These garden apartments all have hardwood floors and fireplaces, leather-pine furniture, and balconies that look out into a courtyard instead of the busy street. It's five long blocks to the beach, but who cares? Closer to the Santa Monica Pier are the **Beach Suites**, housed in a 1910 Spanish-style building that just reopened in 1999 after a full renovation. There are nine suites with rates ranging from $100–$150 a night (based on a minimum monthly rental), as well as hardwood floors, high-speed ISDN lines, 25-inch TVs, skylights, off-street parking, and a free laundry room (they even provide the soap). And you couldn't get much closer to the beach. Loews (whose rates start at $250 a night) is right next door. Unlike that monster, however, the Beach Suites are on a private pedestrian street that is gated. Recent residents include a "well-known" director, an actor working on a feature "with a very famous star," and an ESPN host, plus the usual ad-agency types working on national campaigns. The staff reveals no names, but you get the idea. If you want to stay here, call and make an appointment. Bonus points: You could easily survive here without a car. Down the coast a few miles are the **Venice Beach Suites**, right on the boardwalk. To get any closer to the bladers and crazies, you'd have to be homeless. The suites are in a big masonry building, formerly known as The Potter, that was built in 1908 and was once a vacation home to the Czar of Russia, just before his country's unwashed and unwanted homeless did something about the situation. It was also used by Charlie Chaplin for his romantic assignations. There's a huge Santa Monica Bay view, especially from the top floor. And the windows do open. Bonus points for the large closets built where the old Murphy beds used to be.

26 miles (and 50 years) across the sea... If you really want a taste of that mythical California of the past, when there were more drive-ins than drive-bys and there was only one area code for L.A., come on out to Catalina Island, just a few hours by boat from Long Beach. There are a variety of places to stay here, but the ones with the most charm date from the '50s. The **Villa Portofino** is a recently renovated, three-story European-style resort with great balcony and sun-deck views of Avalon Bay. It caters to couples, but some people actually come here just for the food in the restaurant. While it isn't as cheap as many places on the island, if you're here midweek in mid-winter you'll find rooms starting at $65. The **Pavilion Lodge** is right on the water, but lacks the intimacy of the Portofino. Still, the garden courtyard that dominates the center of the facility is a welcome relief from the endless sun and salt. It's more of a self-enclosed experience, perfect for aging CEOs to take their trophy wives to for a second honeymoon. Bonus points for letting kids under 11 stay for free with their parents, and for labeling all king-sized bedrooms as smokers. On the other hand, better leave the kids home if you really want to enjoy the **Catalina Island Seacrest Inn**. This is a moderately priced small hotel, the kind of place to come to for a sex-filled weekend away from it all. It's designed for lovers with a capital L, people who are here for one reason only: non-stop rutting. The rooms are done up in "romantic Victorian" decor and have whirlpool tubs built for two. They throw in a free souvenir rubber duckie for the tub, but you have to bring any other rubber necessities you might require.

Want to pretend you're William Randolph Hearst? Since you can't stay at Hearst's Castle in San Simeon, the

Santa Catalina home of chewing-gum magnate William Wrigley, Jr., is an excellent second choice. The house, built in 1921, is now known as the the **Inn on Mount Ada** and sits on a perch 350 feet above Avalon Harbor, where you can catch the earliest morning sun and the last afternoon rays. Built back when Wrigley owned 99 percent of the island, it's been the temporary home of both Calvin Coolidge and the Prince of Wales (just before he became the King of England, briefly). Prices start at around $300 and top out at nearly $600 a night. For that much money you expect something more than a chocolate on your pillow, and you get it here—including the sort of service that royalty is accustomed to. The rooms have private decks, private living rooms, and a huge assortment of good wines, beers, and champagnes. In the morning, choose between a big breakfast and a light deli lunch. The Inn gets a huge repeat clientele, from entertainment industry honchos to honeymooners. Be sure of your traveling plans before reserving, though: There's a $1,000 cancellation fee.

Old money and new romance... Around the turn of the century, Pasadena was where snooty Easterners could come to savor the climate, the ubiquitous bouquet of orange blossoms, and the sight of stoop labor working the fields. Some sense of this ambience still exists in South Pasadena, especially in a tree-lined section once known as "Millionaires Row." The houses here are Victorian, and one of the best restored is the **Bissell House.** This bed-and-breakfast has only five rooms, but in each room you get a vision of gracious SoCal living at its old-money best: gabled ceilings, chintz, antique beds, marble sinks, claw-footed tubs, and no graffiti anywhere. It's popular with couples who are out for a weekend of seriously steamy bonding, and business travelers who want something other than another anonymous hotel. The neighborhood is quiet and the overall retro ambience complete—except for the occasional drone of a cop copter searching for the unwashed beyond the borders of South Pas. Old Town, with its crowds, is a comforting mile away. A little too tired to handle the stairs after that big dinner? Take the elevator to the second floor.... Fairly nearby is the **Artist's Inn and Cottage,** a Victorian-era B&B with nine suites, including Jacuzzis, fireplaces, lots of art, and excellent food. High tea is served each afternoon on the front porch, and smoking is allowed only in the garden. This is where the locals come when they just can't take it at home anymore. One guest, a 75-year-old woman, recently came by for four nights, even though she lived just three blocks away. It's that kind of place. From here you can easily hit the Huntington Gardens, check out the spa facilities at the Ritz-Carlton, or, if it's the second Sunday of the month, visit the Rose Bowl Flea Market. The breakfasts are big, too. Over on Fair Oaks Avenue you'll find the **Pasadena Bed and Breakfast,** once the local courthouse and currently a National Historical Landmark. The place is a former hotel built at the turn of the century and is decorated in Victorian furniture, with 12 rooms, five bathrooms that are shared, and central AC. There's also a pleasant courtyard where you can have your breakfast. Unfortunately Fair Oaks is kind of busy, but you couldn't be closer to Old Town, and there are also some great restaurants just a few minutes' walk away. Highly civilized in tone, it's perfect for the semi-retired professionals and international travelers who like to come here.

Icons of Beverly Hills... They call the **Beverly Hills Hotel** the Pink Palace, as much for the decor as the implied sexual innuendo. Want to pretend you're Marilyn Monroe or Yves Montand? Rent either Bungalow 20 or 21, and hump like rabbits (that's where the two stars rehearsed for *Let's Make Love*). Here you'll encounter the culture of Beverly Hills under glass: The place has nearly 200 guest rooms, the Polo Lounge, the pool, the cabanas, and marble bathrooms, all surrounded by 12 acres in which to stroll and make naughty. It doesn't get much better than this, nor should it. Room prices run from $300 to $3,600 a night, but who's counting pennies? This is Beverly Hills! Want a private butler? Just call the front desk and ask them to send Jeeves to Bungalow 20 with a quart of Astroglide and a gallon of Beluga caviar—pronto! The gardens are wonderful, overflowing with hibiscus, bougainvillea, and palm. If you can't afford to stay here, at least come by for a snack at the Fountain Coffee Shop. Or enjoy the afternoon tea in the lobby, and watch people not married to each other check in with no luggage. All in all, the mid-'90s renovation was worth it. The same can't be said for **Lowell's** (formerly L'Ermitage), which had a $65-million face-lift, tummy tuck, and boob job and, after many delays, has finally reopened. Even with all the new modern touches, though, it's the rooftop pool that gets my nod. This is the perfect hotel for reclusive superstars like Whitney Houston—people who want to have their privacy but also want to be close to really prime shopping. The rooms are hiply minimalist, but rely a little too much on presentation and not enough on taste—kind of like the food in the hotel restaurant, which you should not even consider unless you're too drunk to drive anywhere decent. And now to the **The Regent Beverly Wilshire,** an ever-popular movie location (*Pretty Woman*, *Beverly Hills Cop*), and a former home-away-from-home for Elvis, John Lennon, Warren Beatty, the Aga Khan, Emperor Hirohito, the Windsors, and even the Dalai Lama. Can you top that? Lucy Lawless (Xena to you) had her wedding reception here, so you know it has to be classy. The lobby is white marble, the elevator doors are richly carved brown wood, and jackets are required in the restaurants. If you want the Presidential Suite (and who doesn't?), it'll cost you four grand. A night. Up front, thank you.

No money?... Sometimes you simply don't have the scratch, but you're still not ready to sleep on a park bench. That's when places like the **Venice Beach Hostel** come in handy. This is where you come if you 1) have no money, 2) want to be by the beach, and 3) really have no money. There's a communal TV room, lockers, and no curfew, plus it's the only place on the beach where you can cook in a communal kitchen with a lot of cross-cultural advice on your choice of seasonings. Female-friendly, the Hostel has women-only shared rooms for $15 a night. If you need more privacy, consider the private apartments, starting at $325 a week. In between are a range of semi-private singles and doubles, along with the cheapest meals this side of the homeless handouts in Santa Monica. The place is backpack central. You can't get closer to Venice's palpitating heart than this—nor would you want to.

Twin peaks... For some people, L.A. means only one thing: Rodeo Drive, that E-Ticket to the Wonderful World of Mammon. If shop-till-you-drop is your mantra, then the **Summit Hotel** on Rodeo Drive is ideal. The place is done in boutique style and has 86 rooms, the best being the penthouse suite with its outdoor terrace and bird's-eye view of the desperate shopping frenzy below. There are also free shuttles to its sister Summit Hotel in Bel-Air, which is much more enjoyable. The **Luxe Summit Hotel Bel-Air** has twice as many rooms on seven acres, and boasts an outdoor pool, tennis courts, a spa, and rooms that are much larger than at the Rodeo Drive establishment. Added bonus: The only restaurant on Rodeo Drive is the hotel's own Café Rodeo, headed up by the former executive chef at Morton's.

Big newspeople/Small newspeople... What's a big newsperson? Well, here's a hint: it's *not* the guy covering the pileup on I-40 for the local Eye Witless News at Four. He is a *small* newsperson, and he will be staying (if he's in town to talk to the honchos at CBS) at the **GH Guesthouse.** Part of a national chain, the hotel also plays host to tourists and industry corporate types. The place has been newly renovated and is clean and functional, if totally anonymous, innocuous, and characterless. CBS is right across the street, plus you get a free continental breakfast and you're within walking distance of the Farmer's Market and the Beverly Center. On the other hand, if you're a local anchor who just happens to have an exclusive with the doctor who did O.J.'s sex-change operation, then you get to stay at the **Sofitel Ma Maison Hotel,** directly across the street from the Beverly Center. If your room's on the street you may be able to see that stupid Cadillac coming out of the roof of Planet Hollywood, just below the pretentious ticking vanishing-rain-forests countdown (like they don't serve burgers?). The management would like to pretend this is a cozy little French chateau–style inn in Beverly Hills (hence the complimentary bottle of Evian water next to the bed), but actually it's on one of the busiest intersections in West Hollywood. It is conveniently close to Cedars Sinai, however, if you're planning on ODing after you hear that Johnny Cochran's dropped off a subpoena for you at the front desk.

You're queer. You're here. You need a room before you go shopping... What can you say about West Hollywood that will adequately describe its attractions? It's L.A.'s newest city, just a few minutes from the Melrose shopping zoo, Beverly Hills, the Sunset Strip, and Hollywood. It's also probably the largest gay enclave in California outside of San Francisco...but you knew that. Totally in the WeHo mood is **Le Montrose Suite Hotel.** Oooooh-la-la—this is more like it! The place is on a quiet residential street and is so fabulous that it has an astounding 89-percent return rate. You get fruit and mineral water when you arrive, and cookies and milk when you leave. Also sunken living rooms, twice-daily maid service, scales in the bathroom, even in-suite Nintendo! What more could you possibly want? It has a rooftop pool with nice views of the city, tennis courts, plus many rooms have patios, fireplaces, or both. Very private and gay-friendly. The hotel also offers a dog program where guests can get a dog dish and Le Montrose biscuits upon check-in. Now *that's* attention to detail. In a similar vein, just west of La Cienega Boulevard on a pleasantly quiet street, is **Le Parc Suite Hotel,** another gay-friendly and excellently run facility. Music industry big shots who like to keep their private life out of the tabloids come here to unwind in one of the 154 suites, each with a fireplace, patio, kitchenette, and sunken living room. Interior designer alert: It's within walking distance of the Pacific Design Center (a.k.a. the Blue Whale), so, as you might expect, the decor is top notch. Up on the roof is a tennis court, pool, spa, and gym. Meanwhile, over on the East Side in Silver Lake, near gay landmarks like the Crest Coffee Shop and the Detour bar, you'll find the **Sanborn Guest House,** a gay-run apartment in the rear of a well-maintained, Craftsman-style '20s bungalow. The neighborhood is spotty, but the guesthouse is clean, comfortably furnished, and suitable for up to three people, with a full kitchen, backyard, and gated parking. It's also cute, tasteful, has central air and heat, is nonsmoking, and caters to artist/bohemian/alternative lifestyle–type people. Plus, where else are you gonna stay in Silver Lake?

Miracle milers... Just a decade ago, before the riots, Miracle Mile was where film crews would come to illustrate the demise of L.A.'s inner city—the massive, decaying apartment buildings that defined the nonsuburban landscape. It didn't matter that the immediate neighborhood also had the Los Angeles Museum of Modern Art, the La Brea Tar Pits, the Crafts Museum—even the Museum of Miniatures, for god's sake! All the camera saw was that the area was being overrun by immigrants and gangbangers and abandoned by the businesses that had once made this stretch of Wilshire an integral hub to city life. Well, thank you very much, but the Miracle Mile is back. The fact that you can also now get great *bulgolgi* from any number of Korean restaurants in the neighborhood is gravy. Which is the main reason why I like the **Beverly Plaza Hotel** so much. It's not really located on the Miracle Mile itself, but just to the south, on the much more pleasant Beverly Boulevard. The Plaza is a boutique hotel with 98 oversized rooms, a swimming pool in the garden, and, remarkably, complimentary taxi service anywhere inside a five mile radius—a zone that stretches from the Greek Theater to Rodeo Drive, Hollywood, and the Sunset Strip. The biggest draws for some, however, are the Cava Cafe and the tapas bar on the ground floor. This eatery is another of chef Toribio Prado's spin-offs, and is a major hang for the power gays of WeHo as well as industry insiders.

Smells like roach spray, tastes like Marilyn...

Marilyn Monroe supposedly lived on Orchid Avenue— thus its claim to some sort of "historic" status. Right now, though, the only history being made is the construction of the future home of the Academy Awards, over on Highland—a complex that will soon house Armani and Gucci stores, making Orchid "the Rodeo Drive of Hollywood." That's what the locals are betting on, any-way, but I'll believe it when I see it. Meanwhile, there are deals to be had on Orchid, like the **Hollywood Celebrity Hotel,** built in the '80s but not aging well at all. It's deco-rated in that bad Reagan-era Art Deco/Nouveau style, with murals of old-time Hollywood stars thrown in to add some sense of history. *The Hotel* was filmed here, a major feature film that has never been released. It, like the sadly named Celebrity, coulda been a contender. Today, the place is just a down-at-the-heels version of the Roosevelt, with too many mirrors and those grotesque, obligatory star portraits everywhere. You can get a pass to the Magic Castle here though, and there's also free car ser-vice to the Universal Studios and a free, full-continental breakfast, served in your room. The nearby **Hollywood Orchid Suites** is substantially better, but still nothing to write home about. It has larger rooms, suitable for a family, with full kitchens. There's also a nice little swimming pool from which you can watch the gentrification of the neighborhood. Who's in the pool? A stage mother from Finland in town for her daughter's Broadway dance classes, a Goth babe in black lipstick, and a befuddled-looking Japanese guitarist.

Très snotty... The **Standard** is run by the Chateau Marmont people, and is located across the street from its sibling. It used to be a senior citizen's home, and features what they refer to as "mid-century decor" ('50s and '60s moderne to you, stupid). Well, you *will* feel stupid compared with the skinny, Prada-bag-carrying producers, models, filmmakers, and other snotty kids peopling this retro monstrosity. For paying too much money you get beanbag chairs and shag carpet on the ceiling, the overall effect being a hard-to-digest, minimalist ode to those decades that actually are in the "mid (20th) century." The pool area, with its deep blue AstroTurf that matches the rather tiny pool, is quite fabulous, as is the desk "aquarium," which houses a real live human in the p.m. The balconies are wavy Havana-esque numbers, painted baby blue. A cafe featuring sushi as well as other "international" cuisine has just opened as of this writing. There's also a trendy barbershop, newsstand, and piercing parlor on the premises. Don't feel bad if you have to wait 45 minutes to get someone to talk to you—it's all part of the elitist Hollywood thing, man.

Anti-très snotty... Now if you want the *real* "mid-century" feeling, the **Beverly Laurel Hotel** is the one for you. As welcoming as the Standard is alienating (the unloading driveway curves around a pool in the center of the hotel), it's been a location for numerous fashion shoots (starring Kate Moss), and was recommended by those hipsters at L.A. Eyeworks as being the place to stay in mid–West Hollywood. Swing bands also love the place, as does Victor Nuñez, who wrote the screenplay for his Oscar-nominated film *Ulee's Gold*, while staying here. It's clean, comfortable rooms are painted the same deep blue as the attitude, with cool diamond-print bedspreads, half and full kitchens containing all those '50s touches, and mosaic-tiled balconies. All this and the welcoming staff make this a hip, reasonable place to stay. Bonus points for Swingers Cafe next door (open until 4 a.m.), where you can get a groovy breakfast or lunch (okay, and a little bit of attitude).

For international travelers (or people from Florida)... Be afraid. Be very afraid. Or simply come from Europe. The **USA Hostel** is one of several facilities in Hollywood designed strictly for international travelers, but they will admit you from, say, Florida, if you have a passport and/or proof that you will be traveling on within three days. This policy is unavoidable—otherwise the place would be overrun by Hollywood runaways. "Yes," I was told, "drug addicts and alcoholic crazies are discouraged." It also caters to the Music Institute, located just around the corner. The street is "secure," because, well, all of the other businesses here have 24-hour armed security guards. The hostel staff is very friendly and helpful, plus there are Internet hookups, mountain bikes for rent, and cheap tours available. The biggest problem: The rooms are really pretty funky, and the dorms are just a step above a holding tank. People drape serapes or sheets over the lower bunks in a sad attempt at some sort of privacy. With so little space, the center of the room becomes the communal storage area, where you toss your dirty laundry and your daypack. I think I'd rather *be* in Florida, thank you very much. Also geared to the international traveler, on "historic" Orchid Avenue in Hollywood, is the **Liberty Hotel**, where you can feel welcome in the $15-a-night dorm rooms, or throw for your own special private room reeking of Lysol. Between the Saltillo-tiled floors, cottage-cheese ceilings, and cheap chandeliers, the overall ambience is like something out of a Bukowski story or a Pete Wilson–inspired antiforeigner dungeon. **Banana Bungalow** is another "international" hostel in Hollywood, located in a slightly quieter neighborhood, right off the Cahuenga Pass portion of the Hollywood Freeway, but shielded from that sight by lots of vegetation. That, plus a rustic tropical motif-style "club room," makes this a much more acceptable choice for the backpacker set. Included in your room charge is a breakfast of toast, coffee, or tea, as well as use of a pool, pool table, weight room, and a "library" where you can escape from your dorm mates. (Works better than sheets hung over the bottom of your bunk, no?) There are regular shuttles to Universal Studios and Disneyland, as well as a full-day

L.A. city tour for $38, a one-day Mexico (Tijuana) tour for $49, and a four-day tour of the Grand Canyon. The friendly, multilingual staff says you must have proof of international travel to stay here (though that passport from Florida will also suffice).

Beachy keen... Down in Todos Santos, at the tip of Baja, there's a Hotel California that claims it "may be" the place that was the inspiration for the classic Eagles' song about wretched excess and lost innocence. The folks at the **Hotel California** in Santa Monica make no such claims, although they do admit that a lot of their visitors (Europeans and Japanese, especially) come here to have pictures taken of themselves standing in front of the sign. What could say "L.A." more than that? (The photo used on the original album art, by the way, was actually of the Beverly Hills Hotel.) In reality, though, this is not the place for such jaded self-indulgence. The hotel doesn't even allow smoking in the rooms, for example. (Of course, the rules don't say anything about freebasing.) Located in a pleasant, Spanish-style stucco building with a tile roof, the hotel provides mini fridges and nice 25-inch TVs in each room. For chilling, it has small patios and balconies and a very pleasant inner courtyard shaded by banana and Mexican fan palms that is totally ripe with the smell of night-blooming jasmine. It's right next to Loews and costs half as much per night. Unlike most of the places in Santa Monica, this is *not* a European-style beach-resort place but rather something very much of California— hence the name. The rooms were all renovated in 1998. For a wilder feel, check out the **Topanga Ranch Motel**— 30 faded white wooden cottages lined with rambling rose bushes at the nexus of Topanga Canyon and the Pacific Ocean. This is the kind of place that Lew Archer might have crashed in on his way to Santa Teresa. The cottages have mulched into the landscape for so long that they feel more like local real estate than a commercial business, and in fact more than 20 of the little houses have become permanent homes for the hardy breed of Angelenos drawn to this little untamed corner of Eden. Thanks to the Topanga River, which overflows every few years, and the fires that threaten the region the rest of the time, the state's plans to level this area are regularly thwarted by uneasy development concerns. Basically there's still a history here, some-

THE LOWDOWN | ACCOMMODATIONS

thing you can touch and feel. The plant life around the motel is oversized and psychedelic, and the nearby grove of eucalyptus trees blankets the air with an unavoidable California aroma. Across the street the beach is rocky, and a little wild as well, appealing more to surfers than swimmers. You could hole up indefinitely here, buying supplies at the market next door and blissing out on the perfect view of the canyon behind you. It's a perfect setting for a neo-noir L.A. short story, or a new chapter in your life. Just up the road is the **Casa Malibu,** where Lana Turner supposedly camped out. (Presumably she also had a nice bed of her own somewhere else in town.) This "Inn on the Beach" successfully integrates a well-kept hominess with a low-key discreet romantic atmosphere—perfect for private interludes. Unimposing when viewed from PCH, the traffic noise immediately drops off once you enter the lobby and your eyes are caught by the ocean straight ahead, framed by a lovely jasmine-scented inner courtyard. A half wall of glass keeps both the ocean noise and the blowing sands at bay, making for a comfortable, communal lounge area. Each room is a little different, ranging from simple to more luxurious; some have private decks and some face the courtyard. Nothing feels either too fussy or impersonal here. Relaxing where you didn't know you were tense, you'll immediately consider checking in, even if you live only 20 minutes away.

Classic views... The 15-story Art Deco **Argyle Hotel** sits high on the ridge of the Sunset Strip and offers one of the best panoramas of the city. The interior landscape isn't bad either: In fact, the 64 rooms in the recently restored building are drop-dead gorgeous. They've all been done in period style, and in keeping with that more civilized time you can get butler service if needed. On the more up-to-date side, there are also fax machines in every room. The hotel was built in 1927 and became a playground for the likes of Errol Flynn and (of course) Marilyn Monroe. It was reincarnated as the St. James Club for a while, a stupidly haughty "private" establishment, but has now returned to its commoner roots—although there is still something of an attitude about the place. It's hard not to feel privileged with that view. Major bonus point: The 24-hour room-service food comes from the Fenix Restaurant, a super-trendy French-Asian-California fusion slop house on the ground floor.

Rehab: the prequel... It was inevitable that the seedy hotels of Hollywood would serve as temporary homes to those who would later become rich and famous. If you want to follow the bed-linen trail of those with feet of clay and recognizable faces, consider starting at the **Dunes Sunset Motel.** It's located across the street from Channel 5 KCAL-TV, right by the Hollywood Theater and *very* freeway close. Reportedly Tom Waits stayed here for six months—probably researching material for his next CD. Other notable guests include Little Richard and acts playing the House of Blues. The rooms are clean and serviceable, with generic landscape prints screwed into the wall (on the off chance that you may be a kleptomaniac with absolutely no visual taste). Like all of us, however, they've seen better days. Next door is the Dreams Cafe, a coffee shop with comfy blue booths, and next to *that* is a non-threatening bar, a favorite hangout for the KCAL weatherman as well as for techies from nearby film and TV studios, the Kodak Motion Picture Division, and Delux. Down on Wilshire, and owned by the same family as the Dunes Sunset, is the **Dunes Wilshire Motor Hotel.** It's a typical '70s-style hotel, with kitchens available in some rooms. A soap opera star stayed here "for a night," as did Kiefer Sutherland (doing what, I wonder?...). There's a heated pool, and connecting units for families.

The price is right...isn't it? Please?... They claim that one-quarter of the clientele at the **Farmer's Daughter Motel** (so named because of its proximity to the Farmer's Market) are contestants on "The Price Is Right," which is filmed right across the street at CBS Studios. Personally, I couldn't imagine anything more depressing than staying here while debasing yourself for money on national TV. Let's hope they all win big-time so they won't ever have to stay in this ratty, nondescript, vinyl-wallpapered fleabag again. Close by you'll find the **Beverly Inn,** currently under renovation. This place "was a dump," they honestly proclaim, but everything will be much better soon. Honest. And again, the price is right. It's clean and functional, with a tiny, sunless swimming pool in the center. Plus there's CBS across the way—keep trying to get that price right, folks—and the Market. The motel caters to hopeful musicians, actors, and dancers until they find their own apartments—and, as always, those "international" student types. Finally there's the

THE LOWDOWN | ACCOMMODATIONS

Bevonshire Motel, another clean, characterless-yet-serviceable motel with a tiny, sunless swimming pool that you'll never enter. Kudos for the bulletproof glass in the lobby—it really adds to the ambience. Is the place safe? Is life safe? Hey, you could get killed crossing the street; for these prices, who cares? (Plus, there's always "The Price Is Right," beckoning from across the street.)

The Index

$$$$$$	Sky's the limit
$$$$$	to $1,000
$$$$	to $550
$$$	to $350
$$	$100–$200
$	Under $100

Price applies to a standard double room for one night.

Argyle Hotel. Everyone raves about the Argyle: It's one of those special L.A. landmarks that could only exist in the City of Lost Angels. Wonderful Art Deco touches everywhere you look. And it's on the Strip.... *Tel 323/654-7100 and 800/225-2637. 8358 Sunset Blvd., West Hollywood, 90069. $$–$$$* **(see p. 34)**

Artist's Inn and Cottage. Packed with antiques and nice art, you'd never guess that this stately Victorian was once home to a thriving chicken farm. It was tastefully restored in 1989. Nine rooms, five in the cottage, four in the original farmhouse. South Pas living at its turn-of-the-century best.... *Tel 626/799-5668 and 888/799-5668. 1038 Magnolia St., South Pasadena, 91030. 14 rooms. $–$$* **(see p. 25)**

Avalon. If you've got a major interior-design jones, this is the place to go. From its Noguchi-style elevator to the George Nelson geometric bubble lamps, the Avalon has got to be one of the best boutique visual delights in the city.... *Tel 310/277-5221 and 800/535-4715. 9400 W. Olympic Blvd., Beverly Hills, 90212. 88 rooms. $$–$$$***(see p. 22)**

Banana Bungalow. If you've got no money at all, and the choice is between staying here or selling your ass down on Hollywood Boulevard...well, it's a toss-up, I'd say. Dorm rooms, no privacy, backpacker clientele.... *Tel 800/4-HOS-TEL. 2775 Cahuenga Blvd., West Hollywood, 90068. 44 rooms, 10 of them private. $* **(see p. 32)**

Beach Suites. These are truly suites, much closer to a nice condo decked out with all the gadgets than what you'd expect from a "hotel" room. There's a one-month rental minimum and they don't give out the address to the public.... *Tel 310/451-6024. Call for exact street address, Santa Monica, 90402. Eight one-bedroom suites, one studio. $$ per night based on a 30-day rental.* **(see p. 23)**

Best Western Dragon Gate Inn. You get a complimentary breakfast at the Hill Street Cafe, and there are even electronic door locks. Wow! But hey, it's cheap, centrally located, and the rooms are slightly larger than most of its local rivals. Plus it's Chinatown.... *Tel 213/617-3077. 818 N. Hill St., Chinatown, 90012. 50 rooms. $* **(see p. 15)**

Beverly Hills Hotel. There's no easy way to sum up the Beverly Hills Hotel in a few sentences. The Polo Lounge, the cabanas, the endless parade of celebrities...it's just so wonderfully fabulous and part of the glory that is, and will always be, Beverly Hills.... *Tel 310/276-2251 and 800/283-8885. 9641 Sunset Blvd., Beverly Hills, 90210. 203 rooms, 53 of them in the bungalow section. $$$–$$$$$$* **(see p. 26)**

Beverly Inn. It's cheap! Okay? With the money you're saving you can rent a really great car and impress everyone—plus you'll probably be spending more time driving than in your room here anyway. The rooms are depressing, the pool chilly, the neighborhood better than average. Just don't tell anyone you're staying here.... *Tel 323/931-8108/8109/8100. 7701 Beverly Blvd., Los Angeles, 90036. 28 rooms. $* **(see p. 35)**

Beverly Laurel Hotel. This cozy, cheapish WeHo hotel is the digs of choice for those who know all about what's wrong with the Standard. A very comfortable, friendly vibe from the staff, and a very nice, subdued decor and attitude. Popular with bands who don't need to trash the hotel room or OD on the toilet to make an artistic point. Recommended highly.... *Tel 323/651-2441. 8018 Beverly Blvd., West Hollywood, 90048. 52 rooms. $–$$* **(see p. 31)**

Beverly Plaza Hotel. Built for the 1984 Olympics, this boutique hotel was renovated in 1997. It's centrally located and offers some really good promotional packages.... *Tel 323/658-6600 and 800/62-HOTEL. 8384 W. 3rd St., West Los Angeles, 90048. 98 rooms. $$* **(see p. 30)**

Bevonshire Motel. It's clean, and will do in a pinch if you can't find anywhere else nearby. Zero character—but maybe that describes you as well.... *Tel 323/936-6154. 7575 Beverly Blvd., Los Angeles, 90048. 24 rooms. $* **(see p. 36)**

Bissell House. Located on Millionaires Row in South Pasadena, this charming five-room Victorian is perfect for trysting lovers or honeymooners. You get a full breakfast on the weekends, but bring your own condoms and try not to get personal fluids all over the chintz.... *Tel 626/441-3535 and 800/441-3530. 201 Orange Grove Ave., South Pasadena 91030. $* **(see p. 25)**

Carlyle Inn. Close to the heart of Beverly Hills but nowhere near as pricey, this is the perfect choice when you want to be West Side central without busting your budget. It's a great choice for any business traveler. Named after 19th-century poet Thomas Carlyle.... *Tel 310/275-4445. 1119 S. Robertson Blvd., Beverly Hills, 90035. 32 rooms. $$* **(see p. 22)**

Casa Malibu. Okay, it's not really a casa in the Mexican sense of the word, and it's not actually in the Colony—but the price is right, and for a private weekend away with your honey, it beats Vegas. Plus it's close to the beach.... *Tel 310/456-2219 and 800/831-0858. 22752 Pacific Coast Hwy., Malibu, 90265. 21 rooms. $$* **(see p. 34)**

Catalina Island Seacrest Inn. This is the kind of B&B that romance novelists have wet dreams over. If you can't get in the mood here, then there's something seriously wrong with

your relationship. Honeymooner-friendly. Having an anniversary? Leave the kids home.... *Tel 310/510-0800. 201 Claressa Ave., Avalon, Catalina, 90704. Eight rooms. $–$$*
(see p. 24)

Chateau Marmont. Since 1929 this faux-Normandy castle sequestered above the Sunset Strip has been the perfect hideaway for blocked writers and actors desiring to keep a low profile. Includes pool, exercise room, and parking. Small pets allowed. Are you an aging hipster on an expense account who thinks the Skybar is just the shit? Come here.... *Tel 323/656-1010 and 800/CHATEAU; fax 323/655-5311. 8221 W. Sunset Blvd., West Hollywood, 90069. 50 rooms in the hotel, nine cottages, four bungalows. $$$* **(see p. 16)**

Dunes Sunset Motel. Don't worry if you're down on your luck and all your luggage was just stolen at the Greyhound station. They'll understand. Want to absorb that funky Hollywood street vibe? This place is perfect—just make sure you have your Prozac with you.... *Tel 323/467-5171. 5625 Sunset Blvd., Hollywood, 90028. 53 rooms. $***(see p. 35)**

Dunes Wilshire Motor Hotel. Owned by the same family that owns the Sunset Motel, this place is also cheap and way more family friendly, with rooms that connect and a very understanding staff. And there's a pool.... *Tel 323/938-3616. 4300 Wilshire Blvd., Downtown, 90012. $* **(see p. 35)**

Farmer's Daughter Motel. Okay, so it's close to the Farmer's Market and CBS and really, really cheap—but is that your idea of a good time? This is way down on the list of last choices.... *Tel 323/937-3930 and 800/334-1658. 115 S. Fairfax Ave., West Hollywood, 90036. 66 rooms. $* **(see p. 35)**

Georgian Hotel. Small by corporate standards—only 84 rooms, and thus almost intimate. Plus it's close to the beach, the Santa Monica Pier, the 3rd Street Promenade, and Main Street. It has a distinctly pleasing European flavor, and is the kind of place artists exhibiting in Santa Monica galleries might stay if they've just sold a big piece.... *Tel 310/395-9945. 1415 Ocean Ave., Santa Monica, 90401. 84 rooms. $$–$$$* **(see p. 21)**

GH Guesthouse. This is a good alternative to the host of boutique hotels in the area. It's nowhere near as charming as Le Montrose, but then it's also a lot cheaper.... *Tel 323/692-1777. 7721 Beverly Blvd., West Hollywood, 90036. 34 rooms. $–$$* **(see p. 28)**

Hollywood Celebrity Hotel. The name should warn you right away. The last celebrity that stayed here wasn't anyone you've seen on the screen in a long, long time. But it is in Hollywood, and less expensive than the Roosevelt (which it tries vainly to imitate).... *Tel 323/850-6464. 1775 Orchid Ave., Hollywood, 90028. 40 rooms. $* **(see p. 30)**

Hollywood Metropolitan Hotel & Plaza. This is a very good and reasonable alternative to the larger chains in Hollywood. It's clean, affordable, centrally located and safe—and in 10 years it'll look really hiply retro.... *Tel 800/962-5800. 5825 Sunset Blvd., Hollywood, 90028. 90 rooms. $–$$* **(see p. 16)**

Hollywood Orchid Suites. Can you smell the flowers? This is "historic" Orchid Avenue. Some day it may be worthy of that adjective, but right now it's simply cheap, family-friendly, and not in an area I'd send my daughter into at night—but then, that's me.... *Tel 323/874-9678. 1753 N. Orchid Ave., Hollywood, 90028. 40 rooms. $–$$* **(see p. 30)**

Hollywood Roosevelt Hotel. The ghosts of old Hollywood are said to make regular appearances at this landmark hotel, newly restored,　right across from Graumann's Chinese Theater.... *Tel 800/950-7667. 7000 Hollywood Blvd., Hollywood, 90028. 333 rooms. $$–$$$* **(see p. 17)**

Hotel California. Come on. How could you come to L.A. and not want to stay in a place called the Hotel California? It's right next to Loews, costs half as much per night, and brings you much closer to the California feel of things.... *Tel 800/537-8483. 1670 Ocean Ave., Santa Monica, 90401. 26 rooms, six of them suites. $$* **(see p. 33)**

Hotel Carmel. Popular with Aussies and Europeans, and some of the suites have ocean views. This is a limited-service hotel (meaning no room service), but the Art Deco lobby and its proximity to 3rd Street Promenade make it definitely something to consider. A good choice for people with no car.... *Tel 310/451-2469. 201 Broadway, Santa Monica, 90401. 100 rooms. $–$$* **(see p. 22)**

Hotel Inter-Continental. Ideal for CEOs who are here just for business and don't care what it costs. It's less architecturally stunning than the Biltmore down the street, but its sleek presentation and attention to the needs of world travelers used to going first-class is without parallel. Every room has an oversized desk and two dual-line speaker phones with computer hookups, all set up and ready to go, as well as remote-access phone mail.... *Tel 213/617-3300 and 800/442-5251. 251 S. Olive St., in California Plaza, Downtown, 90012. 434 rooms. $$–$$$$* **(see p. 20)**

The Inn at Venice Beach. If you're simply determined to stay in Venice and want to be really close to the beach, this "inn" is suitable but not great. The rooms are generic and clean. They do have a few larger rooms that could conceivably hold a family.... *Tel 310/821-2557 and 800/828-0688. 327 Washington Blvd., Venice, 90291. 43 rooms. $$* **(see p. 20)**

Inn On Mount Ada. The former home of chewing-gum magnate William Wrigley, Jr., this is absolutely the most bizarre and wonderful place to stay on Catalina. Expensive, yes, but it's like nothing else on the island. Amazing service and amenities.... *Tel 310/510-2030 and 800/608-7669. 398 Wrigley Rd., Avalon, Catalina, 90704. 6 rooms. $$$$$* **(see p. 25)**

Liberty Hotel. I'd hoped they were being ironic about the name, but no such luck. If you believe that freedom's just another word for nothing left to lose, then come on in. Scary. Very scary.... *Tel 323/962-1788. 1770 Orchid Ave., Hollywood, 90028. 20 rooms. $* **(see p. 32)**

Loews Santa Monica Beach Hotel. One of the classic Santa Monica beach hotel experiences, featuring great views, a very decent restaurant, and prices that let you know you're in Santa Monica. If you can afford it, it's definitely worth a visit. If not, just stop in to check out the atrium.... *Tel 310/458-6700 and 800/235-6397. 1700 Ocean Ave., Santa Monica, 90401. 341 rooms. $$$* **(see p. 21)**

Los Angeles Athletic Club. It's exclusive, high-class, and the perfect place to scratch that jock itch. If you're a member,

THE INDEX

ACCOMMODATIONS

staying here is rock-bottom cheap, but you out-of-town losers should expect to shell out substantially more. Great basketball courts, volleyball games, pool, and a fitness center that is light-years beyond your local gym.... *Tel 213/625-2211. 431 W. 7th St., Downtown, 90014. 72 rooms. $$$* **(see p. 19)**

Lowell's (L'Ermitage). Recently reopened after a very long renovation, this luxury hideaway has yet to regain the exclusivity and panache it enjoyed in the '80s. Still, if it's top-drawer privacy you're seeking, no matter what the cost, then be my guest. The rooftop pool is truly wonderful.... *Tel 310/278-3344 and 800/800-2113. 9291 Burton Way, Beverly Hills, 90210. 123 rooms. $$$–$$$$$* **(see p. 26)**

Luxe Summit Hotel Bel-Air. Out where the air starts to smell like oxygen, this is a very smart alternative to staying on the West Side, especially if you want to be close to Rodeo Drive or Century City. They have shuttles into the city, and the grounds and facilities are lovely.... *Tel 310/476-6571. 11461 Sunset Blvd., Bel-Air, 90049. 161 rooms. $–$$$* **(see p. 28)**

Metro Plaza Hotel. Clean and safe, and one of the best bargains in Downtown—well, actually, Chinatown—this is an ideal place for the tourist on a budget. Bonus points for the abundance of cheap eats in the immediate neighborhood. Forget about the view, and think of all the money you're saving.... *Tel 213/680-0200. 711 N. Main St., Chinatown, 90012. 80 rooms. $* **(see p. 15)**

Mondrian. You want to know if you've arrived? Then try walking into the Mondrian's Skybar at sunset and see if you get a table. The Mondrian is hip, exclusive, expensive, and dressed to the tits like the celebrity whore it is. Rooms are huge and comfy, the staff is fawning, the views are insane. If you've got the money to spend, why not?... *Tel 323/650-8999 and 800/525-8029. 8440 Sunset Blvd., West Hollywood, 90069. 238 rooms. $$$-$$$$$* **(see p. 16)**

Le Montrose Suite Hotel. It's cozy, they have cookies like Mom used to make, and they don't care what your sexual proclivities are—just don't make a mess, even though the

maids do come in twice a day. We should all live like this....
*Tel 310/855-1115. 900 Hammond St., West Hollywood,
90069. 135 rooms. $$–$$$* **(see p. 29)**

Oceana Suites Hotel. Overlooking the beach in Santa Monica
and quite high on the Hipster-O-Meter, this is the place to
come when you really don't want to drop a bundle for a hotel
in a clean-air environment, but you also don't want to see
roaches flickering across the floor when you turn on the
lights.... *Tel 310/393-0486 and 800/777-0758. 849 Ocean
Ave., Santa Monica, 90403. 63 suites. $$* **(see p. 21)**

Le Parc Suite Hotel. Beautifully run and gay-friendly, Le Parc
offers handsome private suites that are perfect for unwind-
ing.... *Tel 310/855-8880 and 800/5-SUITES. 733 N. West
Knoll Dr., West Hollywood, 90069. 154 Suites. $$–$$$*
(see p. 29)

Pasadena Bed and Breakfast. This wonderfully restored for-
mer courthouse is the ideal place from which to explore Old
Town Pasadena. Great period decor.... *Tel 626/568-8172
and 800/653-8886. 76 N. Fair Oaks Ave., Pasadena,
91103. 12 rooms. $–$$$* **(see p. 26)**

Pavilion Lodge. This is the sort of place tour groups stay at,
maybe because the room rate includes cross-channel transportation. It's okay and will do in a pinch, but lacks the
ambience of places more charmingly funky and cheaper....
*Tel 310/510-2500. 513 Crescent Ave., Avalon, Catalina,
90704. 73 rooms. $$* **(see p. 24)**

Regal Biltmore Hotel. Can't afford a trip to Barcelona? This is
the next best thing. Plus it's right in the heart of the
Financial District. The interior decor is absolutely stunning
and as close to a grand hotel in Europe as you'll find in this
part of the country. And who would have guessed? It's right
next to a subway station.... *Tel 213/624-1011 and
800/245-8673. 506 S. Grand Ave., Downtown, 90071.
683 rooms $$–$$$* **(see p. 18)**

The Regent Beverly Wilshire Hotel. You know this hotel is all
about luxe simply from walking into its creamy-white marble
lobby.... *Tel 310/275-5200. 9500 Wilshire Blvd., Beverly
Hills, 90212-2405. 395 rooms. $$$–$$$$$* **(see p. 27)**

THE INDEX

ACCOMMODATIONS

Royal Pagoda Motel. Right at the end of Chinatown, this is a handy, cheap, and clean alternative to sleeping in the bus station. The area is fairly safe after dark, and there are loads of great restaurants within walking distance.... *Tel 323/223-3381. 995 N. Broadway, Chinatown, 90012. 36 rooms. $* **(see p. 15)**

Sanborn Guest House. Making a gallant effort to improve the neighborhood, this very comfortable, Craftsman-style guest house is perfectly ideal for couples, regardless of their sexual persuasion. It's reasonably priced, and the people who run it are as sweet as can be.... *Tel 323/666-3947. 1005 Sanborn Ave., Silver Lake, 90029. Fully furnished one-bedroom guest house. $* **(see p. 29)**

Santa Monica Suites. These are monthly rental places for people who are in-between residences. They cater to the movie industry and the high-tech community, so you know they're both top-notch and pricey. But, tell me: If you're gonna be here for a month or more, why should you have to put up with plastic flowers?... *Tel 310/459-4243. On San Vicente Blvd. in Pacific Palisades. Call for specific address and to see if you "qualify." (The address is unlisted to protect the "privacy" of the residents—i.e., any TV and movie people whom you might recognize.) Santa Monica. $$$* **(see p. 23)**

Sofitel Ma Maison Hotel. Smells like smog, in a super-busy location but actually cheaper than you might think. It's "Beverly Hills Adjacent," and with a residue of hipness— although it's fading fast. The rooms are clean, plus this is one of the few places you can stay and not need a car to enjoy yourself.... *Tel 310/278-5444. 8555 Beverly Blvd., West Hollywood, 90048. 300 rooms. $$–$$$$* **(see p. 28)**

Sportsmen's Lodge. This is where red-blooded meat eaters come for communal bonding with others of like thinking. Though it's got a Hollywood pedigree (he-man Clark Gable was a frequent guest) and beautiful grounds, the basic vibe—feasting on still-warm flesh—is just a little too creepy for me. But hey, whatever gets you off. Just don't shoot the wildlife in the ponds.... *Tel 818/769-4700 and 800/821-*

8511. 12825 Ventura Blvd., Studio City, 91604. $$$
(see p. 19)

Standard. Are you hip enough? I don't think so. Go wait in the corner, and maybe someone will take notice of you after an hour or so. This place is so of-the-minute, it's already tired and depressing. There, that didn't take long, did it?... *Tel 323/650-9090. 8300 Sunset Blvd., West Hollywood, 90069. $$–$$$$$* **(see p. 31)**

Summit Hotel, Rodeo Drive. Just the place to come if you're interested in the effortless spending of money. It's impossible to be more on Rodeo Drive than this. If that's what works for you, they take every major credit card. Smallish, boutique style, and everyone knows where it is.... *Tel 310/273-0300. 360 N. Rodeo Dr., Beverly Hills, 90210. 86 rooms. $$–$$$* **(see p. 27)**

Sunset Marquis Hotel and Villas. They call it deluxe accommodations, but the rooms aren't really that fab. The best part about this slice of Hollywood High Life is its exterior. It's the perfect package of California living at its best—the gardens, the pools, the security, the Sunset Strip right there at your fingertips.... *Tel 310/657-1333. 1200 N. Alta Loma Rd., West Hollywood, 90069. 115 rooms. $$$***(see p. 17)**

Topanga Ranch Motel. It may be a little closer to the Pacific Coast Highway than you want, but the price is right and the ambience is totally old Southern California. The motel rooms are nice, too. If you want to stay on a nice. clean beach with minimal hassle, you certainly couldn't do better than this. This place is a Beach Bum Special.... *Tel 310/456-5486. 18711 Pacific Coast Hwy., Malibu, 90265. Five rooms. $*
(see p. 33)

USA Hostel. Are you a foreigner? Got a backpack and not quite as much money as you thought? Welcome! Hollywood is your kind of place, and the USA Hostel is where you'll be bunking. Enjoy.... *Tel 323/850-7733. 772 Hawthorne Ave., Hollywood, 90028. 5 private rooms, 7 dorm rooms (6–8 beds per room). $* **(see p. 32)**

Venice Beach Hostel. You're no longer at the zoo, you're in it.

Key advice: Pay in advance. Watch your back. Don't buy any drugs from people you don't know.... *Tel 310/452-3052. 1515 Pacific Ave., Venice, 90291. 14 private rooms, usually 4 beds in each, 11 dorm rooms with 4–11 beds in each. $* **(see p. 27)**

Venice Beach House Historic Inn. Without a doubt, this is the coziest and most charming place in Venice Beach. It's deservedly popular with Europeans, who know a good thing when they see it. The Inn was once the beach home of Venice developer Abbot Kinney, the man who dreamed up the canals. Make your reservations well in advance.... *Tel 310/823-1966. 15 30th Ave., Venice, 90291. 9 rooms. $$* **(see p. 31)**

Venice Beach Suites. This is another of the monthly rental places at the beach. As the boomers age and look toward retirement, places like this are going to become the happening thing. There are huge views of Santa Monica Bay from the top floor and it's right on the boardwalk. Just renovated in the summer of 1999, the main drawback is the lack of parking—always a problem in Venice. Starts at about $55 a night, with a one-month minimum.... *Tel 310/396-4559. 1305 Ocean Front Walk, Venice, 90291. 12 suites. $–$$* **(see p. 23)**

Villa Portofino. Marble baths and an award-winning Italian restaurant. It's a European-style resort, recently renovated, and if you get a room with a fireplace and an ocean view, your loved one will refuse you nothing.... *Tel 310/510-0555. 111 Crescent Ave., Avalon, Catalina Island, 90704. $$* **(see p. 24)**

West Hollywood Hyatt. Once this was where rock superslugs would throw childish fits and toss TVs out of windows. Ah, the good old days. Now it's just another Hyatt.... *Tel 323/656-1234. 8401 Sunset Blvd., West Hollywood, 90069. 262 rooms. $$* **(see p. 17)**

Westin Bonaventure Hotel & Suites. Built in 1976, this conventioneer's wet dream has aged well, especially following a 1994 renovation. The mirrored towers are as close to a landmark as you can find in the Financial District. Warrenlike but still manageable, it's fully self-contained....

Tel 213/624-1000 and 800/937-8461; fax 213/654-9287. 404 S. Figueroa St., Downtown, 90071. 1354 rooms. $$–$$$ **(see p. 17)**

Wyndham Checkers Hotel. This is civilized hotel life at its best. Quiet, very personal and private in tone, and right in the heart of the Financial District. If you need a dose of grandiose splendor, something over-the-top and awesome, the Biltmore is right across the street.... *Tel 213/624-0000 and 800/WYNDHAM. 535 S. Grand Ave., Downtown, 90071. 188 rooms. $$$* **(see p. 18)**

Hollywood Area Accomodations

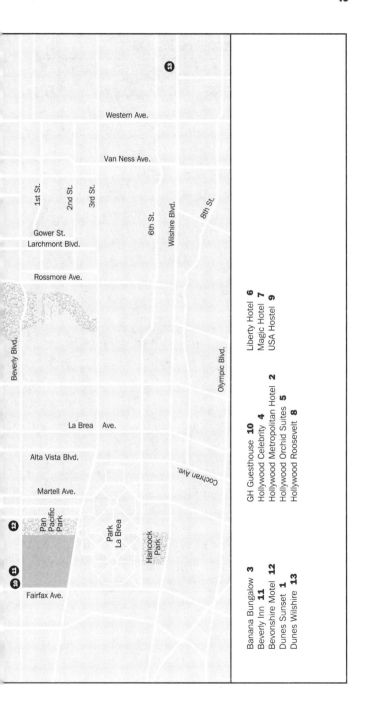

Western Ave.

Van Ness Ave.

1st St.

2nd St.

3rd St.

6th St.

Wilshire Blvd.

8th St.

Gower St.
Larchmont Blvd.

Rossmore Ave.

Beverly Blvd.

Olympic Blvd.

La Brea   Ave.

Alta Vista Blvd.

Martell Ave.

Cochran Ave.

Pan
Pacific
Park

Park
La Brea

Hancock
Park

Fairfax Ave.

Banana Bungalow **3**
Beverly Inn **11**
Bevonshire Motel **12**
Dunes Sunset **1**
Dunes Wilshire **13**

GH Guesthouse **10**
Hollywood Celebrity **4**
Hollywood Metropolitan Hotel **2**
Hollywood Orchid Suites **5**
Hollywood Roosevelt **8**

Liberty Hotel **6**
Magic Hotel **7**
USA Hostel **9**

Downtown Area Accommodations

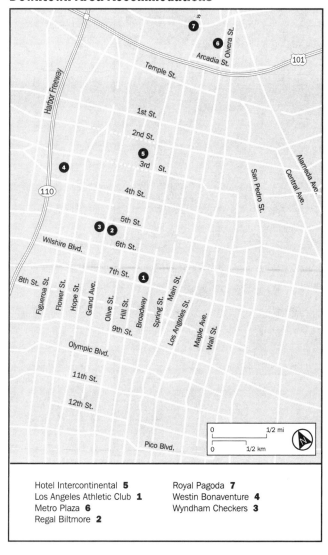

Hotel Intercontinental **5**
Los Angeles Athletic Club **1**
Metro Plaza **6**
Regal Biltmore **2**

Royal Pagoda **7**
Westin Bonaventure **4**
Wyndham Checkers **3**

ccommodations in
.A.'s Westside & Beverly Hills

Argyle **14**	Chateau Marmont **16**	Summit Bel Air **2**
Avalon **1**	Farmer's Daughter **11**	Summit Rodeo Drive **3**
Beverly Hills Hotel **5**	Lowell's **4**	Sunset Marquis **12**
Beverly Laurel **10**	Montrak **6**	West Hollywood Hyatt **15**
Beverly Plaza **9**	Sofitel Ma Maison **7**	
Carlyle **8**	Standard **13**	

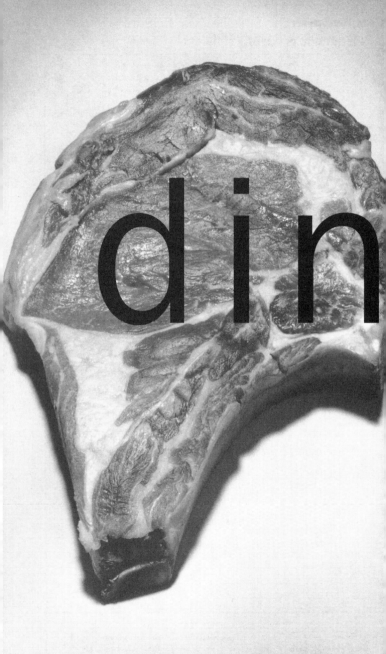

ing

2

Once upon a time,
the culinary
culture of Los
Angeles was
defined by the
city's dominant
midwestern

heritage. We're talking either basic meat-and-potatoes fare, or else bad imitations of what passed for good eating in New York or Chicago. Sure, there was always Mexican and Chinese food around, but ethnic cuisine was only acceptable if it was toned down—the spices reduced and the dishes emasculated to fit in with Angelenos' bland-is-best sensibilities. In fact, for far too long the most reliable meal in the City of the Angels was a burger, a side order of greasy fries, and a drink. And, hey, in some instances, it still is. When the clock strikes 4 a.m. and that last Jaegermeister is starting to bubble uncomfortably in your gut, a trip to **Tommy's** or **Jay's** may be just what the doctor ordered. Happily for those seeking more civilized dining, however, the city's movable feast is now so globally varied, so affordable, and so lacking in San Franciscan pretension that only the most recalcitrant anorexic will have any trouble finding satisfaction somewhere out there on the grid. (Indeed, there are eateries for the eating-disordered as well—just add implants, and you'll get a great table to go with your Pellegrino.)

In other words, thank God for L.A.'s immigrants, legal or otherwise. Thanks to the influx from our Pacific Rim neighbors, we can now tell the difference between *sopes* from Oaxaca and *pupusas* from El Salvador, *soba* and *udon*, Panang versus Mussamun curry.

So, where do you go nowadays when the munchies set in? Answer: Just about anywhere. As you might expect, the culinary cartography of L.A. parallels the metastasized character of our ethnic communities, with flare-ups of great food emerging in the least expected places: tucked away in anonymous strip malls and bracketed by a liquor store and a laundry, or hidden in bombed-out sections of the inner city, where a parked Lexus is like an open wallet lying on the sidewalk. It's no coincidence that the traditional DMZ between the East Side and the West Side, La Cienega Boulevard, is known as Restaurant Row. It used to be that the wealthy gourmands of Beverly Hills and West L.A. would head east for something a little out of the ordinary, a little un-Caucasoid and racy, and this was as far as they'd get. Conversely, when the po' folk of the East Side wanted to splurge and step up for the night, they'd head west, winding up in the same place.

Well, I'm here to tell you that all bets are now off. It seems we've grown up. It all started in the '70s when California Cuisine first hit the streets, drifting south from Alice Waters' Chez Panisse in Berkeley, daring us to put something fresh and foreign into our mouths. Once we capitulated, our taste buds were forever altered. Throw in the cacophony of herbs and spices brought to the city by the Pacific Rim immigrants, and you begin to get an idea of what's currently digesting in L.A.'s collective intestines. Who are our kitchen gods? For starters: Wolfgang Puck, Nobu Matsuhisa, Michel Richard, Joaquim Splichal, Tommy Tang, Nancy Silverton and Mark Peel, Toribio Prado, Mario Tomayo. Good food L.A.-style has gone so mainstream that soon you'll be able get it at Disneyland. The California Adventure, a new Anaheim theme park to be unveiled by Disney in 2001, will include the La Brea Bakery Cafe, complete with its own Craftsman-style building. In the meantime, come on Downtown—or head over to East L.A. or West L.A., Silver Lake or Santa Monica. Your destination depends only on the tickling of your tongue and the amount of gas in your tank (this is L.A., after all).

But remember, according to San Francisco's Union of Concerned Scientists, a drive-through hamburger meal is about the worst environmental action that you can do. Combining industrial meat production with idling gas guzzlers is a killer cocktail for the environment. So turn off the engine, get out of the car, and graze.

How to dress

It's pretty obvious that Angelenos lack the metropolitan flash of New Yorkers or most Europeans. Anything that covers (or exposes) the skin is considered acceptable couture out here. Just wear shoes, that's all we ask.

Still, for you neurotic slaves of fashion, there are some general rules: If you're in the mood to dress up, go to Indochine or Crustacean—people will notice the Gucci and pearls. Understated hipsters on the rise wear khakis, a Hanes T-shirt, and a $1,200 Armani coat when having martinis with the leering producer wearing Hugo Boss—strictly Musso & Frank's. At the Skybar, Fenix, or Fred 62, the dress code is vintage, Bim Sherman, or Prada—though as long as you've got a pair of *really* great shoes, you can get away with anything. For those who haven't changed their underwear recently, you can feel right at home at snack'n'shacks like Jay's Jayburgers. Got a pole up your ass? Try the Ivy.

Getting the Right Table

There's really only one way to be assured of having the best seat in the house, and that's by being famous, notorious, or scandalously rich...or preferably all three. It's fairly obvious

INTRODUCTION | DINING

where the power seats are—they're the ones with the great view. At Crustacean, prime seating is in the banquettes on the raised section at the back. At Cafe Rodeo, the place to be is out on the sidewalk section but in the corner, so you can see without being seen; at Yamashiro you want to be out on the open patio. On the other hand, at Millie's you want to be *inside,* away from the people waiting for tables and the car exhaust on Sunset.

The Lowdown

East Side essentials... There are a handful of places so intrinsically L.A. in their food, delivery, and ambience that corporate cloning is virtually impossible. You want this sort of food, you gotta come here. At the top of the pantheon is **Yuca's Hut**, a humble little shack-stand across from the Lucky's supermarket on Hillhurst Avenue in Los Feliz. There is really nothing else like Yuca's anywhere. Family-run and only open for lunch, they serve the best burritos in the world, with just the right balance of soupy ranchero beans, cilantro, and meat. *Habanero* salsas are on the tables if you need some extra heat. I had a friend in New York who wanted me to air-mail frozen Yuca burritos to him every week, but it simply wouldn't have been the same. Part of their flavor comes from sitting at the tables in the parking lot, gazing at the Griffith Park Planetarium in the hills above, and sipping on your lemonade as you scan *Daily Variety* for jobs. More or less in the same neighborhood is **Cha Cha Cha**, a funky little slice of the Caribbean that appeared here long before Silver Lake was hip 'n' happening, courtesy of chef Toribio Prado. The TV-studio people like to swing by after work, members of my mountain bike team drop in for carbo loads, and gay district attorneys drive over from Downtown on their lunch breaks. The black beans and rice for breakfast are absolutely essential—that, and the soft-shell crabs. They also offer good champagne by the glass or by the bottle. After that, you're on your own—you simply can't go wrong. If you like slightly greasy but way affordable tropicalismo food, you'll be satisfied. Heading east on Sunset you'll find **Millie's**, an oracle of Silver Lake cool. This was originally just a breakfast diner, started by local scene-maker and musician Paul Greenstein, but it has since fed successive waves of punks, post-punks, swingers, and hoards of Gen-Y musicians searching for that elusive big-label deal. It's on everyone's map now, so you'll probably have to wait for breakfast on the weekends, but during the week seating is still easy to get. The food is heavy without being *too* greasy, and the place boasts an amazing jukebox. The clientele is bizarre and nearly as greasy (and tasty) as the food. Someday this place will be named a historic site for its contribution to the arterial hardening of the local music scene.

L.A. icons: safe for eating... Also way up there on the high-colonic list is **Philippe's**, located in Downtown near Union Station. It's supposedly the home of the French Dip sandwich, and while the meat ain't what it used to be (who among us is?), the place is an official historical landmark, with a plaque out front to prove it. The restaurant was established in 1908, and for years this was where the circus folk would hang out. There's still sawdust on the floors, and the long wooden tables and short stools have propped up many a butt grown hefty on the cheap meat dips. It's a deal: The beef is a mere $3.85, the lamb just 30 cents more. If you really want a gooey soggy mess, have your entree double-dipped. For those of you who like to court cardiac arrest before lunch, come by for breakfast. This is just a step above cafeteria food: The coffee is Yuban at nine cents a cup. They also have a decent wine-by-the-glass list. The wine prices aren't great, but who cares? At least it doesn't come out of a box. Then up in Hollywood there's **Musso & Frank Grill**. People come here for the martinis—that, and because it's something you supposedly *have* to do in L.A., especially if you're an aspiring screenwriter. You'd better come in knowing exactly what you want, though, because everything here is à la carte and the menu is encyclopedic. Legendary items include flannel pancakes, anchovy-drenched Caesar salad, crusty bread, and tongue sandwiches. Eat at Manny's counter and you'll hear all the latest Bill and Hillary jokes along with odds on the next big game. He'll also crack your baked potato for you and kiss your date's hand. People rave about the chicken pot pies, but frankly I found the same effect can be achieved by dumping a can of mushroom soup into a cardboard container. Antique food, a friend calls it—and she *loves* the place. Like all of the aforementioned eateries, the **Apple Pan** is part of every Angeleno's formative years. This little West L.A.

diner feels like it hasn't changed since the '50s, which is why it's such a comfortable fit for successive generations of dating couples in the mood for a late-night snack. It's an institution, for sure, but if the apple pie and burgers weren't still happening, this place would have turned into a Starbucks long ago. And please—don't linger over your meal. Others are waiting.

L.A. icons: for drinking only (no eating)... Okay. First there's **El Coyote**, which is an *icon*, God knows why. It used to be that there were only two reasons to come here: Because your parents dragged you in, in a hopeless attempt to destroy whatever affinity you had for Mexican food, or because you wanted to get really drunk really quickly, while nibbling ratlike on tortilla chips. There is nothing truly edible on the menu (the tostadas come with canned beets and peas on top), but the margaritas do the job nicely as long as you *don't* order them by the pitcher. I implore you: *Eat nothing but the chips and salsa*.... When the Health Department briefly closed the **Original Pantry Cafe** in 1998 for the first time in its 75-year existence, enemies (and even some friends) of millionaire owner/L.A. Mayor Richard Riordan just had to laugh. The menu features cheap, fat-loaded food for late-night revelers who can't taste anything anyway, and the graveyard-shift workers who feel like they're dead already. Do your stomach a favor: *Don't touch the food*. Stop by, have a cup of coffee, then tell your friends you've been here so you can prove that you ARE an Angeleno, okay? Really, how much can you trust a restaurant that never shuts its doors? **Canter's** is another one of L.A.'s legendary after-hours eateries, immortalized in film and song. The best things about Canter's are the incredibly cranky waitresses and the 7/24 hours. Plus, they don't mind the occasional food fight. After a certain time of night the management expects all the customers to come in drunk, and will treat you accordingly. The bakery is only so-so, the lights are too harsh, and the food is never as good as the posse of drunk teenagers at the table next to you thinks it is. But like I say, they're open later than you are. Up overlooking Hollywood is the terribly overpriced **Yamashiro**. Want to get your date in the mood without resorting to a date-rape cocktail? Yamashiro has one of the most amazing views in town. The drinks stink and the food is worse, but the vista from the front tables is truly outstanding. Come here at least once. You might even get a chuckle out of the fake *daimyo* castle setting, like something out of Disneyland. Thankfully, the place is only open for dinner.

Back from the dead... For longer than I can remember, the over-the-top decor of the **Formosa Café** was its primary draw. The walls are covered with zillions of 8x10 glossies of celebrities, living and dead. If you've seen them in a movie on TMC or AMC, you'll probably see them here. This old Hollywood glamour, combined with almost sadistically strong kick-ass drinks, has long brought in studio-production drones from all over working Hollywood. But the food used to be, in a word, inedible. I never could understand how anyone could screw up Chinese food so badly. The Formosa was nearly demolished a few years ago, only to be saved at the last minute when legions of alcoholics-in-training rose up in protest. Well, shut my mouth and fill my plate—things have changed at the Formosa. Now there's a new cook dishing out things like seared ahi tuna and—is it possible?—sauces that are actually understated. The pictures are all still there and the drinks will still knock you on your butt before the entree arrives, but at least you can now order something for dinner without leaving most of it on the table.

Late-night grilled meats... Forget Mickey D's, Burger King, or even Jack-in-the-Box. The preference of the current generation of fast-food meat eaters is **In-N-Out Burger**, probably because they also serve vegan garden burgers for the more karmically aware. The franchise outlets are also not easy to find, which adds to the appeal since they're not on every corner. Of course, nobody's fries match up to McDonald's, but these burgers are about the best you could ask for from a drive-through. Meanwhile, **Jay's Jayburgers** on Santa Monica Boulevard is what a burger in L.A. is all about. The food is better than Tommy's, but definitely of the same genre. The place is open all night on weekends, but anytime is a good time for a Jayburger: Hold the chili and order an egg on top, along with a Pepsi, no Coke, and chips, no fries. They're not even a mini chain. If you want a Jayburger you'll have to come clear over to East Hollywood. Bonus point: It's located at the fringes of Silver Lake, across the street from The Garage and just down the street from Akbar's, the Good Luck Bar, and the Dresden Room. You know exactly what you're in for when you walk into a place called **Fatburger,** so don't complain later. You're gonna get a burger, and you're gonna get fat. What you probably *didn't* know is that the various Fatburger outlets around town have great jukeboxes—the only recompense for working around all those simmering lipids. The burgers are freshly fried, the onion rings salty and greasy, and when you walk out of here you'll definitely know you've encountered a primal force that's stronger than you are. Don't fight it. Saving the most famous for last: There are 20 different **Tommy's Original World Famous** burger outlets throughout L.A., as well as a whole posse of Tommy's imitators. But don't be fooled: The original stand is the place to come when it's late and you're feeling a desperate need for a meat anchor. Established in 1946 at the corner of Rampart and Beverly boulevards, Tommy's is known for its incredibly goopy chili hamburgers. They're actually not the best in the city, but try telling that to the 50 million desperate Angelenos who have stumbled in here over the years. It takes about 15 seconds to place your order and pay. Digesting takes somewhat longer. This is also the best place in the city to experience the sensation of heartburn while watching a drive-by shooting....

In the you-may-already-be-a-weiner category...

The name is **Pink's**, and its specialty is frankfurters. That should tell you more than you want to know. Consider for a minute: Who would want a "Pink" hot dog? You have to be either seriously immature, seriously drunk, or both to think of these disgusting little mystery-meat extrusions as "food." If you absolutely have to have one, go for spicy, no chili, and wash it down with something non-carbonated. You *don't* want to be burping this up again anytime soon. Need some more convincing? Check out the losers standing in line behind you. Right in the neighborhood, more or less, is the world-famous West Hollywood landmark known as **Tail O' The Pup**. Now *this* is truth in structural advertising. You've probably seen it in photos, but nothing compares to actually standing next to this L.A. icon: a hot-dog stand shaped like (what else?) a hot dog in a bun. Marvel for a moment at the glory of Los Angeles architecture's Golden Era, and then try keeping down one of their tasty delicacies. Come in the daytime so you can have your picture taken here. And don't worry if your stomach starts rumbling like a mariachi band—Cedars Sinai Hospital is right up the street.

Quivering flesh... There's really nothing like eating with your fingers and playing with your food while buxom women swirl around you jiggling their breasts. It's just like being a baby all over again, which is why people love coming to **Dar Maghreb**. It's not anywhere near as nasty as what you might see in Cairo, more like a PG-17 version of belly dancing. That's okay, though: The food's probably safer here, so that should be worth something. The fare—lemony chicken, fresh pita, grilled meats and veggies—is adequate but not great. But the overall effect, with belly dancers, music, and unrepentant revelers, makes this one of the best party-time dining experiences in Hollywood. You can get the Tunisian version of this experience at **Moun of Tunis** (which always sounds to me like Mound of Pubis, but that's an altogether different spicy eatery). It's basically another North African titillation that you can eat with your hands and come away satisfied, fingers sticky with garlic and lemon, and probably drunker than you intended. I'll also never understand how women with such un-typically L.A. body types can be so seductive and alluring. Paradoxically, this is the perfect place for a girls' night out—since there is nothing as liberating as watching women who weigh far more than you, yet are totally comfortable with their bodies and supremely confident in their appeal.

Places to dine while you watch Malibu burn...
Next to an ocean far, far away, the **Reel Inn** roadside fish shack was once a wonderful slice of Malibu life. Funky, weathered, and frequented by surfers, families, and locals, the fish helpings were big and fresh even though the service was always a little slow. (After sitting in the sun all day, you'd be feeling pretty slow yourself....) But then the prices went up and the serving sizes went down, as did the taste, and the waits grew even longer. Finally, the restaurant opened up a branch on the Turd Street Promenade in Santa Monica—a sure sign of spiritual decay. Now the food at the Malibu establishment is really just a step above a fish fillet at McDonald's, while the one on the Promenade is even worse. If you really don't want to fight the traffic back into town, then stop in and have a beer. But the traffic has to be *really* bad. The Reel Inn was a

DINING | THE LOWDOWN

contender, once upon a time. Too bad. A much better choice is **Neptune's Net**, one of the few places left on this stretch of Pacific Coast Highway that retains the old Malibu feeling, attracting the full range of beach-goers: sunburned kids, surfers, bikers. Although it's a little pricey considering the ambience, it has the freshest steamed fish you're likely to find in the city. Try to snare a table inside—yellow jackets swarm near the trash cans outside in the summertime—and peel the hot shrimp with your fingers. Or just pop 'em in whole. This isn't gracious dining, unless you equate paper napkins with elegance. Up in the wilds of Topanga you'll find the **Saddle Peak Lodge**. This is about as close as you'd want to get to the Super Scooper water drops trying to put out the fires with the Pacific Ocean, thank you. Like an old bear in the woods, the Saddle Peak Lodge must be approached with respect. It is *not* for vegans. The motto here is, as long as it can move and be killed, it can be eaten. The place is just a little bit more than a Frontierland restaurant in Hemingway drag, but not by much. A nice brace of quail, stuffed with onion and sage, roasted in a bacon wrapping, is only $26. And you didn't even have to shoot it! Dead animals on the walls, good wine, park your car in position for a quick getaway in case the fire gets too close over coffee. The best things about **Gladstone's 4 Fish** are the location, and the fact that you can park here. Perched right on the water with spectacular views of the Malibu coast, this is the place you'll want to bring your New York visitors to reduce them to teeth-gnashing envy. *They'll* never know that you never come here otherwise. The food is just barely okay, the prices too high for what you get.

The well-traveled nut... A few miles south down Pacific Coast Highway you'll find **Chez Jay**, which has had the same owner for the last 40 years. Lee Marvin hung out here in his hard-drinking days, and king of the world *Titanic* director James Cameron has also been known to stop in, but this is no star-watching bar. It's basically a neighborhood hangout, featuring steaks and fish. The most interesting edible in the place is the framed peanut on the wall—the peanut that went to the moon and back, carried by astronaut Gus Grissom. Jay gives out peanuts at the bar, so Gus decided to take one along as a souvenir of his lunar excursion. Located directly across from Hotel California in Santa Monica.

Tongue-Thai-ed top list... L.A. is rich with Thai restaurants. They are cheap, ubiquitous, and 90 percent reliable. In fact, they're so common now that you can ask just about anyone to name at least three favorite places and they'll almost never be the same three names. But certainly any Top Ten List of Thai L.A. has to include **Tommy Tang's**, one of the first nouvelleish-Thai eateries to hit the city when it opened more than 20 years ago. Besides being the author of one of the best Thai cookbooks in print—a slim volume that has no bad recipes—Tommy Tang keyed in on a California sensibility that blended traditional herbs, spices, and curries with an appreciation for something a bit lighter, food that was rich without being greasy. This is haute Thai cooking, a clear step above the good-but-not-great Thai fare you'll find just about everywhere. Always a favorite with the Hollywood crowd, Tommy Tang's has never sunk into trendoid self-parody. The food has continued to be honest, sinfully flavorful, and delivered with a sense of humor that's as fragrant as the sweetened iced tea. Come on Tuesday nights for the waiters-in-drag show. Over in Pasadena, **Saladang** is considered by many to be the most Bangkok-reminiscent eatery in town. The space feels like an artist's loft, and the food arrives elegantly styled, but don't let the glossy veneer distract you—this is one Thai restaurant that immediately exceeds jaded expectations. Begin your meal with the Gold Pouch dumpling appetizers and finish it with the wonderful dessert of sweet sticky rice topped with mango. In between, you're on your own. Hint: There are no bad choices. In Silver Lake you'll find **Sompun**, one of the first Thai restaurants to cross Vermont Avenue back in the '70s. Sompun has built a steady and loyal following in the neighborhood. It offers home-style Thai cooking that arrives at the table sweet but never overspiced. Just about everything on the menu is wonderful. The ambience has the feeling of being in someone's home on the outskirts of Bangkok: The tablecloths are white linen, and portraits of the King and Queen hang on the walls. In the summer they have tables outside in the backyard—the best place to sit, as long as the mosquitoes aren't biting. Try ordering the *prik king* and at least one of the appetizers. The beef satay is *outstanding*.

Chan Dara isn't the best Thai restaurant in town at 6 p.m., but at 2 a.m. there's no contest. The place is open way late and is located in close proximity to the Hollywood clubs and recording studios, so it gets a lot of musicians. Maybe that's why it's always so loud here—everyone's a little deaf. **Chao Praya,** in the heart of the music-studio district in Hollywood, is great for late-night après-concert Thai food; the barbecued chicken is a winner.

Living treasures of Little Tokyo... If your idea of Japanese food is limited to tempura and sushi, then a major taste treat awaits you Downtown. While there are other important Japanese communities scattered around L.A., the dominant center for Japanese business, tourists, and culture is at the heart of the city in Little Tokyo. You probably won't be able to find raw horse or whale meat wieners like you would in Tokyo, but just about every-thing else is on the table. Just do me one favor—please, *never* put straight soy sauce on your white rice. In Japan this is simply not done. It's like, I don't know, curry fill-ing in a doughnut (which you can find at Ginza-Ya Bakery [see Shopping], by the way). The amusing Japanese take on curry has been perfected at **Curry House**, a local mini chain that delivers up sauces that are slightly sweet rather than spicy, and are served on pasta as well as on rice. The outlet in Weller Court is a major lunch favorite for *L.A. Times* and city workers. The chicken curry is probably most palatable to the average American's tongue, but me, I like the "Wiener & Spinach-wieners, sautéed spinach and eggs with curry sauce." Yummmm! The most expensive curry entree is the shrimp, at just over $8. Just down the street is **Kokekokko**. If you like yakitori, this is a place you should check out. Yakitori is a style of grilled meat and veggies that are prepared on bamboo skewers, two at a time, like sushi pieces. They cost about the same and are just about as filling. Orders are placed in much the same way, too, by selecting items à la carte as the mood strikes you. The place has a strong charcoal-meat-grill odor, and one whole wall is lined with sake bottles. Yakitori is one type of nomimono, or "drinking food," and a healthy thirst for beer or sake is expected. Here you can get grilled quail eggs, thigh meat, skin, gizzard. The most expensive item? Wings. Best bet is to order the 10-item sampler, $23 per person. For a feeling of what Little Tokyo was like before the Community Redevelopment Agency and the importation of strong-yen money from Tokyo altered the neighborhood in the '70s, check out **Aoi**, on the "preserved" north side of 1st Street. (Some of my friends call it AO-1, but the name is actually the Japanese word for blue.) This is one of the few remaining original storefront restaurants of the kind that used to be everywhere in Little Tokyo—the sort of place that Angelenos take for granted, but shouldn't. It offers completely basic but affordable Japanese working-class restaurant food, and is known for its fast lunches, served quickly and always worth more than you pay. The fare isn't gourmet, but it is very honest. Get one of the rice bowl dishes like katsudon (fried pork on rice, in broth) or the tempura. Just when you thought there was nothing new in Little Tokyo, a few years back, along came **Tot**, short for **Teishoku-Of-Tokyo**. Teishoku means "a regular meal" in Japanese, but the food here ranks far above regular. It's not haute cuisine or some hyphenated blend, but rather everyday restaurant food (noodles to teriyaki to curry to tempura) prepared with a fresh eye and an off-kilter approach. The place is a huge hit with young Tokyo tourists and the downtown artist crowd. Expect to wait for a table at lunchtime. Across the street is **Kagetsu An**, which specializes in noodle dishes, mainly soba and udon. Out of the 30 different noodle dishes on the menu, I like the homemade soba the best. Best of all, it's open late at night—until 3 a.m., Monday through Saturday. The noodles are a little pricey, considering they're just noodles, but if you've ever seen *Tampopo* you know the spiritual talent that goes into making a great broth. Another culinary oddity with a Nipponese bent is the **Mitsuru Cafe** in the Tokyo Village Plaza. It features a variety of snack foods, but the star of the show can be seen right in the front window: little, sweet red-bean pancakes called *imagawaki*, that are cooked up on an old prewar iron griddle. This is typical Japanese festival food, the sort of thing you buy to eat while you stroll. Down on 1st Street in Little Tokyo you'll find **Takoyaki Gen**, a small storefront restaurant that specializes in *okonomiyaki*—basically a griddle-cooked pancake stuffed with fish and veggies and topped with a sweet-yet-tart Worcestershire-like sauce (and often mayonnaise, too). This is popular date food in Japan, where diners usually cook the pancakes at their own individual grills. This way the girl gets to play wife while the boy sits back and smokes approvingly. Here they don't trust you to know what you're doing, so the chef cooks the food on a grill in front of you, instead. For the best view of your meal's preparations, try to get a seat at the grill bar.

Eat it raw... When people picture Japanese food they almost automatically think of sushi—as in raw fish, wasabi, and the struggle to attract the attention of the *sushiya-san* (sushi cutter), like a kid in the third grade trying to catch the teacher's eye. And I agree: Sushi is a unique food, in that it's always better in a restaurant. In fact, you'll never ever be able to make it at home without extensive training and a full-time dedication to browsing in fish markets. That's why I recommend starting at **R-23** on 3rd Street. Can't take the cell phones and boob jobs at Beverly Hills' Matsuhisa? Then head for this downtown artist's alley-side sushi secret. It's easy walking distance from Little Tokyo and the downtown fish and produce markets, so you *know* the food is fresh. The decor is properly minimalist, like one of local artist Carol Kaufman's drawings, layers hidden within monochrome overlays, but the real art here is the kind you can eat. As proof, one of the *sushiya-sans* came from **Shin** in Silver Lake, one of the top five sushi places in the city. Speaking of Katsu, I wish it had retained its former glory as one of the East Side's great unknown and nearly affordable sushi bars. Today it's neither cheap nor unknown. The sushi is still outstanding, though I always feel that I'm paying just a shade too much for it, and that the slabs of fish are a little too big, and that my clothes are somehow just not trendy enough for the waiters. But, like I said, the sushi is still super-fresh and so elegantly presented it's hard to bitch. This is a major hang for slumming Westsiders, TV expense-account drones from ABC just down the street, and Silver Lake bohos with a trust fund. If you really want to drop a bundle for sushi, you can't go wrong at **Matsuhisa**, the flagship restaurant of chef Nobu Matsuhisa. It's in Beverly Hills, so the clientele is about what you'd expect. Absolutely nothing, however, will prepare you for what Nobu's kitchen does with fish, raw or cooked. The cuisine is Peruvian-Japanese, but that really doesn't describe it well. Think of miso-broiled entrees, the intensity of sea urchin innards, the spiky tang of shiso leaf—and then throw in a Latin American influence, and you'll have a sense of the truly bizarre, Continental–Third World–Pacific Rim taste treat that awaits you. Proceed with caution, though—it could cost more than your hotel room.

Forget it, Jake—it's Chinatown... Compared with the Chinatowns of San Francisco or New York, our Chinatown is actually a confused mix of Chinese, Taiwanese, Vietnamese, Laotians, and Cambodians. Most of the second-, third-, and fourth-generation Chinese have long since fled the area for Alhambra and Huntington Park, but they still come back here for essential shopping and special meals. One longtime local favorite is **ABC Seafood**, where both the sweet-and-sour fish and the salt-baked shrimp get major raves. (They've also got a very impressive dim sum menu to go.) The interior is cheesy elegance: heavy glass chandeliers, pink tablecloths, and fake gold everywhere—all ensconced in a windowless, featureless bunker on a Chinatown side street. Waiters hover attentively while your still-living dinner floats numbly in a wall of aquariums by the front door. At the other end of Chinatown is **Pho 87**, situated on Broadway right before it segues into industrial wasteland. This little Vietnamese restaurant is one of the best deals in town, with nothing over $6 on the entire 110-item menu. The house specialty is rice noodles, and their best variation is Pho Dac Biet 87—the special rice noodles with beef combination. Also look for the pork chop rice plate as well as the wonderfully fresh Vietnamese take on spring rolls. To wash it all down, try the red puréed mung bean paste with tapioca and coconut milk (it's much tastier than it sounds). The decor is strictly utilitarian: colored plastic chairs, plastic-covered tables, a dried-up fountain in the front...but on any given weekday morning it's full of Asian men, many just off the graveyard shift, sharing noodle soup and a beer.

Public offices... I don't know if it's the forgiving climate or the incessant desire of Angelenos to perform in public, but all over L.A. it's now considered totally acceptable to be pecking away on a laptop and jabbering on your cell phone while your latte curdles and losers still waiting for a table glare at you. It's part of the power game, dude— deal with it.... Like at the Farmer's Market haven **Kokomo Cafe**, where every screenwriter in town eventually sets up an office. Under new owner Alfredo Diaz (late of the has-been hangout Red) the place is scheduled to be remodeled, in order to make more use of its "backyard" patio space. The food is hearty, modeled on New Orleans cuisine, and while you slop butter on your johnnycakes you can also study closed-captioned reports from ESPN and CNN on the TV screens. Local celebs can still come in sweats and baseball caps without being harassed. It's ideal for taking breakfast story meetings and working out your screenplay pitches. Getting a table can be hard sometimes, but for a power-breakfast location this can't be beat. Warning: The place is a zoo on weekends. Another hot spot for those with a private agenda and a treatment in turnaround is **King's Road Cafe,** where the coffee is mind-bendingly strong, perfect for that extra little bounce right before you pop into a pitch meeting at the CBS offices, just down the street. If the place always seems crowded, that's because of all of the wannabe screenwriters taking up a full table apiece with their laptops, cell phones, and Palm Pilots. The poached eggs are dreamy here. The WeHo version of the pseudo-home office is **Hugo's**, done up in a vaguely retro coffee-shop decor, but with food that's nowhere near as good as Kokomo's (though the juice factor here is much higher). It draws a largely gay crowd, and the windows look out on Santa Monica Boulevard, so you can combine eating with some casual cruising for someone more attractive (or powerful) than your current date. Some people swear by the Pasta Mama blend (pasta and scrambled eggs) but to me it's a little too much this early in the morning, thank you. Order something basic, instead, and start plotting your studio takeove.

Planet Vegan... There's a mini chain of Astro Burgers around L.A., but a drive-through on Melrose, now simply called **Astro,** has reinvented itself as a major vegetarian mecca. It's on the corner of Gower and Melrose by the Paramount lot. Frequented by punk rockers, Mexican day laborers, and Paramount vegans tired of commissary BLTs ("hold the B!"), Astro's menu features garden burgers (no soy, no additives), garden dogs with vegetarian chili, veggie pizzas, even veggie sausages. And you carnivores can relax: There is still plenty of edible flesh to be had, including a Greek corner replete with an "Athenian Astroburger." Astro's claim that it was the first restaurant in California to serve a garden burger hardly matters:

This is one place you can come and stuff yourself with veggie junk food while maintaining the illusion of health. Then up in Hollywood is **Paru's,** a little hidden oasis of excellent Indian vegetarian food overshadowed by the adjacent Kaiser high-rises and the dreaded glaze of acolytes from the Scientology complex just down the street. But don't be dismayed—this is a family-run restaurant, now in the second generation, and the kind of place where they'll remember your name after just one visit. The only meat that sets foot in this restaurant comes in walking on two legs. Vegan dishes are also easily available. The best deals are any of the combo plates, where you get a sample of everything. And as long as that mango chutney keeps coming, so will I. For something totally different, check out the vegetarian pie at the Brazilian eatery **Ipanema.** It's a concoction of hearts of palm, peas, corn, and onions in a tomato sauce. Another noncarnivore favorite on this mainly meat menu is the veggie plate, with black beans, rice, grilled veggies, fried plantains, and a savory Brazilian sauce. Because the Punjab region of India is largely agricultural, and the main chef at **India's Oven** is Punjabi, you can bet that the vegetarian meals here will be good. The interior is done up a little like a Persian disco, with mirrors all over one wall and cozy little leather booths. The best veggie meal is #18, with dal, cauliflower/potato curry, and *saag paneer* (spinach curry with homemade cheese). You can eat an entire meal here for under 10 bucks, and you probably won't be able to finish it all. Bring along your meat-loving buddies, too—all of the tandoori meats are incredible. Highly recommended.

Organic orgasms... Can't stand the thought of all those nasty pesticides ruining your grilled veggies? In that case, consider **Puran's,** on La Brea. It uses only organically grown produce, and the poultry is skinless and hormone-free. The Mediterranean fish specials are another big draw. Puran's has a steady stream of regulars, mostly neighbors, as well as the occasional famous face. The night before I dined there, both Billy Zane and Grace Jones had been in. The place has a French bistro feel, with one wall totally mirrored—so all you Zane and Jones wannabes can confirm your ongoing fabulousness. A longtime organic grocery store, **Erewhon** has a very nice deli with tables out on Beverly where you can sit and inhale exhaust while you purify your colon. It offers the typical roasted veggies, but the sandwich board also includes veggie cutlets, chicken pepperoni polenta pizza, and Ranchero tofu salad. The clientele? Hipsters in cowboy boots, career women gabbing on cell phones, and gay guys in Adidas pants and slides—your typical organic crew. The fellow who brought me my sandwich had waist-long dreadlocks, dyed an unretiring shade of blue—your typical L.A. grocery-store clerk. Parking's a bitch, but on Sundays you can sneak into the Post Office parking lot next door.

Breakfast with bohos... The much-touted **Millie's** is often credited (accurately) with turning breakfast into a power meal for the goateed hoards who have nothing else to do all day. Accordingly, there have been Millie's spinoffs and imitators throughout the Los Feliz–Silver Lake–Echo Park axis. Just west on Sunset from the original is **Cafe Glaxa,** next door to Silver Lake's Glaxa Studios, a long-established performance space. (I saw a guy nail his scrotum to a cedar plank here once—but that's not necessarily a breakfast story.) Magenta, the chef from Millie's, is now here dishing out breakfasts and mainly vegetarian dinners, soups, and salads. The breakfasts are what made Millie's and Magenta into the twin culinary stars of Silver Lake, so that's probably your best choice. It's way less of a scene here than at Millie's, but the kitchen still has Devil's Mess eggs—plus, you may not have to wait for a table. Around the corner from Trader Joe's and the Gayfair is the **Coffee Table,** a place where you can come any time and get a seat, inside or out. (They have a wonderful new patio in the back.) Dogs are welcome as long as they're well behaved. This is a civilized spot for people who enjoy late-morning breakfasts. Go for the good pastries, great fresh fruit plate, and sausage-egg-croissant that is just too rich and wonderful to eat more than once a week. Plus, *big* cups of coffee and zero attitude. Almost to the West Side is **Campanile**, my choice for the best and most consistently tasty California-Mediterranean food in the city. It doesn't hurt that co-owner Nancy Silverton's La Brea Bakery is right next door. The restaurant's clientele range from older wealthy couples to JAPS dressed up in their moms' jewels for a night on the town to just about anybody who loves good food, in a relaxed and architecturally pleasing setting, including the best bread this side of Paris. The

Monday-night family-style dinners are the most fun. Reportedly, Nancy and hubby Mark Peel (the restaurant's head chef) are going to be expanding their place by adding an imported cheese and wine section. Just one more reason to wedge my '63 Beetle in between the SUVs out on La Brea.

Breakfasts with boho wannabees... It's almost a contradiction to imagine bohos on the West Side, since by definition bohemians traditionally live in low-rent neighborhoods and their 30-year-old Ramblers don't always start so they have to walk to their local coffee shop—oh, never mind. Let's pretend: First off, just around the corner from the Beverly Laurel is **Swingers,** and, according to the grunge waiter, "all the movie stars and rock stars come here at *some* point." He didn't seem too thrilled by it. The place is cool-funky, with red mosaic-tiled countertops, lithographed wallpaper, and sparse plaid booths. At 2 p.m. the booths are packed with multi-pierced "bohos" looking bleary-eyed as they try to figure what to have for breakfast. How about some more nicotine? The food is a lighter version of Millie's: très eggy omelets, French toast, and pancakes. If you want something a little more unusual, try the jerk chicken caesar salad. Major Bonus Points for having the most graphically enjoyable menu in town. Over in Santa Monica you'll find **Blueberry,** where you can get eggs every which way, as well as meatless alternatives like tofu scramble. The real stars of the table, however, are the Blueberry's Stacks, which can be either griddle cakes, malted waffles, French toast, or multi-grain pancakes. Equally essential is the Cold Blue Special: blueberry pancakes topped with blueberry ice cream topped with homemade blueberry sauce. Yikes! It's crowded and noisy, and you'll probably have to wait for a table on the weekends. And unfortunately, it's connected to the way trendy Rix. Then for the MTV Generation there's **Networks Cafe,** situated just below the local MTV studios, in Santa Monica. It's open to the public as well as the music channel's employees for breakfast, lunch, afternoon snacks, and general hanging out. The food is good and cheap, the employees refreshingly young and funky, and the dining room is big, friendly, and clean. There's even a large outdoor patio for the midday soaking-up of rays. Medium-loud rock music plays overhead, and the M & Ms, Oreo cookie crumbles, and gummy bear condiments left out to sprinkle over your nonfat yogurt give this spot a great post-college feel—tailor-made for those lucky 20-somethings who have legit jobs where slept-in hair looks cool.

An army shops on its stomach... So you've just dropped a wad on clothes that you'll only fit into *after* your diet? Great—then it's off for a snack. It's only natural that the restaurants around shopping areas like Third Street Promenade, Beverly, La Brea, and Melrose would reflect their retail neighbors. Yes, there's a Johnny Rocket's on Melrose and a Planet Hollywood at the Beverly Center. In L.A., you are what you eat—and what you eat is just another shopping decision. In the heart of Beverly Boulevard's surging retail section you have the **Authentic Café,** where the chicken comes in a tortilla crust and the grilled veggies (for you vegans) are cooked over a wood fire to give them a delightfully smoky flavor. The fried green tomatoes are delectable, but avoid the jerk chicken and the tamales. You can sit out on the sidewalk with all the other shoppers, actors-waiting-for-a-callback, and CBS drones, and watch harried housewives fighting over parking spaces so that they can be closer to Erewhon across the street. Starfucker Alert: Both Babyface and Cuba Gooding, Jr., have been spotted here. On Melrose Avenue you can't do better than **Lala's Argentine Grill** for something well removed from the insanity down by Skeetchers. Enjoy an Argentine empanada worthy of a much fancier place. Also on Melrose you'll find **Mario's Peruvian Seafood,** which some people say has the best ceviche in the city. The egg-and-potato salad (*huancaina* for you Incans) is Peruvian comfort food, but the fish is why you come. I especially like the squid salad. Sure, it's in a faceless little mini mall, but this is the kind of place that locals love and frequent. Down on Third Street, around Zipper and OK, look for **Joan's On Third**. The owner is a caterer with a major jones for high-quality Italian deli meats and antipastos. She goes to Italy four times a year to restock—and the food shows it. The decor consists of exposed air ducts (which gives it a vaguely retro-Industrial feel), and the food comes on paper plates. But that's just fine, considering that the pesto-crusted salmon is only $8 for a big, fat slab. That, along with the three-salad mix, should hold you until you get home to unload the car. Joan still caters as well, and offers special picnic baskets for Hollywood Bowl outings.

Sex food... Have I got your attention? Good. I've never quite understood the theory of raw oysters as raw-sex aphrodisiac. Maybe it's the texture, or the genitalia references an oyster evokes, or maybe it's the salty taste of the ocean. Hey, whatever floats your boat. The raw bar of choice downtown is the **Water Grill,** probably the best place for a huge variety of pollution-free shellfish, harvested in waters from Washington to Maine. The decor is upscale Financial District, so expect to pay a premium. If the interior of a place is less important to you than the taste of its food, check out **Ostioneria Colima,** where you can get raw oysters for $10 a dozen. You park in the lot, order your oysters, and slurp away, mopping up the juicy remnants with fresh corn tortillas. *Heaven.* Should you need something a little more, er, cooked, try the shrimp. They're big and come in a piquant butter-tomato sauce. And if you're dying for a beer to go with this, simply trot over to the supermarket next door.

Long in the tooth but still tasty... For hard-drinking men who like their martinis dry, their steaks rare, their pants full-cut, and a swingin' hangout where it's always 1955, well, ring-a-ding-ding! Starting out at the beach, the semi-legendary **Bob Burns** will draw you in with its piano bar—then the drinks will keep you in your Naugahyde seat, and the very meaty menu will sit in your gut for weeks. The prime ribs are old-style cuts: you can feel the hollandaise sauce hardening into plaque the minute it hits your tongue. Enjoy! Then there's **The Galley,** where not much has changed since it opened in 1934, except perhaps nowadays it has fewer sprinklings of sawdust on the floor. The wooden building kind of resembles the shape of a boat, with a mast on top, portholes for windows, and a mermaid leaning over the front door. The dining room appears very dark when you first enter, lit only by red wall lights and a string or two of tiny Christmas lights flung into a fishing net overhead. Just like on a real boat! Sit in one of the rattan-framed booths, suck on the steamed clams, dip the lobster tail in melted butter, and croon along to a jukebox loaded with Frank

DINING | THE LOWDOWN

Sinatra, Bobby Darin, and…Al Green? The Galley exists in its own time zone, so prepare yourself for culture shock when you emerge and hit the streets again.

Come fry with me… Only in Santa Monica would a tiny community airport become a major foodie trough. The aeronautical theme can get to be a little too much at times, but you can usually find parking, and you'll never have to worry about locating your luggage. In first class we have **The Hump.** The vaguely sexual name refers to a term used by American WWII pilots when they had to fly *through* the Himalayas rather than around them after the Japanese invaded Burma. The feat of "Flying the Hump" is commemorated throughout the room, but most specifically on the window behind the sushi bar, which has an elegant translucent silver cutout of a lone plane flying in the crevice of a steep and forbidding mountain range. The warm wooden tables, ochre walls, bamboo and thatched ceiling, and hanging hurricane lamps make this the most evocative restaurant you're likely to find short of a snack 'n' shack on Pico. The open deck outside is not cluttered with umbrellas, and drinking hot sake here at sunset feels like the beginning of a real, timeless adventure. Absolutely essential order: The Hump Sushi Roll (smelt eggs, salmon, yellowtail, and tuna, sleeping in a bed of cucumber, avocado, and rice). In business class there's **DC3,** located on the north end of the airport at the edge of Clover Park, across the street from Carlsberg Corporation and Spieker Properties. Despite the name, this is the least aeronautically themed of all the restaurants. Inside, the ambience is Upscale Corporate. Everything is constructed on a grand architectural scale, beginning with the long, U-shaped bar in its own room by the entranceway. An extremely large collage on the wall dominates the view, overwhelming even the landing field outside. The entrees are standard and expensive, although new management is working on some changes to the menu. It's best visited at happy hour, or when straggling in after events held elsewhere in the building. And, in the cockpit we have, straight across the street from Carlsberg Corporation and Spieker Properties on the south side of the airport, the **Spitfire Grill** and **Typhoon.** The Spitfire is based in an older wooden building; although it has no view of the runway, it's the likelier pilot-spotting venue of the two. Inside, under a mural of old spitfire planes, a small real propeller, and miscellaneous flying paraphernalia, booths lend privacy to conversations; outside, a shaded patio offers a glimpse of the planes randomly parked in the sprawling lot across the street. A favorite time of day here is breakfast, but the place is open until 10 p.m. for dinner, with the bar serving beer from the local microbrewery Angel City as well as wine. In Typhoon, the noise level picks up once the doors open at noon, sound waves bouncing off the long, semicircular picture windows that face the runway below. Half the floor space is devoted to the bar area, which transforms into a club atmosphere on Monday nights when jazz groups are brought in. Licenses of pilots from around the world cover two posts, lending a taste of history to this stylized room, while the long, mirrored curve of the Pacific Rim behind the bar launches you up into the sky, cruising.

Escape from Saigon... Ever wonder how all those models stay so thin? They feed in places like **Indochine,** where the food is decent and low-fat, and no one eats that much anyway because there's a shoot in the morning. The prevailing tone is green, with banana leaf designs on the walls and comfy leather booths, both of which afford great backdrops for your basic black ensemble. Ideal for up-and-coming director wannabes and the actors they're hoping to get into the sack after coffee and dessert. The lemongrass salmon is a favorite. The cuisine at **Crustacean** is defined as nouvelle Vietnamese, but it's nowhere near as low-cal as the food at Indochine. It's mighty tasty, though. Supposedly the family that runs the place (along with its sister outlet in San Francisco) is descended from royalty; when your check arrives you'll wish you were, too. The crab in garlic-pepper sauce is one of its signature dishes, along with shrimp on garlic noodles. The place is done up like some French Colonial whorehouse in Saigon—it's a tad intimidating, but the pretty little stream filled with koi at the entrance (which you cross to enter) is genius. Starfucker Alert #2: This is a major celeb feeding trough; sightings include Lisa Kudrow, Mel Gibson, Eddie Murphy, Warren Beatty, and Harrison Ford, among others.

Soul-food places for nervous honkies... Most people don't think of L.A. as a place with a sizable African-

American population, not in the same way as New York or Chicago or even St. Louis—even though for decades they were the second-largest minority here. The city's well-established racist history may be one reason why soul food has only recently become something of a trend. The backlash against no-fat food is also helping the resurgence of places like **Harold & Belle's,** a long-time Creole/soul-food eatery where the helpings are huge and dipping sauces will sear your throat. It's popular with a wide range of folks, from bus drivers to members of the L.A. Lakers. The lobster scampi is superb, and there's live music on the weekends. Over on the West Side, right at the beach, is **Aunt Kizzy's Back Porch.** It's sort of amazing to find hush puppies, jambalaya, black-eyed peas, and collard greens in the rarefied atmosphere of Marina del Rey. This is Southern cooking prepared with all the finesse of haute cuisine, so damn the cholesterol—bring on the pork chops! The helpings are so big they'll haunt your nightmares for weeks. Who has the finest African-American food in Downtown? The **Soul Folks Cafe** makes that claim, and they're probably right. One of the chefs was imported from New Orleans, the other from Costa Rica, and the whole melange makes for perfect SoCal soul food. It's a tiny space, tucked inside Bloom's General Store in the sordid armpit of the Downtown artists' loft district. The slacker artists are mainly the ones who come here, lingering at the sidewalk tables over red beans, fried catfish, greens, cornbread, and grits. Goodly portions at starving-artist prices, plus local art on the walls, and, right next door in Bloom's, a huge selection of cigars.

Tired hangouts for the hipeoise... Your so-last-year swinger friends may try to drag you to **Fred 62** for a taste of that edgy Silver Lake buzz, but don't be fooled. This place is just another cynical attempt to evoke that trendy fifties coffee shop shtick using retro decor. The big irony: The food is not much better here (and way more expensive) than the real mid-century coffee shop it displaced. The food, in fact, is terrible, and the service is slow—but it is open all night. Then again, so is the IHOP right across the street, and at least there you have some idea when your food will arrive. The look only fools Westsiders. Maybe it's because they think places like **The Ivy** are the bomb. There you sit in the patio, sniff the roses, and request nonfat cappuccino with Kona beans, decaffeinated in the water process. And maybe a hot fudge sundae? With two spoons? Frankly I don't know why I keep coming here. I guess I enjoy spending too much money to sit next to amoral millionaire producers and their airhead trophy dates. The food is mediocre at best, but you know something? Nobody notices, because they're too busy jabbering on their cell phones, telling their pals that they're calling from the Ivy.

Queer food... You don't have to be gay to enjoy the following places, but it may perk your meal up a bit. First, there's **Basix Cafe,** which draws a clientele of lipstick lesbians and buffed guys with enormous pecs. But the customers are only part of the story. The place has great snacks and salads, plus a thin-crust pizza that is the best for miles. If you're not that hungry, try the scrambled egg sandwiches—they're divine. Right nearby is the **Marix Tex Mex Café.** It has another outlet in Santa Monica, but please, don't bother. If you want the full effect, you have to come here to the WeHo original outlet. The crowd is gay, loud, horny, and ravishing. The fajitas, unfortunately, are only so-so, but the margaritas are pure rocket fuel. It's a major pick-up scene for those packing a condom, or three.

Way, way south of the border... Right in the heart of the retro furniture section of Beverly is **Ipanema,** a little Brazilian restaurant that has huge lunches for less than you'd normally pay for parking. The $5 lunch special includes either a grilled chicken breast or steak covered in chopped tomatoes and chiles, along with rice, beans, fried bananas, and a kind of "Brazilian couscous"—which, mixed in with the rice and beans, is real tasty. The other entrees are similar, some accompanied by Brazilian-style risotto, and go for around 10 bucks. Highly recommended if you're shopping in the area. Another good choice for shopaholics is **Lala's Argentine Grill,** up on Melrose. A lot of its business is takeout, but if you sit in the little out-door glassed-in patio area, you won't be sorry. There's nothing like hot meat served up right from the grill.

Food troughs for trendies... The look of minimalist designer Philippe Starck's white-on-white interior at **Asia de Cuba** goes perfectly with the recently renovated Mondrian Hotel. It's also a statement—an indication—

DINING | THE LOWDOWN

that the Mondrian, like the Sunset Strip itself, has put on long pants and decided to grow up. As the name suggests, this is Cuban-Asian cuisine, a replication of the Manhattan restaurant that bears the same name. The helpings here are huge, your fellow diners often junkie-model thin, and the ambience one of studied sophistication—very anti–*Riot On Sunset Strip*. Except for the excellent calamari salad and the humongous "Bay of Pigs" banana split, the overall feel is reminiscent of too many other Asian-fusion eateries in town. And it's not cheap, either. Dress all in black, and come by for the decor, not necessarily the food...You'll find the same vibe but better food on the West Side at **Hal's Bar & Grill**. This started off as a Venice artist's hangout for locals, the kind of place you could bring your New York hipster friends to without cringing. The food is good, the appetizers inventive and tasty, and there's a good wine list. But even with local artists' work on the walls, this is now the better side of Venice, where the zillionaires who live on the canals come for some safe slumming. It's California Cuisine, with a Caribbean subtext.

You can't go wrong... It's well worth walking into Union Station simply to check out the glorious Spanish Revival architecture of this classic L.A. building. The fact that **Traxx** is here just makes it all the better. It serves classic California cuisine, and while the menu is small, it's totally reliable. Fish is always a good choice here—and the surroundings are like nothing else in L.A. If you really want to touch L.A. Noir and feel its slithery passage, come here for dinner. Union Station is one of the essential L.A. icons, the backdrop for countless films. Close your eyes while you savor your Merlot, and listen for the rumble of trains pulling into the station overhead. The food is much, much better than you'd expect, in a location that doesn't need any extra attractions. Over on Melrose Avenue, the veteran **Angeli Caffe** continues to deliver the goods—including great pastas and pizzas at reasonable prices and the best bread in town (okay, after Campanile). It's no longer the new kid on the block, but it's still noisy as hell—which indicates that, despite its age, Angeli remains a player. Timeless in its minimalist design and deceptively simple in its delivery, this is one of L.A.'s most overlooked Italian delights. I've never had a bad meal here, and, thanks to their cookbooks, I've even been able to duplicate the experience (almost) at home. Also in the Italian mode but on the East Side is **Trattoria Farfalla**, my favorite midrange eatery for the past 10 years. It has better Italian food than I could make at home, caters to local celebs, and is affordable. Although the table positioning is a little too intimate, it's hard to find fault with one of the first good restaurants in the area. Especially since it has continued to deliver reliably great pizzas, pastas, and inventive fresh entrees over the years for very reasonable prices. Plus, there's a great wine list (not quite so affordable, unhappily) and the 50-50 chance of seeing a celebrity. Most affordable can't-go-wrong order is the Farfalla salad and pasta fagioli. Over on the West Side you'll find **Versailles**, one of the first Caribbean restaurants in the city with good prices and a Cuban accent. During the punkish '80s, Versailles was a major hang. It remains popular, and is always crowded with people from all over—Downtown, Venice, even the Valley. It's the place you come when you're really craving Cuban rice-beans-plantain-garlic chicken. But be warned: The birds are small—you can easily eat a half by yourself. It has fish also, but here the chicken is the star.

Cheap eats... When you're strolling down the Third Street Promenade in Santa Monica, the experience is best savored with a hot spud in your mouth, dripping with a garlicky mayonnaise. Congratulations! You've just been to **Benita's Fries**, unquestionably the city's most delightful source for food to eat while you walk. Fries is all they do, but this is Santa Monica, so naturally we're talking. For a treat, check out the gourmet-style Thai peanut sauce. The style is Belgian, not French, but don't let that throw you: This is probably the only french-fry joint in L.A. that consistently gets rated in restaurant guides and "Best Of..." lists. *Highly recommended*. Over on the East Side, in Los Feliz, you'll find the tiny **Maco** storefront, tucked next to Skylight Books and the Los Feliz theaters. It features slightly greasy working-class Japanese food—nothing that will win any Michelin awards, but for the local minimum-wage drones on this mini-hipster strip of Vermont, it's a godsend. Always crowded. But with only five seats, that's not hard to do. The menu is as limited as the seating but you sure can't complain about the prices. Where else can you feel totally full for under $4? On the other hand, you wouldn't ordinarily think of a Bunker Hill lawyer-corporate hangout like **McCormick and Schmick's** as a place to get bloated for pennies, but that's the glory of Happy Hour. This Library Tower institution is legendary among white-collar office workers Downtown. Every office drone in the financial center heads here eventually for the excellent $2 cheeseburgers, served in the evening before the dinner crowd comes in. Unfortunately, you'll have to inhale the appetizers in a sea of cell-phone-jabbering Valley-bound commuter yuppies, but the great wine list more than makes up for it. If you're feeling expansive, the Pacific Northwestern–style seafood here is probably the best in downtown—after the Water Grill, anyway.

Location, location, location... Part of the secret to living in L.A. is knowing about those places just up the block that you don't have to drive to—unlike all the other fools lined up waiting for the parking valet. Such as **Prado**, in the heart of Larchmont Village—a cozy little neighborhood that feels more like Glendale than the south Hollywood it is. Quite in keeping with the area, Prado is a more upscale version of chef Toribio Prado's popular **Cha Cha Cha** over in Silver Lake. The cuisine is still SoCal Caribbean–shrimp in black pepper sauce, blackened sea bass, Jamaican tamales—but the room is far more elegant than its funky-yet-charming East Side cousin. For dessert, you can't go wrong with the raspberry red velvet cake. Elegant is decidedly not the word for **City Pier Seafood**, located in a covered walkway that feels like one of those dreary Penn Station tunnels in New York. But City Pier is one of the only fast, almost-affordable seafood diners in this part of Downtown. To be honest, though, the quality doesn't make up for the prices (just a little too high) and the ambience (just a little too much like a cafeteria). The place is perfect for the State drones who work in the Ronald Reagan Building, across the street, or when there's no time to find a real restaurant, but that's about it. And then there's **Café Rodeo**—the only sidewalk cafe on Rodeo Drive in Beverly Hills. Now *that's* a location with a license for printing money. The food is Californian—the chef used to work at Spago and Morton's—and the views are spectacular. It's like a moving sidewalk of the beautiful, the thin, the rich, and the clueless. Stalker Alert: For those on a celeb hunt, this is an almost guaranteed stake-out situation. Have a nice Alexander Valley white with your grilled tuna and savor the moment.

The Index

$$$$	$40–$50
$$$	$30–$40
$$	$20–$30
$	under $20

Price categories reflect the cost of a three-course meal, not including drinks, taxes, and tip.

ABC Seafood. This longtime Chinatown veteran manages to last because it offers a good return for the money—namely dim sum and just-killed fish in Mandarin sauces that will wow you with their subtlety. Highly recommended by local Chinese.... *Tel 213/680-2887. 205 Ord St., Chinatown. $$* **(see p. 67)**

Angeli Caffe. This Italian restaurant is one of the reasons why people came to Melrose back in the nu-wave days. And it's still good. Stop in, if only to have a pizza and to get one of their excellent cookbooks.... *Tel 323/936-9086. 7274 Melrose Ave., Hollywood. $$$* **(see p. 78)**

AOI. You could spend a lot more in Little Tokyo and get food that isn't half as good as this. Aoi has been here for years, and with good reason—the prices are affordable, the food is good, and the service is fast. What more could you want? *Tel 213/624-8260. 331 E. First St., Little Tokyo.* **(see p. 65)**

Apple Pan. This is an essential part of the L.A. adolescent experience. The food isn't superb, the pies are really only so-so, but the '50s-diner ambience is unquestionably real. Forget Johnny Rocket's. This is the real deal.... *Tel 310/475-3585. 10801 W. Pico Blvd., West L.A. $$* **(see p. 57)**

Asia de Cuba. This is a sister restaurant of the New York original, and Asian-Cuban-Caribbean fusion is the deal. Way too expensive, but it's the Mondrian Hotel, so don't complain. Still, unless you're on an expense account or really want to get into your date's pants, don't bother.... *Tel 323/846-6000. 8440 Sunset Blvd. (inside the Mondrian Hotel), West Hollywood $$$$* **(see p. 77)**

Astro. This is one burger stand that's a huge favorite of vegetarians. The garden burgers taste almost like flesh. It's right across from the Paramount.... *Tel 323/469-1924. 5601 Melrose Ave., Hollywood. $* **(see p. 68)**

Aunt Kizzy's Back Porch. Soul food shouldn't be this expensive, but hey, it's the beach, and rents are high. It's all *too* tasty, and just slightly more healthy than eating a tub of lard.... *Tel 310/578-1005. Villa Marina Shopping Center, 4325 Glencoe Ave., Marina del Rey. $$$* **(see p. 76)**

Authentic Café. Before you drop while shopping along Beverly Boulevard, reenergize yourself at this culinary pit stop; you can't go wrong with the chicken in tortilla crust and fried green tomatoes.... *Tel 323/939-4626. 7605 Beverly Blvd., West Hollywood. $$* **(see p. 72)**

Basix Cafe. Good pizzas, salads, and not-too-distinctive Italian food for lipstick lesbians and their dates. It's run by the gals who started the Marix Tex-Mex place around the corner.... *Tel 323/848-2460. 8333 Santa Monica Blvd., West Hollywood. $$* **(see p. 77)**

Benita's Fries. Unquestionably the best French fries before you hit the Pacific. Go for the whole Belgium experience— mayo, garlic, maybe some peanut sauce. Everything is bad for you, but you're in Santa Monica, so chill.... *Tel 310/458-2889. 1433 3rd St. Promenade, Santa Monica. $* **(see p. 79)**

Blueberry. A decent place for breakfast at the beach. Good pancakes, very rich egg dishes, and not really that cheap. It's full of white people waiting for their first coronary.... *Tel 310/394-7766. 510 Santa Monica Blvd., Santa Monica. $$* **(see p. 71)**

Bob Burns. For Rat Pack cultists, this is the closest you'll get to

the glory days of Sammy, Dino, and Frank. The piano bar and the martinis are why the younger folk like it. The regulars come for the steaks, which are big 'n' beefy.... *Tel 310/393-6777. 202 Wilshire Blvd., Santa Monica. $$$*
(see p. 73)

Cafe Glaxa. The very East Side version of a good breakfast—grease, butter, eggs, bacon, and more grease—is what made Millie's, just down the street, a huge hit. Magenta is the woman who started it all, and now she's slinging hash here at Glaxa. It's way less of a scene than Millie's, which means you'll probably be able to get a table. And don't worry, she serves Devil's Mess eggs.... *Tel 323/663-5295. 3707 Sunset Blvd., Silver Lake. $$* **(see p. 70)**

Café Rodeo. The only place to eat on Rodeo Drive, but really, is that reason enough? If you're shopping on Rodeo and just can't go a single step further without a so-so salad or semi-tasty California cuisine–esque entree, then by all means, stop in and spend. Note: The Café is closed for remodelling until spring 2000.... *Tel 310/273-0300. 360 N. Rodeo Dr. (inside the Summit Hotel), Beverly Hills. $$$* **(see p. 80)**

Campanile. If you're looking for something that is true L.A., not the flavor-of-the-month, it just doesn't get much better than this. It's full of locals—and where else can you get a variety of olive oils for dipping your impossibly tasty bread? The food is California-Mediterranean and a little pricey, but well worth it.... *Tel 323/938-1447. 624 S. La Brea Ave., Los Angeles. $$$* **(see p. 70)**

Canter's. This Kosher deli-bakery is open all night. It's been a West Side institution for successive generations of late-night revelers who don't mind the dry, tasteless pastries, the over-bearing waitresses, and the cheap but unsatisfying pastrami.... *Tel 323/651-2030. 419 N. Fairfax Ave., West Hollywood. $$* **(see p. 58)**

Cha Cha Cha. If it looks too funky from the street, don't come in, because you just won't get it. Established long before Silver Lake became cool, Cha Cha Cha is like a local church where we all come to worship before the indescribable gods of Haiti, the Dominican Republic, and all the nameless sandbars of the Caribbean. Wonderful brunches.... *Tel 323/664-7723. 656 N. Virgil Ave., Silver Lake. $$$* **(see pp. 56, 80)**

Chan Dara. One of the first Thai restaurants to cater to the younger hip Hollywood crowd, Chan Dara stands out as an island of excellence in the sea of fine Thai eateries engulfing L.A. The vegetarian stir-fries are good, but the seafood dishes are great. It can be noisy as hell here, however, so be prepared to shout to your dinner partners. *Tel 323/464-8585. 1511 N. Cahuenga Blvd., Hollywood.* **(see p. 64)**

Chao Praya. It's open way late and does a roaring business with the music studios in the area. The Thai barbequed chicken is the best thing on the menu. Noisy, dark, and a great choice for après concert/dance anchor food. The neighborhood is creepily interesting as well. *Tel 323/466-6704. 6307 Yucca St., Hollywood.* **(see p. 64)**

Chez Jay. It may look like a nothing place from the outside, but this longtime Santa Monica beach-bar shack is something of a treasure for locals. It's close to the waves, and has a funky sensibility that is sadly lacking in most of the area these days. *Tel. 310/395-1741. 1657 Ocean Ave., Santa Monica.* **(see p. 62)**

City Pier Seafood. Its roots go back to 72 Market Street, so you'd expect something a little bit better from this unfortunately situated mid-mall restaurant. It looks like a typical Downtown fast-food outlet until you check out the prices— and excuse me, but the fish isn't *that* good. It'll do in a pinch if you don't have time to make it up to Central Market. Otherwise, forget it.... *Tel 213/617-2489. 333 S. Spring St., Downtown. $$* **(see p. 80)**

Coffee Table. This is one of the best and most comfortable breakfast choices in Silver Lake. Loads of room, good, large cups of coffee, and a great place for morning meetings. It's a quieter, more mature (and far less heavy) version of Millie's.... *Tel 323/644-8111. 2930 Rowena Ave., Silver Lake. $* **(see p. 70)**

El Coyote. Basically cheap, bland mush cleverly disguised as Mexican food. Come here to drink your dinner—*don't* be tempted by the food. A perfect spot for anorectics in love, or relatives from out-of-town whom you don't like. Bring 'em here, and pick up the tab. *Tel 323/939-2255. 7312 Beverly Blvd., Los Angeles.* **(see p. 58)**

Crustacean. Nouvelle French-Vietnamese that is the perfect Beverly Hills Asian restaurant. The interior is incredible, the food rich, and the clientele vacuous. Sure, the garlic noodles are tasty, just not worth the inflated price tag. But if you want to impress a date, this is a sure thing.... *Tel 310/205-8990. 9646 Little Santa Monica Blvd., Beverly Hills. $$$$* **(see p. 75)**

Curry House. The food is a silly Japanese version of Indian curry, but somehow it's incredibly addictive. You can vary the spiciness of the melange—the Japanese like it sweet rather than hot. Highly recommended, especially for lunch.... *Tel 213/-620-0855. 123 S. Onizuka St. (in Weller Court), Little Tokyo. $* **(see p. 64)**

Dar Maghreb. You may not remember your meal, but you will know you had a good time. Belly dancing, sitting on the floor, eating with your fingers. Like Moun of Tunis, this place is party central. Highly recommended for group extravaganzas.... *Tel 323/876-7651. 7651 Sunset Blvd., Hollywood. $$$$* **(see p. 61)**

DC3. Basic California cuisine, unimaginatively prepared. The aeronautical theme is, thankfully, less obstreperous here than at the other Santa Monica Airport restaurants. But even so, this place is still low man on my culinary totem pole. If I couldn't get into the Spitfire Grill, then—and only then—I might come here.... *Tel 310/399-2323. 2800 Donald Douglas Loop North, Santa Monica Airport, Santa Monica. $$$***(see p. 74)**

Erewhon. Primarily a natural-foods grocery store, Erewhon also has a very respectable deli for take-out eats. And if you don't mind sitting on the sidewalk, the place offers tables and chairs out on Beverly—perfect for a quick snack while shopping this retail-heavy section.... *Tel 323/937-0777. 7660 Beverly Blvd., Los Angeles. $* **(see p. 69)**

Fatburger. You're fat. So eat a burger. A Fatburger! Then you'll be even fatter. In a city where hamburgers are considered haute cuisine, these are among the city's very best—a wonderfully greasy slide straight to Cardiac Hell. *Tel 323/663-3100, 1611 N. Vermont Ave., Hollywood; Tel 323/734-7490 301 S. Western Ave., Koreatown; Tel 323/939-9593, 5001 Wilshire Blvd., Miracle Mile; Tel 323/436-0862, 7450 Santa Monica Blvd., West Hollywood. $* **(see p. 60)**

Formosa Café. Once the only reason to come here was for the sheer camp of it all—that and the rocket-fuel drinks. The food was wretched once, but it's all mo' betta now. In fact, the pan-Asian Fusion food is quite edible, even recommended. *Tel 323/850-9050. 7156 Santa Monica Blvd., Hollywood. $$* **(see p. 59)**

Fred 62. It's stupid, it's trendy, it's retro, and the food sucks majorly. So, come on down! There's one born every minute, and why shouldn't it be you? Bad diner food confusingly prepared and only delivered once it's nice and cold and the waiter has nothing better to do.... *Tel 323/664-0021. 1770 N. Vermont Ave., Los Feliz. $$* **(see p. 76)**

The Galley. It may be Santa Monica's oldest restaurant, but don't let the geezer factor keep you away. It's still got that genuine vibe of a place where the melted-butter bowl with your lobster tail is right, proper, expected.... *Tel 310/452-1934. 2442 Main St., Santa Monica. $$* **(see p. 73)**

Gladstone's 4 Fish. Basically just another overpriced, almost-fresh-fish beach-side eatery aimed at tourists cruising PCH who are sick of looking for a parking spot. Well, you can always park here. I won't give the same guarantee for the quality of the fish, but don't worry—you're paying for the view and the parking spot.... *Tel 310/GL4-FISH. 17300 Pacific Coast Hwy., Pacific Palisades. $$$* **(see p. 62)**

Hal's Bar & Grill. It's hard to believe this started out as an artists' hangout. The typical California cuisine/Caribbean-Creole fusion food is still good, and the decor isn't quite pretentious enough to spoil your dinner, but the attitude is just a little too West Side for me.... *Tel 310/396-3105. 1349 Abbot Kinney Blvd., Venice. $$$* **(see p. 78)**

Harold & Belle's. Soul food that comes in helpings bigger than your head. Don't sweat the address. This is an icon, and anyone who appreciates good gumbo makes it here eventually.... *Tel 323/735-9023. 2920 W. Jefferson Blvd., Los Angeles. $$$* **(see p. 76)**

Hugo's. People who should know better flock here for breakfasts of Pasta Mama (scrambled eggs over pasta) and steaming coffee. This is a major entertainment industry power spot, gay subset.... *Tel 323/654-3993. 8401 Santa Monica Blvd., West Hollywood. $$* **(see p. 68)**

The Hump. Without a doubt this is the best sushi you will ever get in an airport—including Narita. It ain't cheap, but the view is totally unusual and the sushi well done and charmingly executed.... *Tel 310/313-0977. 3221 Donald Douglas Loop South, 3rd floor, Santa Monica Airport. $$$* **(see p. 74)**

In-N-Out Burger. Right now In-N-Out is *the* fast-food burger of choice. It's nowhere as good as Steak'n'Shake or even White Castle, but it's still way beyond McDonald's.... *Tel 800/786-1000. Various locations around Southern California. Not enough, unfortunately. $* **(see p. 59)**

India's Oven. Cheap and incredibly delicious, with generous portions.... *Tel 323/936-1000. 7231 Beverly Blvd., Los Angeles; Tel 310/207-5522. 111645 Wilshire Blvd., West Los Angeles. $* **(see p. 69)**

Indochine. Of course it's Vietnamese-centric, but the overall take embraces more or less all of Southeast Asia. It's light, a little pricey, and ideal for a first date with a client or potential squeeze.... *Tel 323/655-4777. 8225 Beverly Blvd., Los Angeles. $$$* **(see p. 75)**

Ipanema. With a name like that, you know it's Brazilian—and even though it's just a little storefront with tables on the street, this is definitely one of the better deals in the neighborhood. Big helpings—and on Saturdays there's *feijoada*, a traditional dish of beans cooked with pork, beef, and sausage. Umm, meaty.... *Tel 323/933-7254. 7912 Beverly Blvd., West Los Angeles. $* **(see pp. 69, 77)**

The Ivy. Want to pretend you're a player? Come here, spend too much for mediocre food, and walk away pissed off. People rave about the crab cakes, but they just made me crabby.... *Tel 310/274-8303. 113 N. Robertson Blvd., West L.A. $$$$* **(see p. 76)**

Jay's Jayburgers. Open until 4 a.m. on the weekends, this is *the* place to come when you badly need something solid in your stomach and it's way too late for anything more civilized. Tommy's is a good second choice, but if you're on the East Side, come here first. The Eggburger is unbelievably soothing.... *Tel 323/666-5204. 4481 Santa Monica Blvd., Silver Lake. $* **(see p. 59)**

Joan's On Third. Good food made from top-quality Italian ingredients served on paper plates in casual surroundings.... *Tel 323/655-2285. 8350 W. 3rd St., West Hollywood. $* **(see p. 72)**

Kagetsu An. If you like Japanese noodles, this is one of the best places to get them in Little Tokyo. Look for the homemade udon, and ignore the fact that it's a few dollars more than you'd normally pay. Highly recommended and open late.... *Tel 213/613-1479 318 E. 2nd St. #A, Little Tokyo. $$* **(see p. 65)**

King's Road Cafe. The panini sandwiches are the thing to eat at lunch, and the coffee is kick-ass strong. You may have to wait for a table if you arrive too close to the breakfast-lunch crowds, so just browse the newsstand next door while you wait. Highly reliable and very popular.... *Tel 323/655-9044. 8361 Beverly Blvd., West L.A. $* **(see p. 68)**

Kokekokko. Eating yakitori at this oh-so-Japanese specialty restaurant is a full-on cultural experience on a par with the best sushi bars in the area—and about as expensive, if you walk out full. The food is excellent and the atmosphere always enjoyable. If you're in the mood for Japanese but want something a little out of the ordinary, come here. You won't be sorry. *Tel 213/687-0690. 360 E. Second St., Little Tokyo. $$$* **(see p. 64)**

Kokomo Cafe. Dying for a nice hot johnnycake like mammy used to make? Come here for a Southern breakfast that will knock your socks off. Ignore the fact that it's in the Farmer's Market and tourists are swirling around you. It's also a major pick-up scene and semi-power lunch spot.... *Tel 323/933-0773. Farmer's Market, 6333 W. 3rd St., Los Angeles. $$* **(see p. 67)**

Lala's Argentine Grill. You could easily drive right past this place without ever noticing it, but it's worth stopping in. It has the feeling of a take-out stand, but it has fine salsas and the most tender cuts of meat you could imagine. If you're shopping on Melrose and just want a snack, pop in for an empanada.... *Tel 323/934-6838. 7229 Melrose Ave., Hollywood. $$*   **(see pp. 72, 77)**

Maco. Totally quirky and still in business while the neighborhood gentrifies around it, this is working-class Japanese food, served at working-class prices. It's not gourmet, but there is no attitude. You won't find almost-decent Japanese food cheaper than this anywhere. If there's no seat, just chill. Few customers linger over their meal.... *Tel 323/660-1211. 1820 N. Vermont Ave., Los Feliz.$*   **(see p. 79)**

Mario's Peruvian Seafood. Really good, cheap seafood served up by chef Mario Tamashiro. The salsa is piquant, the corn snappy, and the seafood stir-fry better than anything you'd find in Beverly Hills, for one-third the price. Highly recommended.... *Tel 323/466-4181. 5786 Melrose Ave., Hollywood. $*   **(see p. 72)**

Marix Tex Mex Café. Just as the name says, it's Tex-Mex. And because it's in WeHo, the clientele is gay and gregarious. The margaritas will knock you out, but the fajitas are a little disappointing.... *Tel 323-656-8800. 1108 N. Flores St., West Hollywood. $$*   **(see p. 77)**

Matsuhisa. Japanese-Peruvian cuisine with smatterings of French savories tossed in for good measure. It's sushi...but more. It's gourmet Latin-American food...but more. Like Wolfgang Puck, chef Nobu Matsuhisa has redefined the way we taste things. If you like seafood, this is an essential stop. It's expensive but unique—and that always costs more. *Tel 310/659-9639. 129 N. La Cienega Blvd., Beverly Hills. $$$*   **(see p. 66)**

McCormick and Schmick's. A lot of Bunker Hill office drones maintain that this is the best Northwest seafood in Downtown—better than the Water Grill. You can decide that for yourself. I come for the wonderful happy-hour specials and the surroundings, right next to the Central Library.... *Tel 213/629-1929. 633 W. 5th St., Library Tower, Downtown. $$$*   **(see p. 80)**

Millie's. Once merely a humble breakfast diner, this has become the epicenter of Silver Lake cool—the place where struggling musicians work part-time, slinging Devils Mess Eggs to cover demo costs. The food is heavy, the clientele too cool for school, the jukebox otherworldly. Highly recommended for a late breakfast or lunch. Forget it on the weekends. You'll wait forever.... *Tel 323/664-0404. 3524 W. Sunset Blvd., Silver Lake. $$* **(see p. 56, 70)**

Mitsuru Cafe. I wanna *imagawa-yaki*. Now! They have other things, too, but this odd sweet-redbean-filled pancake is the only thing I ever get here. Two will fill you up just fine. Three might put you over the edge. Good food for window shopping. *Tel 213/613-1028. 117 Japanese Village Plaza Mall, Little Tokyo.* **(see p. 65)**

Moun of Tunis. Tunisian finger food combined with belly dancers and a party atmosphere that only the North Africans can carry off with such style. This is *not* your typical L.A. dining experience. The lamb is wonderful.... *Tel 323/874-3333. 7445 1/2 Sunset Blvd., Hollywood. $$$* **(see p. 61)**

Musso & Frank Grill. If you come to Hollywood in search of the Golden Era, this is where you'll find it. The menu is absurdly long, the waiters notoriously snotty, the food too bland and overcooked. But you have to come here at least once just to say you've been.... *Tel 323/467-7788. 6667 Hollywood Blvd., Hollywood. $$$* **(see p. 57)**

Neptune's Net. Steamed shrimp is the raison d'être for this great little roadside shack. You eat with your fingers; be careful not to lean on the bikers' hogs out front.... *Tel 310/457-3095. 42505 Pacific Coast Hwy., Malibu. $* **(see p. 62)**

Networks Cafe. Now *this* is the Real World. The Networks is downstairs from the local MTV studios, and in the morning everyone looks like they've been up all night.... *Tel 310/315-0502. 2700 Colorado Blvd., Santa Monica. $* **(see p. 71)**

Original Pantry Cafe. Its still in business, though why and how is one of the great mysteries of L.A. About the only good thing about the place is its hours—it never closes. American food, badly done.... *Tel 213/972-9279. 877 S. Figueroa St., Downtown. $$* **(see p. 58)**

Ostioneria Colima. Raw oysters and fried seafood for just pennies on the half-shell. One of Downtown's hidden treasures. Zero ambience, but a great meal.... *Tel 213/482-4152. 1465 W. 3rd St., West Los Angeles. Open daily for lunch and dinner. $* **(see p. 73)**

Paru's. This easily missed Indian vegetarian restaurant is one of those little treasures that most Angelenos cruise right past. They shouldn't, and neither should you. A major find for vegans and vegetarians. Wonderfully tasty, with a friendly atmosphere.... *Tel 323/661-7600. 5140 Sunset Blvd., Hollywood. $$* **(see p. 69)**

Philippe's. They call it "the original" as if someone else would want to try to usurp the distinction of being the "originator of the French dip sandwich." There's sawdust on the floor, decent wines on the wine list, and a whole variety of meats you can get dipped before they're slopped onto your soggy bun. Plus great breakfasts. *Tel 213/628-3781. 1001 N. Alameda St., Downtown. $$* **(see p. 57)**

Pho 87. One of the best-kept secrets of Chinatown, this no-frills Vietnamese eatery has a huge menu, most of it variations of noodles in broth. Pass the fish sauce. Highly recommended.... *Tel 213/227-0758. 1019 N. Broadway, Chinatown. $* **(see p. 67)**

Pink's. Here's where you come when you're dying for nasty meat whose genealogy you don't want to know anything about. Maybe it's beef. Maybe...or pork? Or whale? Who cares? The bun is sweet and the relish is tart and anyway it's an El Lay experience. If you don't eat this food every day, you probably won't get cancer. Probably.... *Tel 323/931-4223. 709 N. La Brea Ave., Hollywood. $* **(see p. 60)**

Prado. If you like sister restaurant Cha Cha Cha's Caribbean choices, then for sure come here. Crab cakes, green tamales, good wines, easy parking.... *Tel 323/467-3871. 244 N. Larchmont Blvd., Larchmont Village. $$$* **(see p. 80)**

Puran's. Organic produce but meat-friendly. It's hipster heaven without the trendoid factor. Recommended—especially the homemade rosemary bread and the calamari salad.... *Tel 323/933-5742. 142 S. La Brea, Los Angeles. $$* **(see p. 69)**

R-23. There are so many good sushi places in L.A. that it's sometimes hard to separate the great from the stunning. This major oasis for the Downtown artists' community is a little of both. Great sushi from really fresh fish, and a très boho decor. Highly recommended.... *Tel 213/687-7178. 923 E. 3rd St., Downtown. $$$* **(see p. 66)**

Reel Inn. Strictly for tourists or locals who have only been burned a few times and haven't learned. The location is great, the fish is fresh but way too expensive, the service terrible. It was great, once.... *Tel 310/456-8221. 18661 Pacific Coast Hwy., Malibu. $$* **(see p. 61)**

Saddle Peak Lodge. For lovers of freshly killed wild game, this is the place. You can get everything from quail to wild salmon to buffalo to venison—and you don't have to skin a damn thing. Conversely, by the time the bill comes you'll be feeling skinned. Maybe it was worth it—but only your colon can say for sure. Charlton Heston would feel right at home here.... *Tel 818/222-3888. 419 Cold Canyon Rd., Calabasas. $$$$* **(see p. 62)**

Saladang. Very good nouvelle Thai, as gourmet as you're going to find on this side of the ocean. The warehouse-like ambience and enormous flower arrangements don't hurt either. Save room for the mango sticky-rice dessert.... *Tel 626/793-8123. 363 S. Fair Oaks Ave., Pasadena. $$$* **(see p. 63)**

Shin. You can't go wrong if you come here for sushi. The fish is fresh, the presentation perfect. I have my gripes, but it's still my favorite local sushi bar. The decor is minimalist yet tasteful.... *Tel 323/664-1891. 1972 Hillhurst Ave., Los Feliz. $$$* **(see p. 66)**

Sompun. Not the most glamorous Thai restaurant you'll find, and not the rock-bottom cheapest either, but this is honest home cooking. The prik king is superb, the appetizers out of this world, the pad Thai fresh yet mature. I love this place.... *Tel 323/661-5350. 4156 Santa Monica Blvd., Silver Lake. $$* **(see p. 63)**

Soul Folks Cafe. If you want to know what the Downtown artists' community is all about, come here. The very good soul food is lighter than you might think and more reasonable than you'd expect. No dinners on the weekends.... *Tel*

213/613-0381. 714 Traction Ave. (inside Bloom's General Store), Downtown. $$ **(see p. 76)**

Spitfire Grill. Burgers and sandwiches are what I usually get here—although I also like it for breakfast, when the marine fog blankets the runways and adds a level of drama to everything. Almost *Casablanca,* but with a really decent wine list.... *Tel 310/397-3455. 3300 Airport Ave., Santa Monica Airport, Santa Monica. $$* **(see p. 74)**

Swingers. This is more than a West Side version of Millie's. The menu is huge (it'll give you serious vertigo if you're feeling a little woozy), and the food is good, even though it wanders all over the place stylistically. Too bad about the name. For bohos in the area this is a major hang. Best of all, it's open until 4 a.m.... *Tel. 323/653-5858. 8020 Beverly Blvd., Hollywood. $$* **(see p. 71)**

Tail O' The Pup. The only reason to eat here is for the backdrop. Dining at the Tail is a very L.A. moment, something that *must* be captured on film or video—otherwise it's just not worth the heartburn.... *No phone. 329 N. San Vicente Blvd., West Hollywood. $* **(see p. 60)**

Takoyaki Gen. Okonomiyaki may be a mouthful to say, but it goes down so smoothly. You combine cabbage, egg, sweet pancake flour, the meat or fish of your choice, plus pickled ginger, and fry it all up on the griddle. Cheap and tasty. They also have regular Japanese standards, but I wouldn't bother. Highly recommended.... *Tel 213/625-3275. 327 1st St., Little Tokyo. $* **(see p. 65)**

Tommy Tang's. This distinctive version of haute Thai continues to be enjoyable even now, when it seems like there's a Thai restaurant on every corner. Always a favorite with the Hollywood crowd, Tommy Tang's has never sunk into trendoid self-parody. The food continues to be honest, sinfully rich, and delivered with a sense of humor that is as fragrant as the iced tea. Highly recommended.... *Tel 323/937-5733. 7313 Melrose Ave., Hollywood; 626/792-9700. 24 W. Colorado Blvd., Pasadena. $$$* **(see p. 63)**

Tommy's Original World Famous. Haven't eaten here? You're not from L.A. Like Communion, you must pass the chili-cheese-meat Host into your gut in order to fully understand the redemption possible in the City of the Angels. Otherwise you're just pretending.... *Tel 213/389-9060. 2575 Beverly Blvd., Downtown. $* (see p. 60)

Tot (Teishoku-Of-Tokyo). This is one of the best new arrivals in Little Tokyo in some time. It features inventively prepared Japanese standards that have an overlay of California cuisine. A little pricey, but worth it.... *Tel 213/680-0344. 345 E. 2nd St., Little Tokyo. $$* (see p. 65)

Trattoria Farfalla. Light Italian, great pastas, and pizzas that manage to rival Wolfgang Puck's without imitating him. By all means start with the special salad—the dressing is outstanding. And be sure to consider the specials, which are always interesting.... *Tel 323/661-7365. 1978 Hillhurst Ave., Los Feliz; Tel 626/564-8696. 43 E. Colorado Blvd., Pasadena. $$$* (see p. 79)

Traxx. Excellent gourmet California cuisine dished up in the classic noir surroundings of Union Station. The lunch menu is cheaper, but the crowd isn't as much fun. This is sophisticated dining the way it should be.... *Tel 213/625-1999. 800 N. Alameda St. (inside Union Station), Downtown. $$$$* (see p. 78)

Typhoon. Unlike neighboring restaurants DC3, the Hump, and the Spitfire Grill, this Santa Monica Airport eatery is so loud you might wonder if you're out on the runway. The food is Pan-Asian and the menu disturbingly eccentric.... *Tel 310/390-6565. 3221 Donald Douglas Loop South, Santa Monica Airport. $$$* (see p. 74)

Versailles. Part of a mini chain, this highly reliable Cuban restaurant can be a little greasy, but that's the appeal. The roasted chicken is outstanding. For not much money you'll come away satiated.... *Tel 310/558-3168. 10319 Venice Blvd., Culver City. $$* (see p. 79)

Water Grill. When it comes to freshly shucked seafood, there's nothing to match this classy downtown mecca for lovers of the bivalve and all its assorted cousins. The uninitiated might start off with the Fruits of the Sea Platter, an assortment of oysters, crab, shrimp, and lobster. The room is beautiful, the oyster bar a thing of wonder, the wine list extensive. It'll cost you, but it's worth every penny. *Tel 213/ 891-0900. 544 S. Grand Ave., Downtown. $$$$* **(see p. 73)**

Yamashiro. You come here for the fabulous view, not for the mediocre food and watery drinks. It's kind of like Disneyland—everyone has to go at least once.... *Tel 323/466-5125. 1999 N. Sycamore Ave., Hollywood. $$$* **(see p. 58)**

Yuca's Hut. Quite simply, this is the best and most reliable food you're likely to find in L.A. No exceptions. The ranchero beans are heavenly. If they ever go out of business, I'm moving.... *323/662-1214. 2056 N. Hillhurst Ave., Los Feliz. $* **(see p. 56)**

Hollywood Area Dining

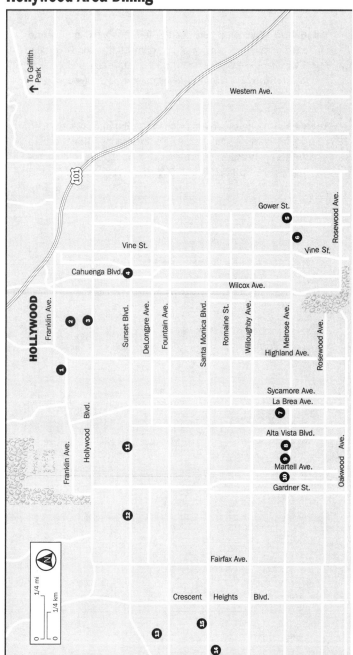

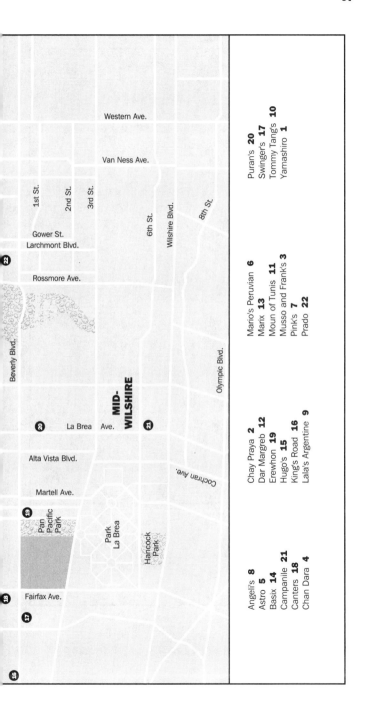

Western Ave.

Van Ness Ave.

1st St.
2nd St.
3rd St.

Gower St.
Larchmont Blvd.

22

Rossmore Ave.

6th St.

Wilshire Blvd.

8th St.

Beverly Blvd.

20 La Brea Ave.

MID-WILSHIRE

21

Alta Vista Blvd.

Olympic Blvd.

Martell Ave.

Cochran Ave.

19

Pan Pacific Park

Park La Brea

Hancock Park

18

17

Fairfax Ave.

16

Angeli's **8**
Astro **5**
Basix **14**
Campanile **21**
Canters **18**
Chan Dara **4**

Chay Praya **2**
Dar Margreb **12**
Erewhon **19**
Hugo's **15**
King's Road **16**
Lala's Argentine **9**

Mario's Peruvian **6**
Marix **13**
Moun of Tunis **11**
Musso and Frank's **3**
Pink's **7**
Prado **22**

Puran's **20**
Swinger's **17**
Tommy Tang's **10**
Yamashiro **1**

Downtown Area Dining

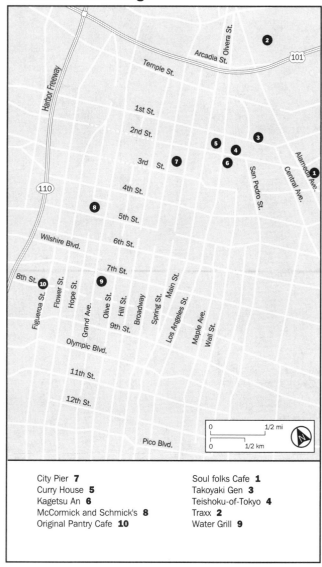

City Pier **7**	Soul folks Cafe **1**
Curry House **5**	Takoyaki Gen **3**
Kagetsu An **6**	Teishoku-of-Tokyo **4**
McCormick and Schmick's **8**	Traxx **2**
Original Pantry Cafe **10**	Water Grill **9**

Accommodations in
L.A.'s Westside & Beverly Hills

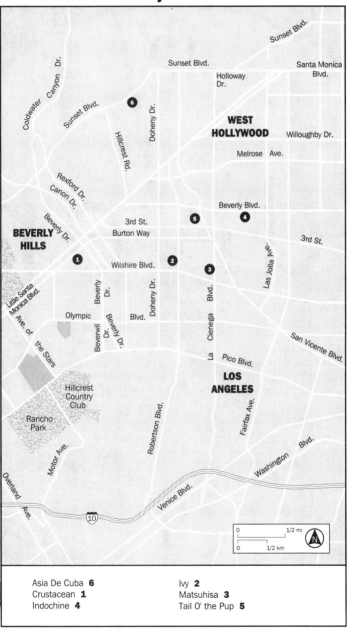

Asia De Cuba **6**
Crustacean **1**
Indochine **4**

Ivy **2**
Matsuhisa **3**
Tail O' the Pup **5**

3

sions

For those of you
who think L.A. is
a culturally vapid
wasteland, where
"nobody walks,"
just consider what
you watched on

television last night. That's L.A., good, bad, ugly, sunny, smoggy, stupid, high-concept, shallow, and working on a very bad sunburn that will result in a nasty melanoma in 12 years. We've got loads of weird and fun places to make that screamer boss an almost tolerable presence. Really. Come on. You know you've always wanted to go to see where "Baywatch" is filmed. Am I right? Consider the reality. The beach is sick, the freeways clogged, and everybody has a gun. We need a place to relax, maybe more than most people.

Getting Your Bearings

Okay, first of all, you've got to know where the hell you are. *Why* is another question, covered in volume II—"Ontology and Automology." Unlike places like Manhattan, where the streets and avenues obey almost logical rules, L.A. is a city that tries (unsuccessfully) to fit itself to a grid. It's curved into the Pacific, hump-backed, and so north is not really north. Its south meanders all over the place, and east-west demarcations are local municipality decisions. Just as in New York City, where people orient themselves by their subway/train stops, in L.A. it's all freeway related. Basically the Santa Monica Freeway (the 10) runs east-west, connecting Downtown to Santa Monica and the Beach. The Hollywood Freeway (the 101), runs north-south, winding through Downtown, Hollywood, and into the Valley before it changes character. These are your two most important freeway lines. From there, everything becomes much easier. The major boulevards (Venice, Pico, Olympic, Wilshire, Beverly, Melrose, Santa Monica, Sunset, Hollywood, Franklin) run east-west. They are crossed north-south by an assortment of avenues, streets, and boulevards: Vermont, Western, Normandie, Vine, Highland, La Brea, Crescent Heights, La Cienega, Fairfax, Robertson. Get these compass points/paths in the proper sequence, and you're ready to roll.

The Lowdown

Wild kingdom... The **L.A. Zoo** has had its ups and downs. At one time the perimeter fence was so full of holes that coyotes were coming in to snack on the flamingos, while the animal enclosures had deteriorated to the point where they were considered "unsafe" for keepers and animals, and the various water areas were universally slimy

and fetid with muck. In 1995 the U.S. Department of Agriculture cited the zoo for hundreds of cleanliness and safety violations, forcing it to clean up its act. Today the zoo is once again a place fit to take the kids. Remember Toshi? The little chimpanzee who was born here under questionable parentage? He was a love child and an instant media star, profiled in *People*. Then, four months after his birth, a couple of adolescent male chimps stomped him to death in what was described as a "gang killing." It's always the innocent who suffer.... Anyway, take the kids over to the warthog area where you can see the original models that Disney animators based their characters on in *The Lion King*. Fun fact: The zoo's biggest python, Baby, is 15 feet long, weighs 227 pounds, and (like all snakes) has no eyelids. Hmm, sounds like an agent to me. From late June through August, you can even spend the night in the zoo. It costs only $75 for adults—cheaper than a motel—and you get to fall asleep listening to the roars of lions, not crackheads. The price includes dinner, a nighttime tour, and breakfast. Also fun are the zoo's outdoor concerts, held all summer long. Meanwhile, a whole generation of animals that were never lucky enough to make it to the L.A. Zoo can be examined—or at least their remains can—at the **La Brea Tar Pits** and **George C. Page Museum**. In the stinky black pools in front of the museum, a family of fiberglass mastodons are getting a little lesson in survival. You can idle by and say thanks to their real-life counterparts for decomposing in such a way that you could have gas in your car. Inside the well-laid-out museum, you'll find hundreds of dire wolves' skulls arranged around the interior of the museum, like some Melrose hipster's idea of goth wallpaper. And in the back, safely behind glass, you'll see living animals/researchers sifting through zillions of tiny bones in the paleontology laboratory. My favorite exhibit is a holographic display of La Brea Woman, a 9,000-year-old female (who still looks pretty good, considering), segueing from bone to flesh. Like Toshi, she was a murder victim.

Ethnics 'R' us... When gangbangers ask a stranger in the hood, "Where you from?" they're not talking about ethnic background or your ancestral tree, and there's (unfortunately) no correct answer. For a less-threatening view of who we are and why we're all together here, however, there are a slew of museums around the city that detail the full range of the immigrant experience, legal and otherwise. The **Autry Museum of Western Heritage** is a good place to start, since it represents the conquerors—the ones who lynched, deported, and decimated as best they could everyone who was here before them. (This country was *built* on ethnic cleansing, bub.) The museum is devoted to the exploration, expansion, and conquest of the west by those saddleback invaders from the east. That's right: Cowboy Culture and all its attendant tools for torturing horses, cattle, and people. The Autry has probably the largest collection of Western memorabilia in all of California, including a very nice assortment of Colt firearms. In the same vein, but dedicated to the ancestors who were on the receiving end of those Colts, is the **Southwest Museum**. This is the best place in L.A. to go if you want to better understand and appreciate the culture of the American Indian. The museum covers Native American history from Alaska to South America, and also has an extensive collection of pre-Columbian pottery and textiles, as well as Hispanic folk and decorative arts. Of special local interest are the exhibits dealing with the Gabrielino Indians, those poor people who happened to be in the wrong place at the wrong time—right in the sights of the Spanish explorers and their missionary sidekicks who came here in the 17th century looking for gold and souls to save. Which brings us to **El Pueblo de Los Angeles Historical Monument**, located at the top of Olvera Street on the site of the Old Plaza, around which the original pueblo settlement was built. The oldest building here is the **Old Plaza Church**, built in the 1820s and still in use. Also check out the **Avila Adobe** structure, halfway down Olvera Street. It's the oldest existing residence in L.A., and has been refurbished to resemble the high-end living conditions a wealthy California family of the time (think Zorro) might have enjoyed. Moving forward in history, there's the **Latino Museum of History, Art, and Culture**, situated in a former Bank of America branch building across the street from Los Angeles City Hall, just a few blocks from Olvera Street. The museum is only a few years old, but its annual *Dia de los Muertos* exhibition has already become a must-see. In fact, the entire 25,000-foot complex is worth a visit for anyone interested in the Latino culture that so vividly defines current L.A. life. Farther down the street (and further forward in time) is the equally new (but much better-funded) **Japanese-American National Museum**, dedicated to the history and experiences of the Japanese immigrants who were so miserably treated by the U.S. government during World War II. Descriptions of the concentration camps used during the war to "relocate" the suspected potential traitors are chilling. The raw open slats of a reassembled Wyoming concentration camp, which housed Americans of Japanese extraction, are reminder enough of the crude and freezing conditions its unjustly interred inmates were forced to endure.

Move your fat a--... If you want to really get a grip on the underlying character of L.A., you've gotta know that its inhabitants like to move around. The city was populated in the first place because the robber barons of the last century needed passengers for their (at-the-time) useless and unnecessary railroads. L.A. signed on to a deal that San Francisco wouldn't accept, and voilà!—instant city. In this regard, a trip to **Travel Town Museum** in Griffith Park is quite instructive. Simply put, this is a "petting zoo" for locomotives, where civilians get a chance to climb over and through the largest collection of steam engines in the western United States, not to mention the museum's antique passenger and freight cars. There are 14 historic steam locomotives in all, the oldest being the ST&E 4-4-0 "American," built in 1864. The oddest item in the place is an M.177, the only AT&SF railcar motorcar ever constructed to operate with a gasoline engine. What a crazy idea! But one that segues very nicely into our second transportation-themed museum: the **Petersen Automotive Museum**. Located on Wilshire Boulevard's Miracle Mile and run by the County Natural History Museum, it has 200-plus vehicles on display, from rare cars to classics. This place is a perfect tribute to L.A.'s car culture, and it isn't just for weekend grease monkeys, either—kids love it, too. Also, don't miss the 24-foot-long, 11-foot-high dashboard display. Now *that's* an instrument panel I can deal with....

Navigating the Getty... The new **Getty Center** is without question the most beautiful public space in Los Angeles. And it's free all year-round—a fact that's especially appreciated at a time when most museums are charging up to

THE LOWDOWN | DIVERSIONS

$15 for special showings. The Getty charges only for parking, provided you're able to snag a parking reservation. Getting there can be a hassle, too: The steep canyon wall by the entrance kiosks makes for frequent backups when you arrive by car, and private tour buses to the Getty are expensive. I suggest you leave your car somewhere in lower Brentwood and hop on the Santa Monica Big Blue Bus 14, which runs every half hour during the week and hourly on weekends. From Bundy at Wilshire, the Big Blue takes only 15 minutes to reach Getty Center Drive and Sepulveda Boulevard. This way, you avoid the frustrating wait in line, so you can approach the museum on the hill with the correct mind-set: that you, personally, have been extended an invitation to the ball. A favorite time of arrival is late afternoon, when the deepening light bounces off the white travertine walls, the sunset to the west glows with smog, and below you crawl the bumper-to-bumper car lights on the 405—lots of folks going nowhere, slowly. What's inside? Lots of pretty pictures and antiquities from all over the world, from classical to modern. But the best art statement may be the museum space itself, high above the freeway. It's a rare view of L.A. that you can only get here. The Getty should be recognized as well for being one of the most generous community-art-directed outreach facilities in the city. It also employed just about every freelance architect in L.A. during its reported $1 billion construction.

Freeway art... L.A. has been called the mural capital of the world. If that's true, it's all thanks to the Chicano political struggle that began in the 1960s. The mural movement grew out of attempts by local activists to educate their constituency, literate and nonliterate alike. Murals were a way to show pride and build a sense of community identity. They flourished first in the barrios of East L.A., but today the art form has spread throughout the city. Unlike the stuff in galleries, this art is open to everyone. **SPARC** (the Social and Public Art Resource Center) is the leading proponent and resource for muralists throughout the city. The center works with hundreds of community groups to promote and protect their artwork, with an emphasis on socially aware, ethnically diverse statements. The organization's best-known project is the ***Great Wall of Los Angeles***, a half-mile-long mural that depicts the history of California from the perspective of women and people of color. The project was conceived and led by SPARC's Judy Baca and was carried out by her art students on a section of wall in the Tujunga Wash drainage canal in Van Nuys. It's a bit of a drive, but well worth the trip. Incidentally, do you know why L.A. has murals all over the freeways? Cynics claim that it's a cheap antidote to road rage: *The traffic is so bad out here, you've got to have something to take your mind off that pistol in the glove compartment.* In reality, the answer may be simply that the huge concrete walls that frame the freeways (built mainly for safety and sound control) present themselves as the biggest canvases in the world, with an ever-changing captive audience. Funded by money from Uncle Sam, local artists first started defacing the sides of ramps, overpasses, and freeway-facing buildings in the mid-'70s. You'll see their paintings everywhere, some of them not so pleasing—like the scary **Buckle Up!** done by an L.A. policeman. It depicts a uniformed cop's face, palm trees mirrored in his reflective dark glasses. No eyes. *Nice*...just what I want to see when I get pulled over. The huge **Olympics mural** on the side of the Victor Clothing building on Broadway in Downtown is typical of the major push for wall art that took place just prior to the 1984 Olympics. It's bright and garish, with Olympics iconography scattered throughout. Apparently Buffy Chandler, part of the family that owns the *L.A. Times*, was so upset by it that she had the new *Times* employee parking lot built in just the right spot to hide the mural from the newspaper's offices. On the other side of Victor is a huge **portrait of Anthony Quinn dancing**. You'll get the best view of it walking on Third Street, south of Broadway. If you want the full Chicano feeling, take a cruise through East L.A., starting at **Self-Help Graphics**, the highly successful art center on Cesar E. Chavez Avenue. You can ask in here for directions or maps to the best local wall art. Plus, the in-store gallery is always worth a visit—some say its Day of the Dead altars are the best in the city.

Neon sights... You won't see any neon in Beverly Hills, because the city fathers there have passed laws to keep the visual blight out of residential areas. But at one time L.A. was Neon City, and there are still pockets of garish lighting left over from the good old days. On Sunset, just west of Echo Park Avenue in Echo Park, above **Jensen's**

Recreation Center, a glowing bowler rolls a red ball toward neon pins. As you're heading south on Alvarado Street to Westlake Boulevard, check out the Wilshire Street corridor signs around **MacArthur Park**, especially at the Westlake Theater and the Wilshire Royale Hotel. (While you're cruising MacArthur Park, consider whether you need an extra green card or fake ID. This is the place to get one, and it only takes a few minutes.) Next, turn north on Vermont Avenue and go up to Third Street to the **Superet Light Church** and its 11-foot-high glowing purple heart. For more modern neon, there's always the **Museum of Neon Art (MONA)** on West Olympic Boulevard. More than 20 of MONA's older, larger pieces can also be seen for free at **Universal Citywalk** in Universal City. And at **Track 16 Gallery** in Bergamot Station you'll find another sizable collection.

Annual events... What's the best thing about being at the **Tournament of Roses Parade** on New Year's Day? Answer: Knowing that in three-quarters of the country people are going around complaining about windchill, slipping on sidewalks covered in frozen urine, and dreading the fact that they have another three months of the same to look forward to (kind of the way Angelenos feel about summer in August—but that's another story...). Anyway, we celebrate the weather everyone else hates us for with a big fancy parade and lots and lots of flowers and celebrities on floats, all topped off with a football game. And just like football, the whole thing is much better when seen on TV, unless you love big crowds and camping out for days to score the best seats. February brings **Chinese New Year** in Chinatown, culminating in the **Golden Dragon Parade**. It's nowhere near as much fun as the festivities in San Francisco (there are *way* fewer fireworks, for one thing), but at least you can find parking. In March, there's the **Los Angeles Marathon**, in which tens of thousands of people run 26 miles through the L.A. streets *without* a cop shooting at them. That in itself makes the footrace a notable spectator sport. The **Spring Festival of Flowers** also debuts that month at Descanso Gardens. Featuring one of the most glorious bulb displays in the Southland, it stays "up" until mid-April, depending on the weather. In April we all head downtown to Olvera Street to get our pets sprin kled with holy water in the **Blessing of the Animals**. Jesus isn't just for people anymore: You'll see dogs, cats, snakes, mice—I even spotted one guy wheeling a Sony console TV through the line. Also in April is the **Fiesta Broadway**, a huge block party throughout Downtown's Central Market: mariachis, drunks, food stalls, drunks, cops on horseback—and drunks. May is **Cinco de Mayo** time in Olvera Street as well as over in East L.A. and the city of Whittier, with lots of parades and food stalls and (again) mariachis and cops. In June the **Playboy Jazz Festival** brings top-name groups to the Hollywood Bowl, while over in WeHo, all Dykes on Bikes and Queers Without Fears come out of the closet for the **Gay and Lesbian Pride Parade**. The **Fourth of July** fireworks displays are held up and down the coastline, but my favorite is launched from Dodger Stadium. Also this month is the **Lotus Festival**, timed to coincide with the blooming of Echo Park Lake's lotus plants. This is an Asian/Pacific Islander event that boasts Cambodian dancers, Thai food stalls, Dragon Boat races, and ducks everywhere. Bonus attraction: This is one of the few times of the year when one is allowed to cross the bridge onto Duck Island. (Watch where you step.) August is the time of the Bon Festival in most of Japan, and over here Japanese-Americans mark the occasion with **Nisei Week** in Little Tokyo. Again, lots of ethnic food from food stalls, plus really cheap bonsai trees, pottery, and kimono cloth. In September the celebration moves out to Pomona for the **L.A. County Fair**, where the 4-H Club meets trailer park culture. If you like watching pigs shit and enjoy crowds, nasty fast food, and getting a headache from the sun, then by all means come on out. (The amateur art shows are a complete hoot.) October brings the **Festival of Masks** to Hancock Park. You'll find ethnic food stalls, as usual, but also theater, free music, contests for the best masks, and a parade down Wilshire Boulevard. It's the perfect lead-in event for Halloween, even though most of these masks are either wonderful folk craft objects or pure works of whimsical art—nothing you'd want to wear out. **Halloween** itself has two special hotspots—WeHo (or West Hollywood), where cross-dressing is celebrated all year long anyway, and Hollywood Boulevard, long notorious for playing host to the weirdest sewer of sickos ever to wear a Ken Starr mask. Then right on the heels of All

THE LOWDOWN | DIVERSIONS

Soul's Eve, at the beginning of November, comes **Dia de los Muertos**—the Day of the Dead! You'll see altars erected all around East L.A. to honor the previous year's departed. As a starting point, check out **Self-Help Graphics** on Cesar Chavez Avenue. At the end of the month is the **Doo Dah Parade**, which used to be a street-guerrilla theater parody of the Tournament of Roses extravaganza, but has since morphed into just another cynical, money-making show. Still, where else can you see the Teenage Alcoholic Precision Projectile Vomiting Marching Band? Then there's the **Hollywood Christmas Parade**, held on Thanksgiving weekend and featuring lots of celebrities you never heard of or thought were dead (maybe they are), marching bands, floats, drunks, cops, and an early appearance by Santa Claus. Just another typical night on Hollywood Boulevard, if you ask me. **Las Posadas**—the candlelight procession out of the San Gabriel Mission at Olvera Street the week before Christmas—is a soothing and authentic reminder of our Spanish-American roots.

Who needs MOMA?... The **Museum of Contemporary Art (MOCA)** and its sister institution, the **Geffen Contemporary,** are L.A.'s most focused statements about the health and vibrancy of the contemporary art scene. MOCA is situated up on Bunker Hill in a wonderful Arata Isozaki postmodern structure that will still look good 50 years from now. The museum has a huge post-1940 permanent collection and mounts more than 20 additional exhibitions each year—historical and thematic shows as well as one-person retrospectives, covering everything from painting, sculpture, and drawing to video, photography, film, music, dance, performance, design, and architecture. Plagiarists' alert: Writing and sketching is allowed in the galleries, but in pencil only (pencils are available at the information centers). The Geffen Contemporary, a.k.a. the TC—so-called because it was the Temporary Contemporary prior to the completion of MOCA's main facility—is down in Little Tokyo. Less stuffy than MOCA, The TC became known early on for throwing wild parties that reflected the vibe and energy of the Downtown art movement. That sense of chaos, fun, and anything-goes art is still alive here. The space was once a police garage until Frank Gehry revamped it, turning it into one of the best warehouse sites for art you'll find anywhere. The museum has a free-form open layout, with an industrial high ceiling, wood and steel beams, and gray-painted cement flooring. The space also houses a reading room and an artist background display center for explanations of what the art means for those who just don't get it. Art *breathes* here.

More free art… Once you get in the habit of seeing art for no charge, it's hard to go back to paying conventional entrance fees. Thursday evenings from 5 to 8 are free at the Museum of Contemporary Art in Downtown and at the Geffen in Little Tokyo, as well as at the new **Japanese American National Museum** next door to the Geffen. During the summer, the Geffen hosts outdoor Thursday-night jazz concerts—also free, with wine and beer available. Since parking in Little Tokyo is easy and starts at just $2, your best bet is definitely to head over here. Normally one museum a day is enough to absorb, but the experiences at the Geffen and the Japanese American National Museum are so different (and they're close to each other) that they make a highly compatible double bill.

Words on paper and in your ear… There is no more glorious testament to the vitality of Downtown than the **Central Library**, a weird Babylonian ziggurat that represents one of the high-water marks of L.A. design, mixing Art Deco with the ancient Middle East. This is the place to come when you need to take the pulse of the city. The chairs are comfortable, the facility clean, and the computers on-line. The fabulous open-air atrium, part of a major expansion and redesign after a disastrous arson fire in the '80s, is a wonderful symbol of appreciation for the power of the word. This is an essential L.A. landmark, free and open to all. The library also hosts numerous readings, storytelling sessions, and photo exhibits. Over in Venice, you'll find the **Beyond Baroque Literary Arts Center**, the main outlet for L.A. poets who are serious about their craft. In existence for more than two decades, the facility has ongoing readings by the hip and famous Thursday through Sunday nights (Exene Cervenka (of X) and Viggo Mortensen, among others), along with free community workshops and readings by developing artists the rest of the week. Complementing the readings are the center's constantly changing gallery of visual art, and the adjacent bookstore—which accommodates the reader with table and chairs, making the center a welcoming hangout for those who still find comfort and meaning in the power of words alone.

Art openings... Being early-evening events, art openings require no RSVPs or costly tickets, and usually come with free drinks, making them the perfect venue for meeting up with a bunch of other poor, thirsty losers whose main sustenance for the night is going to be the accompanying cheese and crackers. Everyone stands around looking for friends and/or scanning the crowd for later-night companionship. Plus, you might even see some good art. And did I mention that the wine is free? First stop is **Bergamot Station Arts Center**, which houses over 30 galleries in addition to the newly relocated **Santa Monica Museum of Art**. The sprawling, seven-acre complex offers an artistic variety not to be found anywhere else in the city. It also has a large parking lot, is wheelchair- and baby-carriage friendly, and is very easy to circumnavigate and sample by whim. Check out the **Gallery of Contemporary Photography**, for its consistently excellent choices, and the lively **Track 16**, where at a recent opening the beauteous Karen Finley writhed naked in a pool of honey while reciting her own X-rated version of *Winnie-the-Pooh*. Openings usually take place on weekends, starting around 6 p.m. Check out the *L.A. Weekly* Openings section for more information. On a warm Friday evening, when movies are being shown on the building walls, and thousands of wine-toting art crawlers are slithering around the galleries, it's like heaven—part '60s happening, part Disneyland for Art. Also in Santa Monica on Main Street (after several years in a Downtown location) is the **Rico Gallery**. It's kept some of that Downtown edge by setting up shop in an old theater. The shows revolve around conceptual themes with lots of participants, so openings are usually very celebratory and lively. Known for providing a supportive environment for emerging artists, the staff are involved, enthusiastic, and accessible. Moving Downtown, we come to **Art Share**, held on the second Thursday night of each month in the heart of the Artist District. This is a 30,000-square-foot "community art incubator" that holds openings for 20 or more artists at a time, with 75 percent of the extremely reasonable sale prices going directly to the artists themselves. The artists change with each show, insuring a diverse and changing crowd month-to-month. Your $3 donation at the door supports the ongoing community programs sustained by this nonprofit organization, and also gets you into a 99-seat cabaretlike theater at the center of the warehouse where seasoned jazz, rock, and world musicians jam for the crowds who drop in between viewings. The art stays up anywhere from a day to a month, so openings are especially recommended here. If you're unfamiliar with downtown geography, just follow the klieg light—it'll take you right to the front door. And if you're nervous about the neighborhood, the security guards will even walk you back to your car. Are you a good artist looking for a showing? Give Art Share a call.... In the same neighborhood, just around the corner from **Bloom's General Store** (a major hang for local artists) is **Action:Space**. This is a rental studio that morphs regularly into gallery events, theatrical presentations, performance art, fund-raisers, and great parties, all overseen by its gracious, soft-spoken interior designer, whose presence alone reassures the ever-changing clientele that a good time on the fringe will be had by all. The art gallery is connected to a performance space by a tunnel-like corridor that passes through a hidden outdoor garden—perfect for meditation, noisy imbibing, or simply sucking up oxygen—so that moving through the space is in itself transforming, as the name suggests. Things get booked at the last minute, and events are usually open to the public, so I recommend just dropping by. If nothing's happening that night, something is sure to be going on at **Al's Bar** next door. And while Bloom's General Store isn't a gallery, it *is* a central meeting place for the Downtown artist district, and is also the best spot to find out what's going on in the neighborhood. Here you can schmooze on a couch at the back of the store; rent a video; get a candy bar, tube of toothpaste, or magazine; or savor the large assortment of fine cigars, including the "Monica #1." At the front of the store you'll find cards, flyers, and free newspapers scattered around the front window describing upcoming events—the clues to your next stop. Two La Brea galleries are also worthy of a peek: The **Jane Baum Gallery**, known for its fun openings (held about every month and a half), carries a lot of international contemporary art, including sculpture, painting, and installation pieces, along with New York artists who are good enough for the local market. There are additional galleries upstairs, so the place has a bit of an art mall feeling, but the scene is a welcome relief from all the snobby salesgirls in the retail shops outside. Just up the street is the **Fahey/Klein Gallery**, also known for party-like openings. The crowd is a little different here, because the gallery represents contemporary photographers as well; in fact, it's probably the best-known fine-art photography gallery on the street. Up on North La Brea Avenue is the **Paul Kopeikin Gallery,** which sells fine-art photography by such contemporary artists as Gary Winogrand.

Community art... Cruising down Crenshaw Boulevard past the Baldwin Hills Mall, you turn west onto West 43rd Street and leave the neon lights of generic shopping venues behind you. You're now in a little-known neighborhood enclave of low-key, single-story, '60s architecture sprinkled with cafes, small and friendly shops, and easy parking. Welcome to **Leimert Park Village**. The quiet, tree-lined streets radiating into this village feel like lower Beverly Hills, but in fact this is a well-established African-American arts community, an area where almost every storefront addresses the needs of the artistic instinct. Up and down the two-block span of **Degnan Boulevard** are at least half a dozen shops featuring authentic African clothing, fabrics, antiques, historical souvenirs, and gift items influenced by the African-American experience. **The Dance Collective**, located mid-avenue, offers free classes in West African dance, drumming, and personal enhancement to after-schoolers. And at night the street transforms itself into a first-rate jazz scene, drawing on superb local talent as well as big names. A neighborhood favorite: the rows of dapper men playing chess nightly outside **Fifth Street Dick's Coffee**, where conversations are thoughtful and unhurried. Day or night, the area is a great place to park and just follow the flow of life. At the top of Leimert Park Village, also on West 43rd Street, you'll find the **Leimert Park Fine Art Gallery**, a beautifully crafted community complex that serves as a showcase for African-American fine art. Embedded in the strips of wood flooring—lovingly laid down by the gallery owners themselves—are hand-painted small portraits. When an envisioned marble entrance proved too expensive to build, cement was painted and polished to give the desired elegant marbleized effect. The gallery fans out in a U-shape, with one wing devoted primarily to African-American portraits and the other featuring African life tableaux in the form of sculptures and bronze statues, including a copy of a tree of life by resident artist Michael Chukes that was recently presented to Archbishop Desmond Tutu. The gallery also rents offices (it even helps start-up community businesses with the paperwork), and offers free children's art classes on Saturdays. Gallery openings rock with local jazz groups, which play into the night—until the owner makes everyone leave so she can get some sleep.

Left of MOCA... It's time for something a little different, the left-of-center art world—WAY left, as in maybe another universe. To start with, there's the wonderful **Museum of Jurassic Technology**. Included in the permanent collection are exhibits like *The Stink Ant of the Cameroon* and *Fruit Stone Carving*, while over in the rotating show a piece is currently on display called *No One May Ever Have the Same Information Again* (made up of letters to the Mount Wilson Observatory, circa 1915–35). You get the idea. Or maybe you don't.... This is a place where parody meets reverence, where the meaning of things, rather than their value, is highlighted. Inside the **Soap Plant** is **La Luz de Jesus Gallery**, an homage to outsider art. Here you'll find Ed "Big Daddy" Roth's Rat Fink–style illustrations and paintings that are halfway between comics and art, usually with a certain trailer park trash appeal. La Luz also hosts the best openings in the city. They're held on the first Friday of the month and are unlike any other. Don't expect white wine and mineral water or snotty West Siders sniffing over the latest de-constructed minimalist offerings dragged out from some Venice garret. Here the refreshment is a keg of beer, and the "patrons" look more like club kids: tattooed, pierced, and sporting crazy-color hair. There's often live music, too, and if the lowbrow aspect wears thin, you can always just wander around the Soap Plant. It's better than a trip to the Louvre. Also in left field, but at the opposite end of the commercial spectrum from the previous two examples, are the galleries at the snooty **Art Center** in Pasadena. This very expensive school is the undisputed leader in producing commercially successful, egoistic drones for the worlds of advertising, illustration, photography, graphic art, and environmental and transportation design. Want to know why your car radio is just slightly out-of-reach, or who dreamed up that latest, offensive junkie-fashion ad campaign? Stop by the students' gallery at Art Center to get a glimpse of where these design horrors come from and what new ones await you. That groovy new Chrysler that looks like a 1940s panel truck but handles like a Miata? Designed by an Arts Center kid. The school was started by an advertising exec in 1930 (what a surprise!)—but, all griping aside, a visit to the galleries is easily as entertaining as going to MOCA, and it's free. Check out the **Alyce de Roulet Williamson Gallery** for a look at established artists and movements. The student galleries are even more interesting—and scarier.

Oddball museums... Trolling through Hollywood Boulevard must include a visit to the **Frederick's of Hollywood Lingerie Museum**. Its undergarment collection isn't as big as, say, Pamela Lee's bra drawer, but where else could you check out the dainties worn by Marilyn Monroe, Madonna, Mae West, Natalie Wood, and Elizabeth Taylor, not to mention cross-dressing regular guys Milton Berle and Tony Curtis? You'll also get to see how women's feelings about what goes next to their skin have changed over the last 50 years. And for pure camp enjoyment, you can peruse a selection of Mr. Frederick's catalogs. At the **Carole & Barry Kaye Museum of Miniatures** on Wilshire Boulevard's Miracle Mile, you'll find perfectly scaled miniatures of the Vatican, King Tut's Tomb, and even O.J.'s courtroom. My favorite is the replica of the *Titanic*'s deck, made out of 75,000 toothpicks and two gallons of glue. Glue sniffing will never be the same.

That's-not-entertainment museums... The **Los Angeles Museum of Television and Radio**, sister museum to the original New York branch, has set up shop right in Beverly Hills. I guess that means *we're* the King of All Media now. Right? This museum is a major research center for the broadcast media, as important to the cultural life of L.A. as MOCA or the Getty. (Too bad about the location, but in this town money talks and bullshit takes the bus. Beverly Hills is not exactly the home of media—it's simply where the money sinks to the bottom of the feeding pool.) It has a collection of over 100,000 radio and television programs and commercials, all cross-referenced on computer and available for private viewing and listening. You sit in the specially designed research stations—some can even accommodate a whole family—and control all aspects of playback yourself. There's also a fully functioning studio in the museum where you can sit in and watch actual tapings and broadcasts (about as exciting as watching grass grow, if you want to know the truth). While the Museum of Radio and Television is geared to serious researchers, the **Hollywood Entertainment Museum**, which opened just a few years ago, is much less intimidating and much more tourist-friendly—more Universal Studios than Library of Congress. They try to cover every aspect of the business called show, from fashion and makeup to special effects and cell animation. Shades of the Frederick's Lingerie Museum: They've even got Joan Crawford's padded shoulders and Marlon Brando's T-shirt. There's also an exhibit that attempts to deconstruct Hollywood into five key words: Glamour, Romance, Comedy, Action, and Spectacle. (Hey, what about *Money*?) Probably the most interesting displays are two complete TV studio sets, one from "Star Trek" and the other from "Cheers." Gee, they looked so much bigger on the tube. Finally, for those who haven't been totally disillusioned by the experience, the museum also has an Electronic Library section with a data bank for Industry jobs.

Griffith Observatory and Planetarium... This is many Angelenos' favorite building/complex in all of L.A., so it gets its own category. Not only is the Griffith Observatory as close to the country as you can get in a 10-minute drive from Silver Lake, but it's also on top of a mountain that boasts a tremendous view of the basin. On a clear winter day you can see Catalina Island to the west, the coast of Malibu to the north, and the snow-capped mountains of the San Gabriels to the southeast—and that's just from the parking lot. The building alone is wonderful, consisting of three large copper domes that hold a solar telescope, a 12-inch Zeiss Refracting

Telescope, and the planetarium theater, respectively. Built in the years 1933–35, the overall style represents Art Deco at its peak. What's a statue of James Dean doing next to a bust of Copernicus and a bunch of famous astronomers, you ask? In fact, major segments of *Rebel Without a Cause* were filmed here. When you go inside the observatory, the first thing you'll see is a slowly moving Foucault Pendulum that provides a physical demonstration of the movement of the earth. The pendulum is a 240-pound brass ball hanging from a wire 40 feet long, which swings in a constant straight line, while the earth (and the building and you and me) is turning underneath it. It's set up each morning and runs all day. Within the Hall of Science, you'll find six-foot-diameter globes of the earth and moon, a large collection of meteorites, one rock from Mars, spacecraft and telescope models, a one-fifth-scale model of the Hubble Space Telescope, live images of the sun (when the sun is shining), a seismograph, a Tesla coil, a camera obscura, astronomy computer games, and loads more. Whether you're a local or a visitor, it's a great place for both kids and adults.

Beautiful buildings we haven't torn down for mini malls—yet... L.A. has a well-deserved reputation for razing structures with more aesthetic appeal than commercial value, especially if a freeway or high-rise is involved or Starbucks wants that corner. Fortunately, they haven't torn down everything worth looking at, at least not yet. Let's start off first with the **MAK Center for Art and Architecture**, formerly the home of Adolph Schindler. (MAK, by the way, stands for Osterreichinsches Museum Fur Angewandte Kunst, or Austria's Museum of Applied Art—Schindler was Austrian.) If you want to really understand L.A.'s non–Spanish Colonial architectural roots, a visit to the studio and residence of this influential architect is absolutely essential. Schindler lived here from 1922 until his death in 1953, and the building reflects his distinctive appreciation for sound, light, and form. It is the prototypical California house: one story, an open floor plan, a flat roof, and a patio entrance that opens into a garden rather than onto the street. Schindler's assistant was Richard Neutra, an architect who went on to surpass his teacher in

terms of local influence: Some call him the most important Los Angeles modernist architect ever. Frank Lloyd
Wright worked his magic here in the '20s as well, and you
can appreciate his striking vision by driving past some of
his houses, sometimes even stopping for a walk-through.
One of his most famous designs is the **Ennis House**, a
massively heavy monument in Los Feliz that has been
likened to a Mayan temple. It was made with "knit-block"
construction, and is in the process of being restored by the
owner. The **Hollyhock House**, inside the Barnsdall Park
complex in Los Feliz, is one of the few Wright homes you
can inspect fairly intimately. The house itself has stylized
hollyhock-motif ornamentation—hence the name—and
has a definite pre-Columbian mood to it. You can also see
Wright's idiosyncratic idea of furniture and interior spa-
tial arrangement. Historical note: Schindler was the fore-
man on this construction project while Wright was away
in Japan.

Downtown: not for skyscrapers only... Los Angeles
City Hall is where we have to begin this section, since it's
the most recognizable symbol of L.A. Clark Kent worked
here, and Joe Friday displayed it on his badge at the start of
every "Dragnet." The building dates from 1928 and
resembles both a temple and a skyscraper. The best views
of Downtown can be seen from the upper floors of the
tower—if you can get up there. Only employees are
allowed into the upper reaches. The interior is Byzantine
dominated by heavy wood, with a rotunda that murmurs
Big-Time Power. Up until the mid-'50s the 28-story
building was the only structure in the city allowed to
exceed L.A.'s 150-foot height limit. Today it's been almost
totally restored. Fans of *Blade Runner* will recognize the
interior of the **Bradbury Building** immediately: it's where
the androids' final battle takes place. The exterior is dull as
a brick, but the inside—which has been wonderfully
restored—is amazing. It's all lacy ironwork and glass, with
open stairways and glazed brick walls, and at the top is a
huge skylight. The Bradbury was built in 1893 and is one
of L.A.'s oldest and best-maintained buildings. Directly
across the street is the **Million Dollar Theater**, built in
1918 by the firm of Morgan, Walls, and Clements, and
boasting a remarkable Churrigueresque exterior. It looks
like a Spanish church from Barcelona, but it's right here on

Broadway. Close by is another sample of the same architects' work at the **Mayan Theater**, which is now a club. Built in 1927, its design includes seven Mayan warriors above the entrance and a wonderfully painted cast-concrete facade. You could plop it down near Chichen Itza, and it wouldn't look all that strange. Well, maybe a little.... For a while it looked as though the splendor of **Union Station** was going to fall into total disrepair as train travel vanished. But the 1939 building has come back from the dead big time: Its cathedral ceilings are all clean and bright, the blend of Art Deco and Spanish decor perfectly maintained. Even the marble inlaid floor shines. It all has to do with our expanding inner-city mass transit system—the MTA, MetroLink, Dash, and Amtrak. They all converge here now, and Union Station is once again a vibrant, living place. It even features a very good California cuisine restaurant (Traxx) that is hugely popular with Downtown executives. Finally, any visit to Downtown must include a drive past the **Coca-Cola Building** on Central Avenue. It was built in the mid-1930s, when Art Deco was still raging. If the portholes, ship doors, promenade deck, and catwalk remind you of the *Titanic*, that's totally intentional. The design was modeled after 1890s-era ocean liners, back when traveling was a glorious experience and Coca-Cola was still made with cocaine. Those were the days.

Hollywood icons... Just up the street from Hollywood and Vine is the **Capitol Records Building**, one of the major landmarks of Hollywood. It was built in 1954 and, despite the denials of its architect, is clearly intended to resemble a stack of 45-rpm vinyl records ("They're like CD singles, son—only black."). Back when the Beatles and Frank Sinatra were on the label, Capitol was the Gold Card of record companies, and its headquarters was the first building of its size (12 stories) to be fully air-conditioned. Today it produces the likes of Garth Brooks and the Foo Fighters. How the mighty have fallen.... And speaking of falling, the **Hollywood Sign** is no longer open for suicide jumps. Perched on the shoulders of Mount Lee in Griffith Park overlooking Hollywood, this "most famous sign in the world" (sez the Chamber of Commerce) was originally spelled HOLLYWOOD-LAND and was erected, appropriately enough, to advertise a housing development in the sticks. It used to be you could easily slip through the chain-link fence that surrounds the sign near the access road on Mount Lee, but the fence has recently been reinforced. It's still possible to make your way through the brush, but I wouldn't recommend it during the summer rattlesnake season.

Buildings built like food... Ever since the '20s, the hokey use of huge buildings shaped like common objects—shoes, hats, a dog—have been a campy part of L.A. schlock. The Brown Derby is gone, but a few choice landmarks remain. One favorite reminder of this genre is **Randy's Donuts** out in Inglewood, which is frequently used as a movie backdrop. Built in 1954, the stand has a huge donut on top of it. It's just so L.A., you know? Deep-fried dough, plus you get to snack on an old-fashioned donut while watching jets glide in for their landing at nearby LAX. You can also buy a T-shirt with the donut on the front. And don't overlook **Tail O' The Pup**—the West Hollywood hot-dog stand built in the form of a giant concrete hot dog. There's more out there to be spotted as you drive around, but all this greasy fast food has made me kind of ill....

Professional sports... Ha ha ha ha ha ha ha!!!!!! Don't! Stop! I can't stand it! Los Angeles professional sports? It's an oxymoron—or maybe oxen morons is the better term. Anyway, we don't have a football team, the **Lakers** have deserted the Forum for the yet-to-be-finished Staples Center, and as I write this, the **Dodgers** are currently in last place. Let's not even talk about the **L.A. Kings.** Or the **Clippers.** In fact, in the last 11 years L.A. pro sports teams (NHL, NBA, NFL, and Major League Baseball) have won no championships. Zero. Zilch. Nada. It's the city's longest overall losing streak since major professional sports came here in 1946 with the Rams (now in St. Louis). In other words, we're Number None! Why do our teams suck so badly now? A sportswriter for the *L.A. Times* says it's because: "Athletes go to places like Detroit or Chicago to work...Athletes come here to retire, make movies, hang out with their families, chill." Hey—it works for me. So we do have pro teams, but I don't think I can recommend any of them for anything other than spending too much money to drink high-priced beer and eat gut-busting fried food while watching a bunch of millionaires struggle to look like they're interested. If you want to see some real athletes giving their all, my advice is to check out the horse races at the **L.A. County Fair**, where you'll find both thoroughbred and quarter-horse racing. And if two-year-old females get your blood going, there's also the **Santa Anita Race Track**, open from December through April. The track is way the hell out in Arcadia, but in the winter the views of the mountains are glorious. The facility is beautiful, too—just try to forget that the stables were used as a temporary concentration camp for innocent Japanese-Americans during WW II. *Much* closer to the real world is the **Hollywood Park** racing facility, which just celebrated its 61st birthday. The park was started by 600 investors, many of them members of the Hollywood elite, fellows like Walt Disney (Uncle Walt, a gambler?!), Bing Crosby, Sam Goldwyn, and Darryl Zanuck. It burned down in 1949 and has seen constant renovation since then, the most recent being the addition of the **Hollywood Park and Casino** in 1994—giving you yet another place to lose your money. Feeling greedy *and* lucky? In 1998 the casino's Pick 6 winners picked up a guaranteed $15-million payoff.

Angelyn, Valentino, and other frights... Ten years ago I passed Angelyn on Sunset, lanquidly cruising along in her pink vintage T-Bird. Our eyes met, and I felt a cold clammy hand placed on my shoulder. I looked away. Quickly. Angelyn is famous for being famous, the ur-celebrity who has made herself recognizable by spending millions (supposedly) on billboards and bus stop shelter posters. They actually advertise nothing but her. Nobody knows how old she really is—the best guess is that she's somewhere in her sixties. Her breasts are in the Kitten Natividad range, and her blank, pursed-lips expression is straight out of Andy Warhol. Reportedly she was so upset at being included in the "Futurama" opening sequence (on a billboard, hooked up to an oxygen tank) that she's moved to New York. Uh-oh. You're in for it now, Gotham. To check out what awaits us all, regardless of how many billboards we've graced, a tour of celebrity graves is always quite instructive. At **Hollywood Memorial Park Cemetery**, off a particularly seedy stretch of Santa Monica Boulevard, you'll find the last resting places of Rudolph Valentino, Cecil B. DeMille, Tyrone Power, and Peter Lorre, among others, plus a fake tombstone for

Jayne Mansfield (put up by her fan club). Finding them can be a bit tricky, but you're in a graveyard, so what's the rush? Over in the **Westwood Village Memorial Park** lie the remains of Marilyn Monroe, Natalie Wood, Truman Capote, Burt Lancaster, Donna Reed, and *Playboy* centerfold Dorothy Stratten. Frank Zappa and Roy Orbison are also buried here, but in unmarked graves. Finally, in the **Holy Cross Cemetery and Mausoleum** in Culver City, you'll stumble across Bing Crosby, Rita Hayworth, Charles Boyer, Jackie Coogan, Rosalind Russell, Al Jolson, Jack Benny, and Manson-family victim Sharon Tate.

Living in concrete... **Mann's Chinese Theater** is where you can put your feet into the cement shoe prints of various stars from yesterday and today. Also handprints. And legs, if you can find Betty Grable. The theater (it used to be known as Graumann' s Chinese) is invariably full of yokels from all over, oohing and aahing as they stare down at the ground in the "Forecourt of the Stars." The sidewalk contains the imprints of more than 180 celebrities, from Gene Kelly and Humphrey Bogart to the entire "I Love Lucy" cast (wasn't that a TV show?). But where's Pee Wee Herman? Tell me that! Well, maybe you can find his imprint over on the Porn Walk of Fame, instead, located in front of the **Tomkat Theater** (formerly the XXX Pussycat Theater, back in the heyday of movie-theater porn). It's now a gay theater, but out front on the sidewalk are the handprints of some of the stars of deep-throated yesteryear: Linda Lovelace, Marilyn Chambers, and Harry Reems. Finally, in front of the Guitar Center store on sunset you'll find the **Hollywood RockWalk**, a "tourist attraction" every bit as crass as Mann's Chinese, but without the history. I mean, Eddie Van Halen? KISS? Dick Clark? Les Paul and John Lee Hooker I can understand, but the Doobie Brothers? Puh-leeeze....

Parks of note... L.A. is filthy with parks. That's one of the advantages of being spread out over such a great expanse of land. The king of them all is **Griffith Park** in Los Feliz. It's the largest city park in the United States; here you'll find the Hollywood sign, the Griffith Observatory, the Greek Theater, the **Los Angeles Zoo**, Travel Town Museum, and the Autry Museum of Western Heritage. You can also choose between a very tricky (and steep) nine-hole public golf course on the park's west side, and a nice, rolling 18-hole course on the east side. The park has two main entrances, one at Western Avenue, the second at Vermont Avenue, both leading onto walkways that meet at the Observatory. There is an additional entrance at Riverside Drive and Los Feliz that takes you to the east-side attractions, as well as a closed access road from Westmoreland that goes around the eastern side of the mountains. This last is a popular hang for gay men trolling in search of a quickie in the woods, but it's also favored by dog walkers, joggers, and bikers. The only traffic is the occasional film crew, and the views of the valley are astounding—plus, in the evening you'll certainly see deer, and maybe even a coyote. The trails coming up from Coldwater Canyon (below the Hollywood sign) are also used by dog people, hikers, and horseback riders. (No mountain bikes allowed.) For the ultimate park view, hike up from the observatory parking lot to the peak of **Mount Hollywood** (it takes about an hour at a very easy pace). Over to the east, **Elysium Park** wraps around Dodger Stadium and the L.A. Police Academy. During the '60s, this was where the hippie be-ins took place. It's both wilder and more parklike than Griffith, with steep shoulders to the east and loads of picnic areas, similar to the picnic areas on Griffith Park's east side. Way less crowded than Griffith, though with fewer attractions, Elysium is especially popular with Latino families. It's a great place to run, bike, or walk your dog. And don't worry—most of those gunshots you hear are coming from the Police Academy's practice range. Out in Pacific Palisades there's **Will Rogers State Park**, where you'll find a polo field—the only outdoor one in the city—as well as the ranch-house home of the late comedian. The interior of the main house is maintained just as it was in the late '20s and '30s when the family lived here, complete with Rogers' collection of Indian rugs and baskets, a stuffed calf (given to Rogers in hopes that he'd rope *it* instead of his friends), and a porch swing hanging in the middle of the living room. The park sits on 186 acres, and is located at the very southern tip of the Santa Monica Mountains, making it the closest available place to the city if you want to park and start walking along the **Backbone Trail**. A steady but not rigorous walk brings you up to **Inspiration Point**, from where you can see the entire Santa Monica Bay, all of Century City, and on into

Downtown. For polo lovers, matches are held here regularly and spectators are always welcome. Admission is free—you pay only for parking. Finally, next to the USC campus, is **Exposition Park**, which is totally unique. Although it's huge and boasts the famous sunken **Rose Garden** with its 16,000 bushes, this is really more of an inner-city entertainment complex, similar to Balboa Park in San Diego. Here you'll find the **Natural History Museum**, the **Aerospace Museum**, the **IMAX Theater**, the **California Science Center**, the **Museum of Science and Industry**, the **African-American Museum**, the L.A. Coliseum (home of the '32 and '84 Olympics), the Olympic Swimming Stadium, and the Sports Arena. If you can't find something to amuse and educate you in all this diversionary diversity, then you might as well head out to Figueroa Street and score some crack, 'cuz you're brain-dead already.

Behind the scenes... To really get an appreciation for the utter, stifling boredom of people working in the TV and film industries, you have to take a trip to the studios. **Paramount Pictures**, the longest continuously working studio in Hollywood, is probably the most visually pleasing of the lots. For $15 you get a two-hour walking tour that's guaranteed to persuade you of the wisdom of becoming an agent, not an actor. You should remember that this is a working business: Unlike the Universal Studios tour, there's no canned activity here. What you see will vary from day to day, and sometimes you may not see anything other than the outsides of buildings and a fleet of beaten-up bikes. No cameras or recorders allowed, and no kids under 10. If you want the full sheeplike experience, sign up at Paramount for a TV taping. Tickets are available five working days in advance of each scheduled show and are distributed on a first-come, first-served basis. **Warner Brothers Studios** also has a two-hour tour, which some people say is the best of all the working-studio tours. (The tour may or may not include filming.) TV studio tours at **NBC Television** are one hour long and are the only ones offered by a genuine network. They'll even let you see things like the "Tonight Show" set and special-effects labs. You can try to get "Tonight Show" tickets while you're there—the show tapes in the afternoon—but they go fast. For a truly low-rent experi-

DIVERSIONS | THE LOWDOWN

ence, check out **KCET**, our local PBS station. They give free (of course) one-hour tours, but only on Tuesdays and Thursdays. Stop in to see how a real TV station functions, even one that is perpetually strapped for cash, thanks to Strom Thurmond and his ilk.

Ringside seats for the circus... The real name of the **Venice Boardwalk** is Ocean Front Walk, but then nothing in Venice is quite what it seems. The Boardwalk has earned a well-deserved reputation as a throwback to an earlier, crazier time, when playing guitar while skating backwards with an amp strapped to your back seemed perfectly normal—a career choice, almost. The vendors and the performance artists are what bring people here, so when the local bureaucrats decided you had to have a permit to sell or perform on the boardwalk, naturally there was a stink. These aren't the kind of people who dutifully report to some faceless office, chain saw in hand, to ask for government approval of a juggling license. Today the program has been amended, and even so, there's little enforcement of the regulations. Those suits just don't get Venice: A few years ago, the Pavilion area—long a canvas for graffiti artists, and one of the truly great public art attractions in the area—was painted over by a confused city-works crew. They'd been told to clean it up, so they did. Maybe some of the upper crust who live just a few blocks inland on the canals in their multimillion-dollar homes complained. At any rate, it's claimed that more people come to the boardwalk on a daily basis than go to Disneyland—perhaps because Minnie Mouse doesn't skate around in a thong with her buns hanging out. You'll see all types here, including Angelenos of every hue, class, body shape, and sanity level. Everybody's watching everybody else, except for the roller-blading body beautifuls who skate through the crowds like wisps of fog through a forest. Some people think that the boardwalk is the best place in L.A. to buy sunglasses. Maybe—if by that you mean cheap sunglasses. Out on the sand there are volleyball nets, swing sets for the coulda-been Olympic gymnasts to show off on, and the basketball courts just opposite Muscle Beach, on the Venice Boardwalk, where some of the best pick-up players this side of the NBA will kick your ass free of charge. And then there's Muscle Beach, which for my money is better than a trip to the zoo. This is a public weightlifting area right next to the boardwalk, where the bulked-up men and women go through their reps, serenely ignoring the audience. You'll never look at your own body the same way again. There are also tons of shopping, dining, and drinking possibilities in the area. One caveat: I wouldn't go wandering out on the sand after dark, whether you're a man or a woman, alone or in pairs. The **Santa Monica Pier**, on the other hand, is totally (well, almost totally) safe after dark. There are always lots of crowds, plus low-key cops riding around on bikes, and really nowhere to run to unless you don't mind jumping into the foul waters underneath the pier. When you walk down from Colorado Boulevard onto the causeway, the first thing you see (and hear) is a spiffy renovated 1922 carousel, with bells clanging and the most beautiful antique wooden horses charging up and down. At the far end of the pier, anglers hang their lines over the railing, obviously unconcerned about the beach's consistent "F" rating from local environmental groups. The real "Baywatch" headquarters are also here, perched in a raised structure. There are also restaurants, gift shops, carny-style arcade games, a tiny roller coaster, and a Ferris wheel. During the summer the pier hosts free concerts by name bands.

Garden spots... The **Theodore Payne Foundation** is a nursery and bookstore out in the Valley that is a must-visit for anyone who's interested in that green-gray-brown stuff that covers Southern California's hills and burns so nicely every September. This vegetation, known as chaparral, is actually a mixture of different wild native plants. The nursery here cultivates these various plants and sells them in containers as well as in seed packets. The foundation also has a 24-hour Wildlife Hotline during the springtime bloom, which can be used to locate where the poppies are in full, brief glory. Many of the 400-plus species cultivated here are ordinarily difficult to find, since they're rarely sold at normal nurseries. Even if you're not shopping for your garden, however, this is a great place to stroll on your own or take a walking tour through the five-acre grounds, especially during the spring. The **Huntington Gardens** started off as a rich man's toy, installed in 1903 by millionaire Henry Huntington. The gardens now cover nearly 150 acres and contain more than 15,000 species of plants, most of them landscaped into theme gardens that are living testaments to the

DIVERSIONS | THE LOWDOWN

botanical sciences: The landscape categories include sub-tropical, desert, and jungle flora; Japanese plants, Australian plants, roses, camellias, palms, lily ponds, and herbs. There are also more specific displays such as the North Vista Landscape Project, the Zen and bonsai courts, the art gallery and its rockery, and the desert garden conservatory. The **Descanso Gardens** are much the same thing, only wilder, slightly bigger, and less stuffy—basically the difference between the rich ambience of San Marino and the more middle-class La Canada suburb. Here you'll encounter wandering peacocks, huge lawns, wonderfully manicured flower beds, pools and waterfalls, a toy train, statues and benches interspersed at regular intervals, plus 25 acres of live oaks that are the backdrop for a four-acre rose garden and thousands upon thousands of camellias. The *Camellia japonica* collection is considered the best in the world: It was originally developed from some 50,000 plants bought in the 1940s from Japanese-American gardeners and nursery owners who were locked up in internment camps at the time.

Action:Space. Performance art, openings, and parties. It's a good place to check out what's happening in the Downtown-artist loft scene. It's always interesting, and the audience and participants are genuine. If you're curious about L.A. art, street level, but you don't know where to go, come here.... *Tel 213/680-4237. 734 E. 3rd St., Artist District, Downtown.* **(see p. 113)**

Al's Bar. It's a bar, a performance space, a punk landmark, and the primary watering hole for the downtown artists who still drink. Bonus points for the outdoor smoking patio.... *Tel 213/626-7213. 305 S. Hewitt St., Downtown.* **(see p. 113)**

Art Center. This is an art school—a professional, commercially oriented art school. It's hugely expensive to attend, and its graduates influence an inordinate quantity of contemporary American design, from cereal boxes to the layout of dashboards. The student galleries here are amazing.... *Tel 818/396-2200. 1700 Lida St., Pasadena.* **(see p. 115)**

Art Share. Very exciting and strange happenings can take place here. You pay to get in, which seems a little weird for an "opening," but the art is priced so reasonably that it's hard to pass up. It's one of the few galleries that considers the concerns of the artist as a primary directive, hence the always interesting rotating show of local work.... *Tel 213/687-4ART. 801 E. 4th Place, Artist District, Downtown.* **(see p. 112)**

Autry Museum of Western Heritage. The Wild West is presented here in all its seedy glory. Lots of artifacts, from lariats and guns to photos, cowboy-culture junk and a life-sized bronze sculpture of the "Singing Cowboy" himself, Gene Autry.... *Tel 323/667-2000. 4700 Western Heritage Way (opposite the L.A. Zoo), Griffith Park.* **(see p. 104)**

Bergamot Station Arts Center. This is a huge arts complex situated in a former industrial space, with way more galleries than you could ever slog through in a single evening of cheap wine and "art".... *310/829-5854. 2525 Michigan Ave., Santa Monica.* **(see p. 112)**

Beyond Baroque Literary Arts Center. Poets of the world...rewrite! They come here to read and listen, gossip and snipe. Always underfunded but still fighting, this bookstore/performance center is an essential local literary outlet. If you're looking for an L.A. writer who's not on a major publisher's list, come here first.... *Tel 310/822-3006. 681 Venice Blvd., Venice.* **(see p. 111)**

Bloom's General Store. The primary hangout for artists in the loft district. Come here for directions and info regarding gallery openings, happenings, fistfights in progress.... *Tel 213/687-6571. 716 Traction Ave., Artist District, Downtown.* **(see p. 113)**

Bradbury Building. They call it futuristic Victorian, and the elaborate ironwork, skylight, and dark wood—combined with its *Blade Runner* legacy—do make a good case for that paradoxical genre. It's a high-toned office building now, but they'll let you in to walk around. Well worth a visit.... *Tel 213/626-1893. 304 S. Broadway, Downtown.* **(see p. 119)**

La Brea Tar Pits and George C. Page Museum. It's not exactly Jurassic Park, but for the fledgling paleontologist in your family, this is the next best thing. Most impressive exhibit is the life-sized mammoth skeleton. Great gift store as well.... *Tel 323/934-7243. 5801 Wilshire Blvd., Miracle Mile.* **(see p. 103)**

Capitol Records Building. This famous company headquarters looks like a stack of 45s on a spindle. Also check out the mural on jazz, just off the parking lot.... *323/462-6252. 1750 N. Vine Ave., Hollywood.* **(see p. 120)**

Carole & Barry Kaye Museum of Miniatures. Let's get small! Tons of very teeny-weeny depictions of large objects, buildings, and scenes.... *Tel 323/937 MINI. 5900 Wilshire Blvd., Miracle Mile.* **(see p. 116)**

Coca-Cola Building. Shaped like an ocean liner that's been stranded in the warehouse district of Downtown. Drive-by only.... *1334 S. Central Ave., Downtown.* **(see p. 120)**

The Dance Collective. Offers classes in dance, drumming, and personal enhancement.... *Tel 323/292-1538. 4327 Degnan Blvd., Leimert Park.* **(see p. 114)**

Descanso Gardens. A huge garden that verges on wilderness, with big lawns and more camellias than you'll ever be able to sniff. It's a wonderful place for an afternoon out with the kids. Check out the Tea House.... *Tel 818/952-4400. 1418 Descanso Dr., La Canada.* **(see p. 128)**

Ennis House. One of Frank Lloyd Wright's biggest efforts in L.A. Drive-by only.... *2607 Glendower Ave., Los Feliz* **(see p. 119)**

Exposition Park. There's just about everything you could want here for a day in the park—provided it's an uplifting educational experience you're seeking. Besides the L.A.

Coliseum, the 1984 Olympic swimming and cycling venues, and its extensive Rose Garden, the park contains four museums.... *Natural History Museum, Tel 213/763-3515; African-American Museum, Tel 213/744-7432; and the California Science Center, which includes the Aerospace Museum and the IMAX Theater (323/724-3623). Figueroa St. at Exposition Blvd., Exposition Park.* **(see p. 125)**

Fahey/Klein Gallery. This is L.A.'s premiere outlet for vintage and contemporary fine-art photography.... *Tel 323/934-2250. 149 N. La Brea Ave., Wilshire.* **(see p. 114)**

Fifth Street Dick's Coffee. This cozy little hangout in Leimert Park is where you come to get whomped at chess by some crusty old men. It's shady, the coffee is great, and the jazz and blues coming over the P.A. are soothing. Parking's easy.... *Tel 323/296-3970. 3347 W. 43rd Place, Leimert Park.* **(see p. 114)**

Frederick's of Hollywood Lingerie Museum. The master of nasty lingerie has built his own museum to show off the undies worn by famous celebrities. No, he doesn't have Monica's thong—but I'll bet you never knew there were so many things you could do with crotchless panties.... *Tel 213/466-8506. 6608 Hollywood Blvd., Hollywood.* **(see p. 116)**

The Geffen Contemporary. Formerly known as the TC, or Temporary Contemporary, this is (and has been for more than a decade) Ground Zero for the local art scene. It has the best installations and openings of any museum in the city.... *Tel 213/621-2766. 152 N. Central Ave., Downtown.* **(see p. 110)**

Getty Center. This Acropolis-style complex, perched high above the 405 Freeway, is more than a museum, less than Disneyland. It features incredible vistas, a computerized tram, and, oh yeah, a bunch of pictures by dead guys. The art is off-and-on fabulous, sometimes overwhelmed by the sheer beauty of the setting. Open until 9 on Thurs. and Fri. Admission is free, but call ahead for parking reservations. Since the opening crush, things have calmed down, and it's possible to get a reservation during the week easily. If they've got a big show coming, however, you should call weeks in advance. Westside Limo Service is another good way to get close to the tram without worrying about the major parking problem.... *Tel 310/454-1173 or 310/440-7300. 1200 Getty Center Dr., Brentwood.* **(see p. 105)**

Griffith Observatory & Planetarium. Great Art Deco architecture, views of the sun and the L.A. basin, and there's a piece of Mars inside. Also, historical links to *Rebel Without a Cause* and other classic movies. And the Laserium show is pretty cool too.... *Tel 323/664-1191. 2800 E. Observatory Rd., Griffith Park.* **(see p. 117)**

Griffith Park. The kingpin of L.A. parks, Griffith Park contains the aforementioned Observatory, the Los Angeles Zoo, the Greek Theater, and Mount Hollywood.... *Tel 323/664-1181. Los Angeles.* **(see p. 123)**

Hollyhock House. A Frank Lloyd Wright house you should park by and visit on foot. Located inside the Barnsdall Art complex, the house itself has stylized hollyhock ornamentation. And, unlike most houses that Wright built in L.A., you can actually inspect its interior and furniture.... *Tel 323/662-7272. 4800 Hollywood Blvd., Los Feliz.* **(see p. 121)**

Hollywood Entertainment Museum. This long-awaited museum showcases Hollywood's entertainment industry, and features such attractions as sets from the television series "Star Trek" and "Cheers." It's more hype and industry promotion than you'd expect from a "museum" but still worth a visit.... *Tel 213/465-7900. 7021 Hollywood Blvd., Hollywood.* **(see p. 117)**

Hollywood Memorial Park Cemetery. Where you can meditate on the remains of Valentino, DeMille, et al. This is probably the most popular graveyard for trolling goths and punks, not because of its interred celebrities, but because it's right in Hollywood and easy to break into.... *6000 Santa Monica Blvd., Hollywood.* **(see p. 122)**

Hollywood Park. This is the most venerable and historic of the local racetracks. Plus, in between races there's now a new card casino where you can lose even more money. Beautiful grounds, and cooler than Santa Anita.... *Tel 310/419-1500; scratch and results line.... Tel*

310/419-1470. 1050 South Prairie Ave., Inglewood.
(see p. 122)

Hollywood RockWalk. Handprints, signatures, and memorabilia from some of rock & roll's greatest players, inventors, and hacks. Located in the entrance to the Guitar Center store.... *Tel 213/874-1060. 7425 Sunset Blvd., Hollywood.*
(see p. 123)

Holy Cross Cemetery and Mausoleum. Walter Brennan, Mario Lanza, Michael Landon, Lorne Green, Jack Benny—they're all here. No autographs, please.... *5835 W. Slauson Ave., Culver City.* **(see p. 123)**

Huntington Gardens. Its full name is the Huntington Library, Art Collection & Botanical Gardens, but you're really here for the plantings—some 15,000 different species, landscaped into highly specific botanical zones, from Japan to the desert.... *Tel 626/405-2141. 1151 Oxford Rd., San Marino.* **(see p. 127)**

Jane Baum Gallery. This is one of the largest small gallery spaces around. It's known for great opening parties. Come by, grab some wine, and deconstruct.... *Tel 323/932-0170. 170 S. La Brea Ave., Los Angeles.* **(see p. 113)**

Japanese American National Museum. This brand-new, $45-million pavilion is a wonderful open space of sandstone and yellow granite and neatly frames the Japanese American Museum, which resembles a glass ocean liner. The museum's artifacts of this immigrant group's early American experiences are so sincerely presented—including photos secretly taken of the interior of the camps—it'll make you weep.... *Tel 213/626-6222. 369 East 1st St., Little Tokyo.* **(see p. 111)**

KCET. Free one-hour tours of this headquarters for L.A.'s Public Broadcasting System station are offered on Tues. and Thur.... *Tel 323/666-6500. 4401 W. Sunset Blvd., Hollywood.* **(see p. 126)**

La Luz de Jesus Gallery. Unquestionably the most interesting and party-like openings to be found anywhere in the city. Mingle with scene-makers, hipsters, grunge artists, musicians, and the dregs of Hollywood/Silver Lake/Echo Park.

They're punks, not patrons, and you'll be drinking beer, not wine. First Fri. of the month, 8–11.... *Tel 323/666-7667. 4633 Hollywood Blvd., inside the Soap Plant, Los Feliz.*
(see p. 115)

Latino Museum of History, Art, and Culture. This fairly new museum is still getting established, but it holds great promise for becoming a much-needed definitive resource for the Latino heritage, past and present. The primary emphasis is on Mexican roots and influence, but all of the Latin-American cultures are being explored. This year's Day of the Dead show, for example, comes from Guatemala.... *Tel 213/626-7600. 112 S. Main St., Downtown.* **(see p. 104)**

Leimert Park Fine Art Gallery. The most active and interesting African-American gallery in L.A. Like Self-Help Graphics, it serves its community admirably, giving local artists a platform from which to declare their sensibilities, regardless of their commercial appeal.... *Tel 323/299-0319, 3351 W. 43rd St., Leimert Park.* **(see p. 114)**

Los Angeles Central Library. More than a library. If El Pueblo is the historical heart of L.A., then this is its intellectual center. Plus, it's quite clean, has awesome architecture, and is the third-largest library in the country. Totally accessible to everyone, and always busy.... *Tel 213/228-7000. 630 W. 5th St., Downtown.* **(see p. 111)**

Los Angeles City Hall. This is the epicenter of L.A. bureaucratic power, where the mayor and his minions do battle with a usually confrontational council. Fabulous interiors, incredibly dull hearings, Fascist guards.... *Tel 213/485-2121. 200 N. Spring St., Downtown.* **(see p. 119)**

Los Angeles County Fair. An annual extravaganza held every September, it includes horse races, a carnival, farm husbandry competitions, folk arts and crafts, and lots and lots of heartburn-inducing food. Pig out, ride the Ferris Wheel and spew.... *Tel 909/623-3111. 1101 W. McKinley Ave., Pomona. Approximately 30 miles east of Downtown Los Angeles and 10 miles west of Ontario International Airport, where the 10, 210, and 57 freeways meet.* **(see pp. 109, 122)**

Los Angeles Zoo. No, not Venice or Hollywood—I mean the

literal zoo. This is the closest most people outside of the entertainment business will ever get to a snake. Angry chimps in the Great Ape Forest, gay pandas, and free music in the summer.... *Tel 323/666-4650. 5333 Zoo Dr., Griffith Park.* **(see p. 123)**

MAK Center for Art and Architecture/Schindler House. You can't get into most of the houses around L.A. designed by the famous architect Adolph Schindler, so paying a visit to his original home is a highly instructive treat. For serious architects, this is the Rosetta Stone, where the climate was dealt with sensibly, mixing indoor-outdoor living in a seamless format that is still popular.... *Tel 213/651-1510. 835 N. Kings Rd., West Hollywood.* **(see p. 118)**

Mann's Chinese Theater. This used to be Graumann's Chinese, but now it's just Mann's. The footprints and handprints remain, out in the courtyard. Everyone has to come here—once.... *Tel 323/464-8111. 6925 Hollywood Blvd., Hollywood.* **(see p. 123)**

Mayan Theater. It's not a movie theater but rather a wonderful downtown space for all kinds of performances, usually cutting edge, ethnic, and expensive. But just dropping by to check out the exterior design is worth it.... *Tel 213/746-4674. 1038 S. Hill St., Downtown.* **(see p. 120)**

Million Dollar Theater. Located just a stone's throw from the Central Market, the Million Dollar Theater was one of the original movie palaces of the golden age of cinema. Now it's been revamped and presents a variety of live shows, from child mariachi stars to evangelical prophets.... *Tel 213/473-0720. 307 S. Broadway, Downtown.* **(see p. 119)**

Museum of Contemporary Art (MOCA). Twenty years ago, no one ever imagined that L.A. would have a contemporary art museum this complete and this important. Among the permanent collection are works by Ed Rushea and Lari Pittmann. The building itself is a work of art, and the openings are super classy—if a little stuffy.... *Tel 213/626-6222. 250 S. Grand Ave., Downtown.* **(see p. 110)**

Museum of Jurassic Technology. This is the strangest museum in the city. Not recommended for people lacking a sense of humor or perspective. Is it art or a joke on you, the audience? Usually it's both.... *Tel 310/836-6131. 9341 Venice Blvd., Culver City.* **(see p. 115)**

Museum of Neon Art (MONA). It's the nature of neon art that it be large, so some of the museum's collection rotates over to the Universal CityWalk—but this is a much more educational place to view this most L.A. of art styles. The museum also offers classes in making neon art, and conducts nighttime tours of the bright lights of this big city.... *Tel 213/489-9918. 501 W. Olympic Blvd., Downtown.* **(see p. 108)**

Museum of Television and Radio. Catering to heavy-duty broadcast students and professionals, this L.A. version of the New York museum is stunning in its variety of television and radio programs, all available here for the public to re-live in private viewing booths. It's the home of never-ending summer reruns.... *Tel 310/786-1000. 465 N. Beverly Dr., Beverly Hills.* **(see p. 116)**

NBC Television. This is the West Coast headquarters for the network, the place to come for tours or tickets to TV tapings. Wow, I'm so excited. Be warned, though: TV studios are kept freezingly cold, so bring a sweater.... *Tel 818/840-3537; ticket information: Tel 818/840-3537. 3000 W. Alameda Ave., Burbank.* **(see p. 125)**

Paramount Pictures. Two-hour tours of the working studio are available here, as are tickets to TV tapings (handed out on a first-come, first-served basis). A limited number of advance "priority admission" reservations for TV tapings can be obtained by calling Paramount Guest Relations.... *Tel 213/956-5000; Paramount Guest Relations 213/956-1777. 5555 Melrose Ave., Hollywood.* **(see p. 125)**

Paul Kopeikin Gallery. Selling fine-art photography by people like Gary Winogrand.... *Tel 323/937-0765. 138 N. La Brea Ave., Melrose–La Brea.* **(see p. 114)**

Petersen Automotive Museum. It's all about internal combustion—something that every Angeleno deals with on a daily basis. L.A. and the automobile are joined at the head and groin: Out here you are what you drive, functionally and sexually, and to fully appreciate this zeitgeist, a visit to Petersen's is essential. Loads of cars—rare, modern, historical, and just plain weird.... *Tel 323/930-CARS. 6060 Wilshire Blvd., Miracle Mile. Los Angeles.* **(see p. 105)**

El Pueblo de Los Angeles Historical Monument. This is where it all began for modern Angelenos. The Plaza was the symbolic heart of colonial California, in the days when the Spanish ran the place. Today it leads directly into Olvera Street, where Tijuana-style merchants are hawking Mexican arts and crafts. Attractions include the Old Plaza Church, the Avila Adobe house, and the Pico House, all built in the 17th century .... *Tel 213/628-1274. 130 Paseo de la Plaza, Downtown.* **(see p. 104)**

Randy's Donuts. This is where you come for the big donut on the roof, but stay for the smaller, deep-fried variety.... *Tel 310/645-4707. 805 W. Manchester Blvd., Inglewood.* **(see p. 121)**

Rico Gallery. Finally, a spunky Downtown-style art space in Santa Monica. Good openings, usually held on Friday nights.... *Tel 310/399-5353. 208 Pier Ave., Santa Monica.* **(see p. 112)**

Santa Anita Race Track. A wonderful horse-racing track amid great surroundings and stupendous views. Harness racing is the big attraction.... *Tel 626/574-RACE; for results and scratches: Tel 626/446-8501. 285 W. Huntington Dr., Arcadia.* **(see p. 122)**

Santa Monica Pier. Pacific Ocean Park is long gone, but that sense of a carnival on the beach is still here. A great stroll destination after a day of bloating and buying on 3rd Street.... *Tel 310/260-8744. Colorado and Ocean avenues, Santa Monica.* **(see p. 127)**

Self-Help Graphics. This is the place to come to find out about any sort of art project in East L.A. They also have art classes, a gallery, and a great *Dia de los Muertos* altar every year.... *Tel 213/264-1259. 3802 Cesar E. Chavez Ave., East Los Angeles.* **(see pp. 107, 110)**

Southwest Museum. Absolutely the best collection of Native American artifacts and historical reference material in L.A. Pottery, baskets, clothes, weapons, and the lifestyle detritus of the original inhabitants. Plus the facility, based in a hacienda on top of a hill in Mt. Washington, is a stunner.... *Tel 323/221-2164. 234 Museum Dr., Highland Park.* **(see p. 104)**

SPARC (Social and Public Art Resource Center). SPARC is the best place for getting a line on the murals and public art that dot the walls of Los Angeles. They were the ones who painted the awesome Great Wall of Los Angeles mural at the Tujunga-drainage canal in Van Nuys. The group also conducts bus tours of the city's murals, sometimes led by the artists themselves.... *Tel 310/822-9560. 685 Venice Blvd., Venice.* **(see p. 106)**

Tail O' The Pup. It's a food stand inside a stucco hot dog. No, it's art! The aesthetic experience comes with relish and onions.... *Tel 310/652-4517. 329 N. San Vicente Blvd., West Hollywood.* **(see p. 121)**

Theodore Payne Foundation. This all-native-plant nursery and resource center is a great place to come for a better understanding of Southern California flora. They sell seeds, books, and various kinds of local plants in pots. You can also get a tour of the estate.... *Tel 818/768-1802; Wildflower Hotline: Tel 818/768-3533. 10459 Tuxford St., Sun Valley.* **(see p. 127)**

Tomkat Theater. The porn walk of fame is just outside—don't step in that! Inside it's gay hard-core. Gee, I can't seem to make up my mind.... *Tel 323/650-9551. 7734 Santa Monica Blvd., Hollywood.* **(see p. 123)**

Track 16 Gallery. It's not easy standing out in the gallery petting zoo that is Bergamot Station, but Track 16 manages to draw attention. The punk retrospective, in spring '99, was the best the city has ever seen. It can be hit or miss, like all galleries, but it has a great bar area in the back.... *Tel 310/264-4678. Bergamot Station, 2525 Michigan Ave., Santa Monica.* **(see p. 108)**

Travel Town Museum. Restored railway cars and steam engines, even a miniature train for the kiddies. Ever wanted to play engineer? Come on over. Maybe they'll even let you blow the whistle.... *Tel 323/662-9678. 5200 Zoo Dr., Griffith Park.* **(see p. 105)**

Universal CityWalk. Most people come here for the restaurants, movies, shops, and clubs, or because they're on their way to the Universal Studios Tour. Me, I come just for the neon display: It's free, it's big, and it totally fits in with the bizarre architecture.... *Tel 818/622-4455. Universal Center Dr., Universal City.* **(see p. 108)**

Warner Brothers Studios. A working movie studio that also gives the best tours of the filming process in action.... *Tel 818/954-1744. 4000 Warner Blvd., Burbank.* **(see p. 125)**

Westwood Village Memorial Park. Marilyn Monroe is buried here. What more do you need to know?... *Tel 310/399-5353. 1218 Glendon Ave., Westwood.* **(see p. 123)**

Will Rogers State Park. Part historical tour, part polo park, and part jumping-off point for walks into the Santa Monica mountains. This is one of the best and least discovered parks that's still close to the city. Great for a day when you can't find parking at the beach.... *Tel 310/454-8212. 1501 Will Rogers State Park Rd., Pacific Palisades.* **(see p. 124)**

DIVERSIONS | THE INDEX

Hollywood Area Diversions

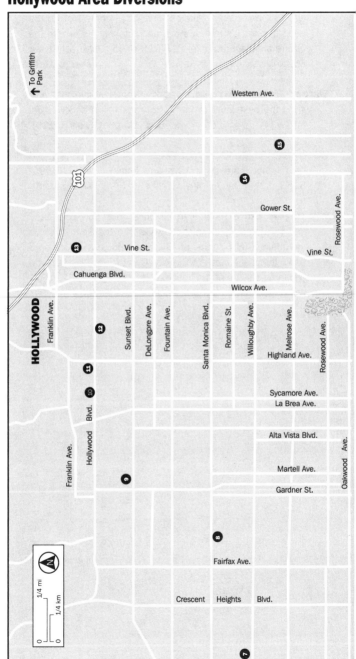

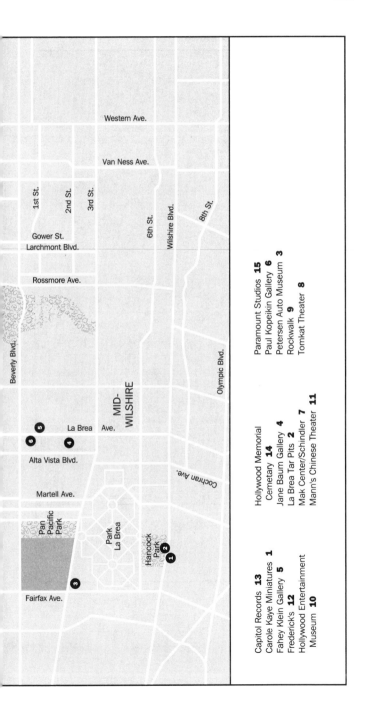

Western Ave.

Van Ness Ave.

1st St.

2nd St.

3rd St.

6th St.

Wilshire Blvd.

8th St.

Gower St.
Larchmont Blvd.

Rossmore Ave.

Beverly Blvd.

La Brea Ave.

MID-WILSHIRE

Olympic Blvd.

Alta Vista Blvd.

Martell Ave.

Cochran Ave.

Pan Pacific Park

Park La Brea

Hancock Park

Fairfax Ave.

Capitol Records **13**
Carole Kaye Miniatures **1**
Fahey Klein Gallery **5**
Frederick's **12**
Hollywood Entertainment Museum **10**

Hollywood Memorial Cemetary **14**
Jane Baum Gallery **4**
La Brea Tar Pits **2**
Mak Center/Schindler **7**
Mann's Chinese Theater **11**

Paramount Studios **15**
Paul Kopeikin Gallery **6**
Petersen Auto Museum **3**
Rockwalk **9**
Tomkat Theater **8**

Downtown Area Diversions

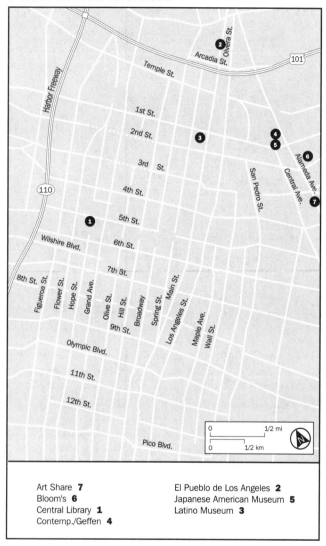

Art Share **7**
Bloom's **6**
Central Library **1**
Contemp./Geffen **4**

El Pueblo de Los Angeles **2**
Japanese American Museum **5**
Latino Museum **3**

Diversions in
L.A.'s Westside & Beverly Hills

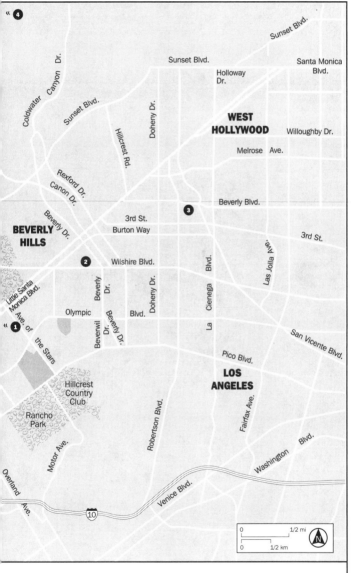

" **4**

Sunset Blvd.

Sunset Blvd.

Santa Monica Blvd.

Holloway Dr.

Coldwater Canyon Dr.

Sunset Blvd.

Doheny Dr.

WEST HOLLYWOOD

Willoughby Dr.

Hillcrest Rd.

Melrose Ave.

Rexford Dr.

Canon Dr.

Beverly Blvd.

Beverly Dr.

3

BEVERLY HILLS

3rd St.

Burton Way

3rd St.

2 Wilshire Blvd.

Las Jolla Ave.

Little Santa Monica Blvd.

Beverly Dr.

Doheny Dr.

La Cienega Blvd.

" **1**

Ave. of the Stars

Olympic

Beverwil Dr.

Beverly Dr.

Blvd.

Pico Blvd.

San Vicente Blvd.

LOS ANGELES

Hillcrest Country Club

Fairfax Ave.

Rancho Park

Robertson Blvd.

Blvd.

Motor Ave.

Washington

Overland Ave.

Venice Blvd.

10

0   1/2 mi

0   1/2 km

N

Getty Center **4**
Museum of TV and Radio **2**
Tail O' the Pup **3**
Westwood Village Memorial Park **1**

getting

4

outside

That's not smog
obscuring the
mountains, it's
haze. This is one
of the first things
you learn here.
Only tourists

call it smog—the rest of us understand that the delicate chemical dance of carbon monoxide, nitrogen dioxide, and ozone is what makes this city so special. Just as leaves turning red-yellow signals the arrival of fall to Easterners, for us Angelenos the sky turning brown heralds the beginning of summer. And fall. Despite a long list of anti-pollution measures, L.A. still has the funkiest air in the country. The AQMD, the government agency that monitors such things, estimates that about 1,600 people a year in the greater metropolitan area die prematurely simply from breathing the stuff. But that's not you. Is it? Anyway, the air is getting better, believe it or not. Twenty years ago the city had 116 Stage 1 alerts and 12 Stage 2 alerts, the latter meaning everyone stays inside, no exercising, no kids in the playground, industry must shut down, and so on. There *is* no Stage 3. Last year we had only 23 Stage 1s and zero Stage 2s, so *something's* getting better.

The thing is, a pollution emergency is about the only thing that can keep Los Angeles residents indoors on the weekends. In some ways, the summer is actually the worst time for outdoor sports, even though rain stops around May and doesn't begin again until November. During El Niño years, the winter is especially wet and the summer milder than usual. Except for all those who just like to sit on the sand and soak up rays, fall, winter, and spring are the best times. So just about all year long, when Saturday comes we grab the blades, load the Cannondale onto the bike rack, lace up the Air Jordans, slather Sex Wax on the short board and hit the boardwalk/mountain trails/courts/waves. In L.A., anytime is playtime—so come on, what are you waiting for?

The Lowdown

Child's play... The thing about little kids is, you've got to run 'em around. Most commercial establishments do not appreciate the clatter and chaos that accompanies this fact of life. Parks and the beach are good sports for kids in theory, but in these settings it's the parents who get bored after half an hour or so without a coffee break, magazine stand, or other adults to divert them—to say nothing of those long trudges to scary bathrooms. For short breaks during the day, what works best for everyone involved are kid-friendly, indoor-outdoor combos. A few lucky neighborhoods have this sort of thing built into the local real estate, and if you don't live in one of these areas, you can always visit. Let's start with the **Malibu Country Mart.** The mart extends on either side of Cross Creek Road, and each side has something to offer a family outing. On the north end is a daisy chain of boutiques, restaurants, and free parking, all surrounding a play area for young children containing two large, well-maintained sandpits with swings, slides, and bouncy animal rides. Wraparound wooden benches border the sand for hands-on parenting or time-out periods, but the grassy areas and umbrella-shaded tables nearby still let you keep well within visual reach while also giving you room to spread out your stuff and relax. The semi-fast-food establishments located just a few steps away are all locally run. Particularly recommended is **John's Garden** (tel 310/456-8377) for its healthy take-out sandwiches; you can also pick up a few fruits and vegetables at the stand out back. If you wanted to you could even get your car washed and detailed at the car wash next door while you're here—but then again, there's the sand to consider. On the south side of the mart you'll find more service-oriented businesses than across the road, but there are a few notable stops for families out on a walk. Heading the list is **Pet Headquarters** (tel 310/456-7029). This pet store smells exceptionally fresh, and the diverse selection of animals are extremely well cared for, reminding you that Malibu is still a semi-rural community at heart. By the front door, small playpens house puppies for petting, and a bank of glassed-in cages along the wall displays a veritable zoo of animals, ranging from domestic (hamsters, bunnies, cats, more dogs, turtles) to the more exotic (tarantulas, garter snakes, green anoles—"eats crickets, great for kids"—lovebirds, and a bearded dragon the day I was in here).

At the **Ocean Park Farmer's Market** (on Main St. and Ocean Park Blvd. in Santa Monica), Saturdays are for the tourists, but Sundays are family day. Around brunch time, Dads in flip-flops can be seen pushing baby carriages in the direction of the **California Heritage Museum,** where the parking lot has been taken over since early morning by an outdoor market that features not only organic produce but samples from local restaurants, delicious prepared foods, clothing, and gift items. By noon the lawn in front of the museum is covered with blankets, picnic baskets, and babies, as families meet up with friends to hear the live music groups that change each week. Sometimes the mood is jazzy, sometimes more folk, but it's always casual. By early afternoon everyone wanders back home or to the beach, which is only a block away. Finally, what five-year-old could resist a trip to the **Santa Monica Recycling Center**? A few years ago an observant father of a three-year-old boy made a million dollars marketing a home video of big trucks he saw on the street, just doing their thing. You can score similar points with your preschoolers and teach them about ecology at the same time by taking them with you to the recycling center. You'll see rows of city trucks, tractors, and scoopers moving and mashing small mountains of wood, lawn trimmings, trash, and various broken things. It is, in fact, endlessly fascinating. To illustrate the general point of it all, Eva Cockcroft's block-long colorful mural outside the center depicts how materials break down and travel through every layer of life on earth. The Center is located between Cloverfield and the 10, right under the waving black-and-white flag reading "POW and MIA— You are not forgotten" (2500 Michigan Ave., Santa Monica).

Inner-city beaches... When the temperature reaches the high nineties Downtown and you know there's bumper-to-bumper traffic heading up Pacific Coast Highway, don't despair: There are alternative water sources right here in the concrete heart of the city. You can't actually go swimming, of course, but a refreshingly cooling effect is produced simply by strolling along big expanses of water. The newest such beach is the **L.A. River**. It's hard to imagine that L.A. has a river—not just a huge drainage ditch—but it does, and in a few sections where the "soft bottom" is left intact you can get an idea of what it was once like. More than 250 species of birds live on the waterway from Tujunga Wash to Long Beach, along with more than 150 types of vegetation. When the Gabrielino Indians inhabited its banks, floods were expected and were considered good omens for the next year's crops. It used to be a healthy, flowing river for its entire length, but the flood of 1938 killed nearly 50 people and did $40 million in damage—so in anger the city fathers called upon the Army Corps of Engineers. Ten thousand workers poured three million barrels of concrete (all applied by hand), and by 1940 the Sepulveda Flood Basin and Dam was finished. It was and is as ugly as sin. Now the Friends of the L.A. River are trying to bring the last semi-wild section back into public awareness, leading walks along the basin on the third Sunday of every month (tel 213/381-3570). There's a bike path and a walking trail that runs 3.2 miles (with lighting), plus new artistic wrought-iron gates that welcome you in (entrances are at Los Feliz Boulevard in the south, and on Riverside Drive at Victory in the north). Plans for the future include a greenbelt that will run along the west side of the river from the Sepulveda Basin all the way to Long Beach. It wasn't so long ago that this was strictly gang land, a place to dump a body or put your tag up. Up in the Hollywood Hills you'll find **Lake Hollywood**. This is a hugely popular dog-walking and jogging area for the mid-level Hollywood executives and drones who live in the neighborhood. You'll see lots of *very* attractive people of both sexes getting all toned up for that audition. The water in the "lake"—it's actually a reservoir—is deep blue-green. It's a very similar scene (although much younger and more boho in tone) around the **Silver Lake Reservoir** in Silver Lake. Unfortunately, there's traffic right next to the jogging path, so walking or running here is hardly a transcendental experience. If you want to walk your dog, it will be safer hanging around the Dog Park at the south end of the reservoir.

Guaranteed O.J.-free golf courses… I won't guarantee that you won't be playing with wife-killers, but I can assure you there won't be a Heisman Trophy winner on the next tee. At the top of the list are the two 18-hole **Griffith Park** courses, **Wilson** and **Harding** (tel 323/664-2255, 4730 Crystal Springs Dr., Griffith Park, east side). These are two very popular regulation courses, built in 1914 and 1933 respectively. The Wilson course, a par 71 and 6,610 yards long, has small greens and narrow fairways. The Harding, a 6,945-yard par 72, has trees and water hazards and is considered the more difficult of the two. You can play either course for a buck a hole. Both are always loaded with dressed-to-the-nines Koreans; unless you have a reservation card (available from the pro shop), you won't be able to get in on weekends, but getting a tee time on weekdays is usually fairly easy. There's also a clubhouse, lockers, and electric-cart and club rentals. If you have the next Tiger Woods in your family, they also offer a special 10-week course for kids, ages 6 to 17. Also in Griffith Park on the west side is the **Roosevelt Municipal Golf Course** (tel 323/665-2011, 2650 N. Vermont Ave., Griffith Park). This is a very tricky, nine-hole par 33 that involves lots of precision shots because of the narrow fairways. It's the closest nine-holer to Downtown, and probably one of the cheapest anywhere at $10 per round. It's the classic duffers' hangout, a place where retirees meet up and gossip while they play. Another very tricky nine-hole course is the one at the **Catalina Island Golf Club** (tel 310/ 510-0530, 1 Country Club Rd., Avalon, Catalina). It was built in 1925 and has the most amazing views you can imagine. The greens fees are $23 for 9 holes and $40 for 18 holes. Working downward in difficulty, there's **Los Feliz Municipal** (tel 323/663-7758, 3207 Los Feliz Blvd., Los Feliz). This is practically a miniature golf course, consisting of nine holes that are all par 3s. You come here mainly to work on your pitching and putting. It costs $4 to play the course, which takes about an hour. There's easy parking, no hills to climb, and the "clubhouse" is EAT, a snack-shack that, if they only served beer, would be the ideal place to finish an abbreviated tour of the links. Who comes here? Slackers with no real job but not enough time on their hands to play a real golf course either. If you work up a sweat, then you're doing something wrong. Finally, for those of you who like the idea of golf but hate the thought of lugging around all those clubs, consider playing an 18-hole game of frisbee golf at **Hahamonga Watershed Park** (tel 626/744-4321, 1042 Oak Grove, La Canada). It's a full course that requires controlling your hook, slice, and distance so that you get your disc to land in the "hole" (actually a basket). There are no greens fees, no silly clothes, and you can use your dog for a caddy. If you feel the need to work on your drives, check out **Lakes of El Segundo** (tel 310/322-0202, 400 S. Sepulveda Blvd., El Segundo). It's open until 11 p.m. and has seven PGA pros there to talk to about your swing. One bonus: The wind is always with you. Over in Griffith Park, at the pro shop for the Wilson and Harding courses, you'll also find a double-decker driving range, where the wind is never a problem since you're driving into a box canyon. The range is open until 10:30 p.m. and charges $7.50 for a bucket of balls.

Feets do your thing... Although the beaches get all the press, most of the people I know agree that the mountains are the most glorious aspect of living here. There are trails everywhere, varying in walkability from easy to impossible. Let's start off with something mild, like the **Griffith Park Night Hikes,** sponsored by Griffith Park Sierra Club (tel 213/387-4287). Conducted every Tuesday, Wednesday, and Thursday evenings starting at 7 p.m., they can attract as many as 500 people on a warm summer night. The hikes range from a 90-minute four-miler to a two-hour eight-miler that's considered slightly strenuous. You first have to pay $35 for an annual membership (which goes to the Sierra Club), then you meet up with your fellow hikers behind the old carousel on the east side of Griffith Park. Wednesday nights are now called Love Hikes, aimed at singles looking for a mate. No flashlights or dogs are allowed. You don't have to have a guide to walk the park, of course: there are 53 miles of trails, and maps can be obtained from the **Griffith Park Ranger Station** (tel 323/665-5188). Open fires and smoking are prohibited. Be warned, though: This isn't a Hollywood set. You can easily encounter fox, coyotes, and rattlesnakes out here. For real cross-country types, there's **La Jolla Canyon**, an 11-mile hike with a 2,000-foot elevation gain. The starting point for the hike is **Point Mugu State Park** (tel 805/488-5223), and the route takes about six hours to complete (be sure to carry plenty of water during the summer). You'll get incredible ocean views while walking through one of the few remaining tallgrass prairies. This is true California coastline vegetation: The canyon is very uncrowded and is dotted with 10-foot-high coreopsis plants that sport brilliant yellow flowers during the spring. It's also the western edge of the 65-mile **Backbone Trail**, which runs through the Santa Monica Mountains all the way into Pacific Palisades. From the peaks of the trail you can see all the way to the Channel Islands off Ventura. If you make it to **La Jolla Valley Camp**, you'll find piped water, restrooms, and picnic tables under the live oaks. Just to remind you that you're not completely in the wilderness, you may hear gunshots coming from a nearby military shooting range— and don't be startled if an F-16 goes screaming over your head, departing from Pt. Mugu Naval Air Station a few miles away.

One of the most popular (and easy) hikes in the **San Gabriel Mountains** is the **Mount Lowe trail** (Mount Lowe Arroyo Seco Ranger Station, tel 818/790-1151). The trail is just over three miles round-trip, but it takes about 90 minutes to climb up and over the 500-foot elevation gain. To get there you park on the Mt. Wilson Road and then head up the fire road under San Gabriel Peak. Mt. Lowe was once the upper end of a scenic funicular that crawled along the side of the mountains up here. The railway was a huge tourist attraction around the turn of the century, even giving rise to a tavern that ultimately burned down. Some artifacts from that era remain, including sighting tubes propped on stands that describe what part of the basin you're looking at. Walking from **Point Dume** to **Paradise Cove** on the Malibu coastline (Santa Monica Mountains National Recreation Area, tel 818/597-9192) hardly ranks as a hike, since the route is totally flat and only about two miles long, but it's the best tidal-pool trip in the area. When the tide is very low you'll find an amazing assortment of sea life at your feet: periwinkles, tube snails, sculpins, mussels, shore and hermit crabs, sea anemones, barnacles, and starfish. The best seasons for these extreme lows are in the afternoons, two or three times each month, from October through March. Park at Westward Beach on the west side of Point Dume, then walk around the point heading south. The rock here is volcanic and very craggy and sharp, and at times you'll be climbing over it, so wear good sneakers. Don't be surprised if you come across a naked person or two along the way.

Pollution's a beach... The L.A. Department of Public Works is building new storm-drain diversion channels because there is so much nasty stuff in the runoff. Every summer, Angelenos come down with Surfer's Flu—stomach upset, respiratory infections, skin rashes, and coughs, all caused by the choice mixture of motor oil, fertilizers, pesticides and animal feces that provide the backdrop to our bathing experience. And the nasty stuff isn't just in the water—it's also in the sand. Last year the county spent $1.3 million just scraping the crap off the top layer. Thank goodness for Heal the Bay, the environmental group that monitors pollution levels at the area's beaches, giving them a grade based on either weekly or daily measurements. To be safe you should stay at least 100 yards away from any flowing storm drains, and avoid going in the water totally for at least three days following a rain. The worst beaches for pollution are Malibu, Will Rogers, the area south of the Santa Monica Pier, and the coastline close to the Basin H boat launch in Marina del Rey. That was as of *last* week, anyway. (Check the group's web site at healthebay.org for updates.)

Okay, now just forget about all that. Los Angeles has 72 miles of coastline: sand bottoms, rock bottoms, reef bottoms, coves loaded with tide pools, wide expanses dotted with volleyball nets, and always convenient, overpriced parking lots nearby. You can always get to the beach, except around Malibu, where they don't like the masses using *their* beach. Of course you know about Venice and Santa Monica and Will Rogers beaches, all just minutes from Santa Monica. But the closest beach to the city itself—and the least used—is Dockweiler State Beach, south of Santa Monica Bay and directly under the LAX flight path. There's lots of parking there, plus dozens of concrete fire rings for your evening barbecue. At the northern end of the beach, near Playa del Rey, college kids play pick-up volleyball games. Fishing is allowed, but I don't think I'd want to eat anything that swims in the Bay, thank you. If you've got small kids with you, try the aptly named **Mother's Beach** (officially called Marina Beach) at Admiralty and Via Marina in Marina del Rey. This is a small sand beach with no waves and no pebbles in the shore break. The only problem time is after it rains, when the area can get an F rating. For families, Valley teenagers, and treasure hunters, **Zuma Beach** (30050 Pacific Coast Hwy.) is the best choice. No decent surfing here and no snorkeling, but plenty of parking, lifeguards, fast food, and volleyball. It's a bit of a drive from the city, but it's the closest decent beach with something of a wild feel. The three best **Point Mugu State Park** beaches are **Malibu**, **County Line**, and **Leo Carrillo**. If you plan to bring your board along, however, only **Surfrider Beach** (named after the slew of '60s Gidget movies that were shot here) in Malibu (tel 310/456-8432, 23200 Pacific Coast Hwy.) is a rival for the breaks in San Diego, Santa Barbara, and the South Bay. Forget about the funky water in the Lagoon—

it's *Malibu*, and when it's pumping here the waves are truly magical. **Leo Carrillo State Beach** (805-488-5223; 35000 Pacific Coast Hwy.) is good for families and worth the hour's drive from Santa Monica. There's easy parking and access to the beach, plus great tidal pools loaded with sea hares and starfish. It also has sometimes-decent (though very crowded) waves.

Skimming the surface... With the advent of lighter, more maneuverable kayaks, the sport has taken off big-time here. When you're kayaking, you're on the water but not drinking it, getting an incredible upper-body work-out and working on a skin cancer from the reflected glare. The best place for novices and intermediate paddlers is Malibu. **Malibu Kayak** (tel 310/457-3181) has rentals and tours (a single kayak costs $30 for four hours, while tours start at $45 for two hours). The rental includes kayak, backrest, paddle, and life jacket. Starting out from the beach opposite the store, go around the pier, heading north beyond the surfers toward the Point Dune head-lands. That way the wind will be at your back coming in. For a kayaking experience on a totally different level, consider a trip to Catalina. **Catalina Island Expeditions** (tel 310/510-1226, on the sand on Descanso Beach, west of the Casino) has easy and hard trips, depending on your pain-pleasure threshold. Their wildest trip is a full island circumnavigation (four days, three nights for $295), and is for experienced paddlers only. You'll never get a better look at Catalina's 54 miles of coastline. Much more basic is their Goat Harbor overnight trip for beginners ($195), which involves a six-mile paddle to a campsite on a pri-vate beach where there's good snorkeling, fishing, and hiking. They have loads of other guided tours as well, some only 90 minutes long. The most unusual short trip is the "Full Moon Paddle," which happens once a month and involves paddling into the channel in open-deck sea kayaks to watch the moon rise. All gear is included: lights for evening paddles, dry sacks for cameras, paddle pants and jackets if the weather dictates, binoculars, snacks, and bottled water. And be sure to bring snorkel gear, because Catalina also has a prime snorkeling-only spot: **Lover's Cove Marine Preserve**.

Where to be humiliated in pickup basketball games... Now that Michael Jordan has retired, maybe there's room for you on the team. Refine your swish at one of the many pickup basketball games that occur at recreation centers or parks all over the city. There are scores, but the following are especially notable. At the **Jim Gilliam Recreation Center** (tel 323/291-5928, 4000 S. La Brea Ave.), you'll find some of the best amateurs around, city to college, bumping up against one another. The games happen Monday to Friday, from noon to 10 p.m., and on Sunday from 9 a.m. to noon. At the **Rogers Recreation Center** (tel 310/412-5504, 400 W. Beach Ave., Inglewood), you'll have the privilege of getting elbowed by some of the very best players in the city, perhaps even a pro or two. They offer games daily, but the hours vary depending on who's there. The **Westwood Recreation Complex** (tel 310/473-3610, 1350 Sepulveda Blvd.) is more casual. The players are older, and there are two full courts, both indoors. Where did the Lakers and the Clippers go to stay sharp during the NBA strike? To the **UCLA men's gymnasium** (tel 310/825-1135, just east of Wooden Center, UCLA campus). There are four courts in the two-story complex, and who knows who you'll bump into? If you see Shaq, ask him if he'd like to play HORSE.

Swimming the yellow river: pools for kids... There's nothing quite so dispiriting as an overheated, sweaty child who's bored, bored, bored. My advice: Send him/her to the pool right away and give both of you a break. First choice is the **Echo Park Pool** (tel 213/481-2640, 1419 Colton St., Echo Park). This indoor pool, right next to Echo Park Lake, is a major hang for the mostly Latino and Asian kids of the neighborhood. You may see lots of furtive glances as the kids check each other out, but there's zero gang feeling. They leave their attitude in the lockers here. The pool is big and very family-friendly, with lap lanes, water aerobics classes, and water polo leagues. After your dip you can go over to the lake and watch the ducks doing *their* workouts. The **Griffith Park Pool** (tel 323/664-6878, 3401 Riverside Dr., Los Feliz) is a great outdoor facility that is jammed with kids in the summer. Finally, there's the pool at the **Ketchum Downtown YMCA** (tel 213/624-2348, 401 South Hope St., Bunker Hill). It's a lap pool, but it also has great water fitness classes for elders and swimming classes for kids. This is one of the premier Y's in the city, and it has a wonderful outreach program for the disadvantaged children of Downtown.

GETTING OUTSIDE | LOS ANGELES

Calling all gym rats... My favorite gym is also at the **Ketchum Y,** not because I'm a disadvantaged youth (although I could be, if the price is right), but because they have great machines, lots of classes, and a great mix of Bunker Hill lawyers and executives rubbing elbows with ancient Japanese retirees from Little Tokyo and just plain neighborhood folk. Plus, there's a wonderful view from the second-floor exercise rooms, looking out over the high-rises of Bunker Hill all the way to the mountains when the air is clear. They also have a very clean steam room, a dry sauna, a massage service, the pool, an indoor running track, squash courts, and a fairly relaxed pickup basketball court. Parking is only $1; lots of the conventioneers staying at the Bonaventure come here over the Sky Bridge for their daily fitness fix. When you're finished exercising you can go to the Central Library, just a block away. Work your body and your mind—get it? The **Spectrum Club** (1815 Centinela Ave., Santa Monica) is where the racquet freaks come to play, since it has more racquetball and squash courts than any other club on the West Side. The place echoes with the sound of hard little balls being slapped against sweat-streaked walls—kind of like the Detour Bar in Silver Lake. People rave about the Sunday-morning Gospel Moves classes at **Crunch** (tel 323/654-4550, 8000 Sunset Blvd., West Hollywood), when you feel not just the burn but the Lord as well. This club has live deejays playing funk and hip-hop, techno, even a stand-up comedian to make you laugh while you're gasping for air. They also have the best and newest machines in the city. The facility here has been rated one of the cleanest gyms in L.A. One caveat: A new trend of gym thefts has been noticed, especially in women's locker rooms. The thief cuts off the lock from a locker and steals ATM cards, cash, and credit cards. Then the thief or her accomplice (usually a man) phones the victim while she's still working out and tells her that her wallet was found, and that he works for the bank's fraud unit and needs her PIN numbers to cancel her ATM card. The victim is so flustered and stressed that she often blurts it out.

Fat-tire fanatic... The L.A. basin is surrounded by mountains, and we have some of the best mountain biking this side of...uh...Fresno, no matter what those gearheads in

Moab say. For beginners, the **Arroyo Seco trail**, behind the Jet Propulsion Laboratory (JPL), in Altadena, is the perfect place to get your feet wet—which you will if you ride it in the winter or spring. It's 12 miles, in and out, with only a 600-foot elevation gain, but there are a lot of water crossings. The trail is used by lots of people, including hikers, dog walkers and horse riders, so be cautious coming around blind turns. Although the biking isn't strenuous, it can be technically tricky, especially after a wet season. Not only will the water crossings be deep, but there will be a lot of rocks in the trail, so you'll probably have to dismount and walk in some sections. To get there, take the 210 East and the Windsor exit, then turn left and look for the parking area that overlooks JPL—it'll be full of cars with bike racks. Looking toward the mountains you'll see a road going toward JPL and a gated road next to it. This is the trailhead. It starts off as pavement, but turns into hard pack and then sand and then water and then rocks at the end. Always bear to your left, and you'll never get lost. If you're looking for something that will really burn your thighs, follow the Arroyo Seco trail as described, but take the **Brown Mountain Turnoff**, marked by a sign about a half mile in from the entrance gate. This is a relentlessly steep uphill climb of about four miles to a saddle where the trail meets the fire road going down to Milliard Camp Grounds—where you could also start from and sweat a lot less. If you've still got the energy after you reach the point, continue on up to your left and you'll finally dead-end at the top of Brown Mountain. Your reward will be one of the most amazing views in Los Angeles—all the way to Catalina. To the north, you'll see cars and motorcycles whipping along Angeles Crest. From Arroyo Seco to the summit takes about two hours if you pump the entire time. The return trip is a screamer of a downhill; make sure your brakes are in good shape, because you're going to need them. Also be mindful of deer and mountain lion up here, especially at twilight. If you have lights on your bike, this is a great ride to do at night during the summer.

Out just beyond Malibu is **Sycamore Canyon**, which is the mountain-biker's version of the La Jolla Canyon Hike (which does *not* allow bikes). If you are with people who are not riding or are beginners, this is the ideal location to visit. There are showers and picnic tables, the beach is right across the road, and the hiking trails here are fantastic. For this ride, park your car at Pt. Mugu State Park and then bike through the campgrounds into Sycamore Canyon. Beginners should simply continue straight into the canyon. There are some small water crossings, but the trail is a very gradual uphill, gently rolling and shaded by sycamore and oak (plus lots of poison oak in the underbrush—so if you get off the trail to pee, be careful). There are no horses on this trail, and the farther up you get, the fewer hikers you'll see. If you want a challenging climb, take the first left as you come out of the parking lot and head onto **Overlook Trail**. As the name suggests, you'll overlook the entire coast once you get to the top, about 2,000 feet up. As you descend on the other side, watch for a single track off to your right. This is a fairly new trail and full of switchbacks—very tricky, and lots of fun. It'll loop you back onto the main Sycamore trail in the valley below. Total riding time: about three hours. There are hundreds of other trails within an hour's drive from Downtown L.A. in the Santa Monica and the San Gabriel mountains. For maps of them all as well as advice on what's new and happening, stop in **I. Martin Bicycles** (tel 323/653-6900, 8330 Beverly Blvd., West Hollywood). All the salespeople here are avid riders and very chatty. You'll probably walk out having spent more than you expected to: The store has a huge selection of biking gear and some of the most tricked-out (and expensive) bikes you've never ridden. They'll also tell you there that this is not a good town for road weenies. There's something about the sight of a bike in front of a driver's car on city streets that produces rage. I've had automobile drivers try to force me into the curb, open doors in front of me, and screech to sudden stops with no warning. The bus drivers are even worse. The only place I feel safe is riding around the traffic-free back roads of **Griffith Park**. You get a climb out of it, and can also do some fairly high-spinning muscle-building, especially off Riverside Drive or up Commonwealth Avenue. Road bikes can be rented at **Woody's Bicycle World** (tel 323/661-6665, 3157 Los Feliz Blvd., Los Feliz). They're not the greatest bikes in the world, but they'll do. There aren't many other places to rent either road or mountain bikes here, except for beach bombers out on the Venice Boardwalk. There you'll find shops every 20 feet or so, renting bikes and in-line skates.

Going postal... Sometimes working out or even getting a good massage can't relieve that stress building up inside of you like a tightly wound spring. That's when you need to grab your gun and go hunting for humans. For boy-men who just can't stop playing war (or women with a secret agenda), the action game of the moment is paintball, the "sport" that involves firing pneumatic air guns loaded with gelatin bullets containing blood-colored liquid. Relax, it's just a game. The "hunts" typically last about 20 minutes and are refereed. You don't need muscles—just good aim and a thirst for revenge. **Close Encounters Paintball Field** (tel 805/255-5332, 22400 The Old Road, Newhall) features 157 acres of war, along with picnic tables so your loved ones can watch as you get wasted. Twenty-five dollars gets you in for the whole day. Paintballs and CO_2 for your guns are extra, and you can also rent weaponry camouflage outfits and safety headgear. For an added touch of realism they also hold night games every Friday. If you'd rather do your human hunting in a more real-world environment, check out **SC Village Paintball** (office; tel 949/489-9000, 27132A Paseo Espada, Suite 403, San Juan Capismano). This place has 11 different themed fields spread over 60 acres and modeled after film sets, which is why movie stars like Wesley Snipes drop in for practice from time to time. Where do you want to fight today? Beirut? Bosnia? Vietnam? They don't have a set that looks like Columbine or a CAA agent's office *yet*...but they should. There are two categories of play, beginner and advanced. It costs $20 for a half day and $25 for a full day, but you have to bring your own gear. If you're unarmed and really need to do some damage, go for the Semiauto/Pump Rifle Package ($45), which gives you protective gear, 200 rounds of ammo, and a weapon that will satisfy those murderous urges nicely. They do a lot of corporate outings here on the premise that shooting at each other "promotes team building." Yeah, right.

Smells like fish... There are basically three different ways to go after fish here: From the shore, from a pier (or barge), or from a party boat. Surf casting gets better the farther you get from the city, of course, and the fish will be marginally less polluted. A lot of people fish from the rocks near **Big Rock** on Pacific Coast Highway, but I think it's best to go at least as far as **County Line** before you unpack your long pole and your pyramid sinkers. If you use worms or ghost shrimp or sand crabs with a #4 hook or smaller you'll most likely catch sculpin, surfperch, and maybe corbina. Then there are the city piers in Santa Monica and Venice. **Venice Pier** (right next to Muscle Beach) was badly damaged by the '83 El Niño storms, and it was totally rebuilt in the 1990s. The pier is wheelchair-friendly (and disabled people get a free fishing license). There's an artificial quarry rock reef around the end of the pier, which draws rockfish. During especially warm years yellowtail and white sea bass can also be caught here, but I wouldn't start planning your cookout just yet. Depending on where you're standing on the pier—even with the wave line or out on the end—you could land stingray, sand sharks, halibut, mackerel, bonito, barracuda, kelp bass, yellowfin croaker, and even thresher shark. You can get frozen bait at **Nick's Liquor Store**, across the street. The pier is open from 6 a.m. to midnight and has benches, restrooms, fish-cleaning stations, and parking (which fills up quickly). There's also a shuttle to the pier if you need to park farther away.

The **Santa Monica Pier** was also heavily damaged in the '83 El Niño, which resulted in a $30-million renovation that turned this into one of the state's most angler-friendly piers. It goes out nearly 2,000 feet into the Pacific, half of this over the ocean, and has lowerlevel sections that put you just a dozen feet above the surface of the water. Again, depending on where you are and what bait you're using, you can reel in mackerel, white croaker, surfperch, sculpin, bonito, and sand sharks. Out on the end of the pier some fishermen go after full-sized sharks using heavy tackle (120-pound steel leaders and 8/0 hooks) and live bait. Thresher sharks in the 70-pound range are not rare, and in 1996 someone caught a 185-pound, seven-gill shark here. There's a bait-and-tackle shop by the end of the Santa Monica Pier. The pier is open 24 hours a day and has benches, lights, and fishcleaning stations. Major caveat: The Department of Fish & Game recommends against eating "an excess" of fish caught from either of these piers.

Okay, so far you haven't caught anything you can— or at least should—eat. To fish for your stomach you'll have to get onto a boat and head out for blue water. If you want the closest possible sportfishing facilities, talk to

L.A. Sportfishing (tel 310/822-3625, Dock 52 on Fiji Way in Marina Del Rey). The parking is free here, but nothing else is. They have a variety of boats going out, but your most productive day trip will be a three-quarter-day surface trip, leaving at 7 a.m. (cost, $30). Possible catches include sea bass, halibut, sculpin, sharks, barracuda, and kelp bass. The company will also rent you tackle and clean your fish for you if you wish. Of course, whether you catch anything or not all depends on the season, the water temperature, and if it's an El Niño year or not. Basically the winter months are better for halibut and cod, while the summer favors barracuda, yellowtail, and albacore. Those last two are the ones that most local fishermen drool over, partially for their fight but also for their good eating. If you want fresh fish but don't want to bother fishing for it yourself, come to Dock 52 around 3 p.m. when the boats return, and see if anyone wants to sell part of their catch.

For people wearing funny clothes... Of course, not every outdoor activity has to be about improving your body. Sometimes you just want to live out some odd Dungeons & Dragons obsession. That's why we have **Pleasure Faires**. If your idea of a great afternoon is dressing up like Friar Tuck and talking funny while you stroke your staff suggestively at the passing wenches bearing ale, then prithee come on down, dude. The **Tudor Fayre** is held at Fair Oaks Park in Pasadena (South of Madison Ave. on Fair Oaks) and has some 100 booths and three stages. It's held in June and attracts about 20,000 people. This year the Fayre was set in the English Renaissance town of Bridgewater in the year 1536, when good King Henry VIII ruled. The biggest of these truly retro events is the **Renaissance Pleasure Faire of Southern California** (tel 800/52-FAIRE, Glen Helen Regional Park, 2555 Glen Helen Pkwy., Devore, out near San Bernardino). It draws some 200,000 visitors, and has been going on for 40 years. It's held from late April through late June, and the theme is always Elizabethan. Any costume is allowed, although they do advise that "common decency applies," which I assume means no transparent codpieces.

For people wearing no clothes... Sometimes, I don't know, you just want to get nekkid. Y'know—strip, disrobe, let it all hang out. And down, of course, sagging and drooping as gravity exerts its unstoppable force. Well, maybe not. But if you're comfortable with your body type and simply find these day-to-day clothes too confining at times, then a trip to **Elysium Fields** (tel 310/455-1000, from 9 a.m. to 7 p.m. PT, 814 Robinson Rd., about a mile north of Topanga Village) is just what you need. This is the only clothing-optional resort in Los Angeles (although there are a ton in Palm Springs now). It's in Topanga, which is the perfect setting for getting rid of that bikini line once and for all. The resort offers yoga sessions, t'ai chi, even karate classes (which must be seen to be believed). Most people come just to laze in the sun, play tennis, swim, or hang in the hot tubs. It's a family-oriented facility, which means kids are welcome; long horny stares and suggestive behavior aren't. It's clothing-optional, which means you don't have to be nude if you don't want to. But why else would you come here? The clientele is mainly in their thirties and forties, a cross section of humanity ranging from plumbers to doctors to bartenders to ballet dancers, in all shapes, sizes, and colors. If you're curious, there are free introductory tours every Wednesday, Saturday, and Sunday at 11 a.m. If you want to stay for the day it's $25 for one person, $30 for two people coming together. For those who don't want to spend money to enjoy the sand-in-the-crack sensation, there are a few nude beaches relatively close to the city. Be warned, however, it's a $150 fine if you're busted. The most private stretch is probably the trio of beaches **El Pescador**, **El Matador**, **and Piedra at Robert J. Meyer State Beach** (32000 Pacific Coast Hwy.). There are parking areas at all three and trails down to the beach. On a typical day about half of the crowd is nude, male and female. **Dockweiler State Beach**, south from Marina del Rey, is also a fairly deserted beach where you can go naked since the lifeguard patrols are fairly infrequent. Down on Palos Verdes Peninsula there's **Inspiration Point** and **Smuggler's Cove**, both very small and reachable only by fairly slippery trails. Park at Abalone Cove and head south about a half mile. Wear a pair of protective shoes, since the rocks are jagged and the tide pools are loaded with sea urchins.

The recovery process... Now that you've exercised, baked your skin, and sweated the toxins out of your gut, it's time to take care of that poor bag of water you call your body. Better yet, hire someone to do the job for you. Around the turn of the century, a wildcattter looking for oil dug a hole near Beverly Boulevard. and only found water. *Hot* water. Disgusted, he capped the well and left. Today that hot water has been uncapped, and it's the reason people come to the **Beverly Hot Springs** (tel 323/734-7000, 308 N. Oxford Ave.), a luxury facility midway between Downtown and Beverly Hills. It's not just a tub soak palace, either. You can get body scrubs, shiatsu massage, and a variety of facials and body wraps. But the soaks, at $40 for 90 minutes, are some of the best de-stressers in town. The entrance features a baby grand piano positioned in front of a two-story enclosed waterfall. To experience the European approach to body care, stop into **Brooks Massage Therapy** (tel 323/937-8839, 7619-21 Beverly Blvd.). If you're expecting a soothing, Alpha-wave rubdown, then guess again. Brooks has been in business for nearly half a century, and the mainly Russian staff is strong and forceful. It also has shiatsu massage and reflexology, but the Swedish and deep-tissue bodywork is what brings in the crowds. There's also a "live steam" sauna and a dry rock sauna that are a deal at $15. The best package is a 90-minute massage and sauna for $100. You'll come out three inches taller and ready for a long nap.

Facials aren't just for women anymore. Anyone who spends any time exposed to the salt, exhaust, wildfire soot, and smog of the L.A. basin has to have some seriously clogged pores. You've got some real gunk down there, but that's why you come to **Fayces Salon** (tel 310/313-3223, 11373 Washington Blvd., Culver City). They'll pop those blackheads that you just can't reach. Bonus points for the end-of-session glycolic masks, so your face doesn't look like a truck ran over it. It's all part of the L.A. ethos: A face is a terrible thing to waste. **Tawa's Shiatsu Spa** (tel 213/680-9141, 362 E. First St., Little Tokyo) is one of the best deals in town, offering an hour massage for about $60. And don't think for a minute that this is going to be some sensually stimulating, possibly erotic experience. The masseuses will pop and prod and reroute your chi energy flow so that everything is back in balance again. It may even hurt. There's also a small spa for men only.

shop

5
ping

Consumerism is
what L.A. is all
about, right?
That's what they
say up in Yuppie
Central—a.k.a.
San Francisco.

After all, having more stuff is the carrot of the American Dream. Why else would we work at terrible jobs for bosses we hate? It's not just the *having* that's a pleasure, it's the whole dance of foreplay and climax—of shopping, then shopping some more, and, finally, buying. Without it, we might as well all be living in trailers out in the desert, sucking on stones. Shopping also fills an existential need, giving Angelenos something to do when they leave the tanning salon and have an hour to kill before their appointment with the cosmetic surgeon.

Target Zones

Unlike many other megacities, Los Angeles is not obviously a walking city. Instead of strolling, your best plan is to drive the grid of streets and do destination-point shopping. In L.A., think of the car as simply an extension of your grasp, a convenient way to pluck that hard-to-reach fruit hanging outside your neighborhood. Once you've incorporated this concept into your subliminal filters, everything becomes much easier, as long as you ignore that recent study showing that people driving in cars breathe much worse air than anyone else, even when the windows are rolled up and the AC is on. Doesn't help. Better yet, since you're getting poisoned anyway, just grab the credit card with the most left on it and head out to buy something you don't need!

The short list of destination shopping extends from the foothills of **Pasadena** to the **3rd Street Promenade** in the seaside town of **Santa Monica**. The buying zone winds through **Downtown**, then heads west along **Melrose Avenue**, **Beverly Boulevard**, 3rd Street, and **La Brea Avenue**, straight through the heart of **Beverly Hills**. Each area has its own character, its own attractions, and headaches. **Pasadena's Old Town** is really just a San Gabriel version of the **3rd Street Promenade**; **Melrose** is now well into middle age and looking very tattered around the edges, about to reach that stage of **Hollywood** funkiness where only tourists can ignore the squalor; **Beverly Boulevard**, 3rd Street, and **La Brea** are the new happening locales, where you can shop with some sense of ease without being upstaged by either the soundtrack or the hoards of know-nothings, pierced and otherwise. Beverly Hills is Beverly Hills—so it was and so it ever shall be. Consider yourself warned—this golden village is strictly Suckerville, appropriate mainly for movie moguls, gazillionaire foreigners, and trophy wives. You can shop here, certainly, just like you can visit Main Street in Disneyland and feel you're someplace real. Although the parking is cheap (there are public parking structures), everything else is overpriced. Conspicuous consumerism is the *sine qua non* of Rodeo Drive. Morals, ethics, humanism—they carry no value. Snotty shopgirls with silicone implants do. The idea of shopping here, other than as an exercise in camp, has become grotesque. If that doesn't make sense to you, then maybe you should immediately head there. Abandon all hope, the rest of you. If you want to spend real money and have fun doing it, go to **Montana Avenue** or **Main Street** in Santa Monica instead. The air's a lot better, there are more crazies and good-looking people, and shopping suddenly becomes a way of life, less a symptom of neurosis than an entire philosophy, coffee by Starbucks, postcards from Urban Outfitters, fiction from Midnight Special, local indie CDs from Penny Lane. Plus the parking is pretty cheap and convenient here, too.

That being said, you also don't have to head for neighborhoods to get a full culture fix. It's lifestyle shopping now, from bath mats to pickled fish, retro furniture to "That '70s Show" bell bottoms; from how-to salsa instructional videos to candles. Think globally, shop locally.

Looking for sales? Try cruising the high-traffic, overpriced neighborhoods, especially **Montana Avenue** in Santa Monica. The handful of landlords who own the street raise the already astronomical rents so often that any imaginative, risk-taking store doesn't have a prayer and soon goes belly up. That's when you can swoop in and get all kinds of treasures, up to 85 percent off. Just drive along at a leisurely speed and keep your eyes peeled for the "Everything Must Go" signs. Sooner or later, you'll find what you're after.

Also, don't ignore the "previously owned" option. There's nowhere else in the country with so many large-scale regular swap meets. Mark your calendar: The first Sunday of each month brings with it the **Pasadena City College Flea Market**, featuring tons of free parking and fairly cheap prices (though it tends to be a little too heavy on the bad CDs and horrible homemade art). This is followed on the second Sunday by the **Rose Bowl Flea Market**, acknowledged as the original Big Bang of all swap meets. This is where Japanese buyers come to buy used clothes by the ton. The farther out you go from the main area, the hipper the scene. This is the outsider zone. If you're serious, you'll be there with your flashlight at 4 a.m. On the third Sunday is the **Long Beach**

Antique & Collectible Market, which is more on the down-and-dirty side. Used porno tapes and unused home exercise equipment and other mass-market items predominate. It's held in Long Beach's Veteran's Stadium, a 40-minute drive south of L.A., and if you've got the stamina to withstand the heat, you're certain to pick up some bargains. At the other end of the spectrum is the **Santa Monica Antique & Collectible Market**, held on the fourth Sunday of the month at the Santa Monica Airport (a so-very-Santa Monica touch). There are collectibles to be had, but both the crowd and the sellers are more chichi, reeking of the moneyed West Side. Everyone is clutching a Starbucks cup, looking as if they've actually dressed up for the occasion. Even if you don't buy anything here, you'll at least have had some sort of encounter with all those shiny happy people you pass on the freeway every day.

An even more personal shopping experience can be had by checking out some of the hundreds of weekend garage sales advertised each week in the newspaper. Check the classifieds in the *L.A. Times* or the *Recycler*. Hot neighborhoods include **Santa Monica**, **Silver Lake**, **East Hollywood**, **Los Feliz**, and **Glendale**. You'll find a lot of the same crap, but every now and then you'll come across the odd Hollywood prop person or the divorcing couple or the old folks who have lived in the same place for 50 years with their Airstream trailer in the back yard—mainly folks who don't know the true value of what they have. You'll go through a lot of junk, but then you stumble across some treasure, usually for under a dollar. A garage-sale expedition is the antithesis of the mall experience, tucked away in the midst of the ultimate mall culture.

The Lowdown

Ethnic one-stops... East Hollywood was once a major Armenian neighborhood, which is why you'll still find **Bezjian's** there, just a half-block from the new Red Line station on Vermont Avenue. It's a corner Armenian grocery store, specializing in Middle Eastern and Indian spices, teas, nuts, and chutneys. They've got everything from dry curries and Iranian pistachios to cookbooks, olive oils, perfumes, and Turkish coffee urns. Similarly, Santa Monica has become home to a generation of expat Brits, and now there's the **Continental Shop**, on Wilshire Boulevard, to show for it. Here you can find videos of last year's British TV shows that never made it over here, as well as jams, newspapers, racks of teas, a huge selection of English candies, and all the Marmite you could ever want. Looking for a close encounter of the Japanese kind? **Yaohan**, in Little Tokyo, has ready-cut sashimi, ivory chopsticks, Japanese magazines, rice cookers, Shiseido soaps, kimonos, *Anime* videos, plus all the ingredients you need to make a 20-course gourmet Japanese meal. If you're in the market for a well-maintained used car, there's also a wonderful bulletin board here for Japanese kids who are returning home and trying to unload their cars, usually at bargain prices. On Sunset Boulevard you'll find the **A-1 Grocery Warehouse**, which caters to the large Chinese-Vietnamese-Cambodian population residing around Echo Park. A-1 contains a huge fish market, along with other exotica such as fresh rice noodles, spiky durian fruit from Indonesia, aluminum Thai serving bowls, incense, and every type of curry paste and fish sauce imaginable. From cognac to rice, the prices for everything are among the best in town, and everything is super-fresh. It's impossible to park in their lot on Sundays when the place is traditionally jammed. Other days, catch the eye of the lot guard (he's the one dressed up like the last soldier out of Saigon, in full-flak jacket and camouflage), and he'll help you find a space. **Thailand Plaza**, in Hollywood, serves the Thai community in much the same way that Yaohan caters to local Japanese. Its wide-ranging inventory includes videos, fresh coconuts, dried noodles, serving trays, and packages of condiments that smell icky and taste great. Upstairs is a quirky Thai restaurant that features karaoke singing at night. You can park in the store's own garage, off Sunset (turn in the driveway just before the gold-plated shrine out front). **Grand Central Market**, in Downtown, is really the northernmost suburb of Mexico City. Multileveled, with sawdust on the floor and the omnipresent odor of *sopes* simmering in hot oil, it's jammed all day long with shoppers. Here you'll find fresh produce and fish, goat meat, pig heads, *liquados* (fruit and veggie drinks), a terrific traditional herbal/homeopathic pharmacy, tequila—from rot-gut to Reposado—spicy, greasy fast food, and more. One caveat: The produce throughout is cheap, but you're better off paying a little more at the stalls in the back and making your own selection for top quality. Another caveat:

Parking is expensive. Your best alternative (unless you're really going to shop for the month) is to park down in Little Tokyo and take the Dash. **Govinda's International Imports** is a must for *pukka sahibs* who crave a taste of the subcontinent. Follow the music and incense up the stairs of the faded pink temple housing the International Society of Krishna, and you'll come upon a community store featuring beautiful Indian clothing and accessories for men, women, and children—all sold at a fraction of what they cost in local department stores. Although it's open to the general public, this treasure trove has been a well-kept secret of the stars until quite recently (the day I visited the shop Sharon Stone had been by a bit earlier). The store is best known for its Pashmina shawls, made from the soft undercoat of capra hircus goats, which are found only in Kashmir and Nepal. To top it off, the carrot cake at Govinda's vegetarian buffet downstairs is the best I've ever eaten. Hare Krishna! Finally, for a slice of true L.A. culture (though some people might call this an oxymoron), try one of the many **Trader Joe's** outlets scattered around the city. This Pasadena based mini chain specializes in boutique wines and beers, almost-organic food, dried fruits and nuts, olive oils, and frozen fish, everything at reasonable prices. The best part of Trader Joe's is that you don't feel you're in a huge warehouse full of other desperate shoppers who are just dying to get out the door and back in their cars. It's an alternative-lifestyle grocery, and your fellow shoppers are far more enticing than those you'll run into at the local Ralph's. Best deals: wine by the case. Worst deals: the produce.

Tokyo prose... In Weller Court, in Little Tokyo, you'll find **Kinokuniya**, the largest outlet for things Japanese in the city. This bookstore covers every aspect of Japan's culture, language, and history. If you're looking for a Japanese writer translated into English, modern or ancient, they've got it here, along with kanji flash cards, visual dictionaries, and even a series of numbingly dull government white papers. For the benefit of fashion victims they also carry a massive selection of current Japanese magazines, from *Popeye* to *Hot Dog Press* as well as huge stacks of fat *Manga* starring your favorite *Anime* character. Best news for kids: they have a wide assortment of Pokémon paraphernalia up at the front. Like any big bookstore in

Tokyo, Kinokuniya is totally silent and always full of pasty-faced Tokyoites rooting about for news of home. Also in Downtown, just on the other side of the 101 Freeway, is **Great Wall Books & Art**. As the name suggests, this is the Chinese version of Kinokuniya. All conversation stops when a foreign devil walks through the door, but just amble over to the English-language section and the regulars will quickly forget all about you! Here you can get a superb six-volume comic-book version of Sun Tsu's *Art of War* ($60 a pop), which teaches the theory of combat by showing examples from Chinese war history. They also have books geared to students of Mandarin and Cantonese, as well as an impressive (and pricey) selection of Chinese medicine and acupuncture tomes—including books on Yuanbao Qigong, the controversial exercise sect.

Armchair travel... So you're heading out of town and need another *Irreverent Guide*? In West Hollywood, the **Traveler's Bookcase** has a massive selection of travel books, travel literature, and a variety of gadgets intended to make the traveler's life easier (that leopard-pattern barley-filled neck pillow, for example). In Burbank, near Warner Brothers Studios, **Geographia Map and Travel Bookstore** carries much of the same selection but features an easier browsing format. This is also the place to come if you're looking for weird maps of places most people never heard of. If they don't have the map you're looking for, they'll know where to find it. If you find yourself in Pasadena, head for **Distant Lands Travel Bookstore & Outfitters**, which is half bookstore, half travel-supply shop. In addition to the usual books and travel accessories like passport holders and money belts, they also sell backpacks, language materials, globes, and walking sticks.

Produce supreme... If you spend any time at all in L.A., you will discover that even in this concrete-asphalt hell there are garden spots where you can savor the bouquet of baby carrots, organic elephant garlic, and "fat-free" tamales that will curl your toes. There are farmer's markets in Culver City, Glendale, Hollywood, and Beverly Hills, but the **Santa Monica Farmer's Market** is the one that gets the most press. Open on Wednesdays from 9–2 and Saturdays from 8:30–1, this is one of the largest produce markets in the state and extremely popular among all those California-Asian-fusion-whatever chefs forever in search of the freshest, smallest, most expensive, and hardest-to-find veggies. Have an aversion to sprays and pesticides and weird waxes on your food? Then do your shopping here. There's also a no-name Latin-flavored market in Santa Monica on Saturdays at Pico Boulevard and Cloverfield Avenue, from 8–1. Note: Don't confuse the Santa Monica Market with the Farmer's Market complex on 3rd Street at Fairfax Avenue—which is also worth a visit, but for different reasons. The Farmer's Market complex on Fairfax is the closest thing the city has to a theme park for foodies. It has a carny atmosphere but with great little gewgaws and a wild assortment of boutique foods, both prepared and fresh. It is L.A.'s first mall, our version of a Turkish bazaar. People hang out here over coffee, shop for hot links, gorge on chocolate.

High-end cocooning... **East Meets West**, located on La Brea Avenue in Hollywood, near Melrose, is the largest antique quilt retail store on the West Coast. Everything here comes from the East Coast and the Midwest—hardly surprising since we Californians make a habit of trashing our history. The owner is from Pennsylvania and frequently returns back east on buying trips. After 20 years in the business, he has developed some deep contacts in the quilt trade. They also have country furnishings and 18th-century painted furniture, but the quilts are the main attraction. They range in price from an affordable $295 up to $15,000 and beyond. Don't even think about asking for a "new" quilt. Vintage is all they carry now that the Chinese are flooding the market with imitations. Who would spring $50,000 for something to throw on the bed? How about movie-industry folks, quilt collectors from around the world, and investors looking for collectible art, for starters. Designer Mimi London just snatched up a vintage braided rug that I'd had my eye on. **Not So Far East Trading**, on South La Brea Avenue, has mostly Indonesian furniture hand-built from recycled wood. The furniture makers take old houses apart and then reconfigure that wood (along with its intricate carvings) into new designs. The results are very versatile: some pieces are very simple, while others are quite ornate, appropriate for Mediterranean- or Mexican-style houses. The store carries armoires, daybeds, tables, chairs, dressers, and a full line of upholstered products. Prices range from $195 for a side table up to $3,900 for a full-sized armoire. You'll see lots of young celebs browsing here—they enjoy the earthy teak smell and like to believe that it's somehow environmentally correct to buy coffee tables made from refurbished pieces of Third World people's homes. **Chestnuts & Papaya** is the group effort of a photographer, a fashion stylist, and a model who used to pick things up on her fashion shoots around the world. You'll find furniture here from Japan, Vietnam, Thailand, and China. The items, including clothing, accessories, shoes, and dishes, range from affordable to stupidly expensive. You can get a hand-painted lantern for $24 or drop $25,000 on a screen/room divider. C & P isn't limited to Asian goods—they also have baskets from the Andes and a large selection of African art, sculpture, and masks. If you're looking for unusual fixtures, drop by **Hardware Antique**, on La Brea Avenue, where only losers ask how much it costs. They boast more than one million pieces of antique hardware in their inventory, procured from across the world. Need something a little out of the ordinary for a doorknob? How about a pair of 1860 glass Pairpoints, for a mere $395? Or you can throw for a tasty Spanish Revival thumb-level handle—a steal at $4,300. Buyer Liz Gordon plunders the world in search of these must-haves, and her efforts have turned Hardware into the ultimate wet dream for people with too much money who want to spend it all restoring an antique home. If you're looking for knobs for that Idaho farmhouse you got from Bruce and Demi after they broke up, come here. Or you can just send in pictures of the knobs and Liz will track them down like a bloodhound. Even if you're not seriously shopping, stop in to check out the extensive Bakelite knob and handle collection. In the same vein, but with a Continental twist, is **Maison Midi**, where everyone from Nancy Reagan wannabes to celebs with crazy-color hair come to satisfy their urge for French housewares. You can get everything from tea towels to a $6,000 antique wood-topped table with a wrought-iron vase. There are Moroccan lanterns, glassware from France and Italy—even North African tea glasses.

Nice buns... In the heart of Silver Lake you'll find the **Back Door Bakery**—so named because for the longest time it didn't have a permit to sell retail, and customers had to come around to the back door. Now it's the happening breakfast and take-out spot in the neighborhood, where everyone within walking distance eventually comes to sample the "lemon sex" bars, gourmet ding-dongs, and fresh bread. Right across from the nightclub that defined Silver Lake cool, Spaceland, the **Back Door** is the neighborhood's closest thing to a community center. They have the best bulletin board in the area, and they don't care if your dog comes in while you shop. Celebs of note include pulp actor Tim Roth and O.J. courtroom star Kato Kaelin. While you're down in Little Tokyo you must pay a visit to **Ginza Ya Bakery**, a typical Tokyo outlet for the particular Japanese take on French breads and pastries. It has the same huge thick-sliced bread packages you can see in every mom-and-pop Tokyo market, as well as potato donuts, curry donuts, and Western-styled, totally tasteless rolls and danishes. For takeout it sells those horrible crustless sandwiches similar to the ones you can purchase on the high-speed bullet train *Shinkansen*.

Mid-century mania... Everything old is new again. Or at least that's the current theme along Beverly Boulevard, 3rd Street, and La Brea and Melrose avenues. The architectural wizards who defined L.A.'s post-war style were Neutra and Schindler, and the houses they designed were filled with Eames chairs, Art Deco revamped for the post-nuclear age, a sort of Palm Springs Lite. It's not modern; it's *moderne* with an *e*. Like pornography, you can't define it, but you know it when you see it. It makes you...wet.

And what better place to start mining this vein than **Modernica**, where you'll find both vintage mid-century furniture and new knockoffs? Here you'll find '50s and '60s antiques, Noguchi-designed lamps, Danish modern tables and chairs in mint condition, and prices to match. How about that coconut chair ($3,700), or the grasshopper chair, the egg chair, the womb chair, or the garden egg (encased in plastic for outside pleasures)? Down on 3rd Street you'll find **OK**, which has tons of glassware, most of it new, made from old designs that are still in production from Scandinavia. The old stuff all has a new feel to it, the kind of things you'll find at the Standard Hotel (with whom OK has worked extensively). The store has a core following of influential designers who appreciate things like the classic Vespa motor scooter and Erico phones. The latter you can find here, along with what is probably the best selection of design books of this genre anywhere in the city. The glassware can run into the $1,200 range, but most are priced a grand less. Working the same side of the street, but situated across town in Silver Lake, is **Rubbish**, which has a continually shifting collection of modern and Asian furniture. The prices are better here than on the West Side, although the selection is not quite as extensive. Shopping here is a much more low-key experience. For more high-end decor, there's **Fat Chance**, which has been selling mid-century furniture (mainly '30s–'60s) for the last 21 years. The pieces are all originals, even the new ones, like a coffee table by Australian sculptor Peter Michael Adams, which goes for $6,800. Adams only makes about 10 pieces a year, so that's not really too high for a genuine work of art. They also have a lot of Herman Miller, Italian glass, lamps, and artwork from the mid-century. Fat Chance is a major source for studio set stylists, collectors, and architects, and of course celebrities with way more money than you. Its patrons include Tommy Lee Jones, Bette Midler, and Barbra Streisand, among others.

Habitat... **Shelter**, on Beverly Boulevard, is run by an architect and designer who designs contemporary furniture and home accessories. Their Thonet chairs are similar to Eames but more comfortable and durable. Got a yen for that David Design laminated-birch ply side table? You'll find it at Shelter. A lot of the furniture is manufactured by craftspeople in Silver Lake and South Central, so you're supporting the local craft scene when you shop here. Other hot items include Japanese kiri-wood boxes, beds, and sofas. If you need inspiration, they also have books on design and photography. **In House** is another showcase for local furniture makers, offering designs by Richard Montgomery Lawton (a professor at Otis School of Art and Design) and his partner Mark Zuckerman. Check out the "Circle 3" magazine table, which is included in the permanent collection of the Baltimore Museum of Art. It's yours for a paltry $450. Or the very cool TV cabinet with a window shade to hide the offending media center, just $3,000. Little touches like these are what bring in New York zombies, design professionals, photographers, and the more "sophisticated" celebs like Margaret Cho and Christopher Lambert. Also high on the Modern Hollywood list is **Zipper**, where you'll find a mix of new takes on retro designs along with futuristic 21st-century bizarro-world accoutrements. This is the kind of place you can walk into and find 10 things you weren't looking for, but simply *have* to have—like recycled vintage milk bottles with words etched into them, Prada-esque pet carrier bags, votive candles with pulp magazine covers plastered on, gummy-bear lights, or that cardboard rocking chair, which only costs $850 and will last a really long time as long as you don't have a cat. **Arte Design Imports** is a "custom ironworks" store specializing in mosaic-topped wrought-iron tables, Mexican tin full-length mirrors, iron chairs, and outdoor lounges. **Outside**, on La Brea Avenue, is a retro niche outlet that focuses on nothing but classic garden and patio furniture—everything from deck chairs to picnic tables and benches. You'll find ironwork and wood, both new and old. If all this mid-century stuff is just driving you crazy, buzz over to **Burkes Country Pine**, on the corner of Melrose Avenue and Crescent Heights Boulevard. Thirteen years in this outdoor location, they feature—you guessed it—country pine furniture. Best bet: their new shipment sales, featuring merchandise from all over Europe. You buy it right off the truck, so they don't have to unload. They have antiques as well as reproductions, with prices ranging from $80 for a CD rack up to $2,600 for a three-piece armoire.

Used (or refused)... If you don't mind seeing someone else walking around in your old jeans—or vice-versa—come by **Buffalo Exchange**, where you can trade or sell your used clothes. It may feel a little odd having a sales clerk make a critical judgment on your sense of style (you get 30 percent of the anticipated retail value or 50 percent in trade), but think of all those disco fools who've made a mint selling treasures left over from their *Saturday Night Fever* days. This isn't the Salvation Army: The buyers for the store are very selective with the vintage stuff—it has to be in good shape. Bonus points: They'll knock five cents off your purchases in lieu of providing a plastic bag, which they then donate to local charities. **Waste Land** runs a similar operation but also hawks a variety of mid-century furniture, mainly chairs. The store is cavernous, confusing, and basically overwhelming—and the sight of a line of losers, nervously clutching their trade-ins as they wait for a buyer to pass judgment, is truly depressing.

High-end vintage... **Golyester** is also a vintage clothing outlet, but you'd never know it by the prices. The items are all high-end and in perfect condition, like nice rayon dresses for $485, or a Hawaiian suit (skirt-blouse-jacket combo) for $125. They also deal in textiles, and have the best selection of '20s-through-'50s curtain fabrics you'll find anywhere. Complete sets can go for as much as $2,500 (though most are way cheaper). Along with Chinese shawls and embroidered silk kimono sleeve bands, you'll find paintings, colored photos, and prints. The decor is very warm and homey, especially compared with the cooler, more modernist, stores on this street. The sales girls range from ex-hippies in pajamas to young punker girls with tribal tattoos. The clientele are collectors, older Beverly Hills couples in Panama hats, and other tattooed punker girls with tribal tattoos. Their stock remains strong, but you're going to pay through the nose. They also have new items, including some cool hats and shoes (see below). The salesclerks have plenty of attitude, but the hoards of Japanese tourists don't seem to notice. The store looks like a New York loft, with columns, exposed rafters and ducts, and distressed concrete floors. Over on the West Side you'll find **Vintage Vintage**, which specializes in impeccable '40s couture. Their window displays, which are often of museum quality, are a standout on Montana Avenue. Once inside the door, softly swinging jazz draws you further into the era, until you find yourself wondering why clothes have gotten so boring over the last decade. It's a good place to buy evening gowns cut on the bias, colorful prints with a waist, a fine Hermès wool suit, and the sparkling costume jewelry to go with it all. Prices? If you have to ask, you shouldn't be here. **Framm Ltd.** occupies a specialized niche in the vintage world, managing to survive for 22 years by selling nothing but antique wedding dresses and one-of-a-kind special occasion wear. Ask for a closer look at the evening gowns locked in the glass armoire. The soft colors, intricate hand-beading, and subtle layering of diaphanous materials on these female-form-flattering

SHOPPING | THE LOWDOWN

draped gowns will make you wish you had some place to wear all this. A good source for hard-to-find mother-of-the-bride outfits.

American Rag CIE was one of the first to recognize the fine-wine appeal of vintage clothing. It offers classic European designer clothes and shoes, as well as vintage martini shakers and cigar accoutrements for the ring-a-ding-dinger in you. One of the most unusual vintage stores is **Shabon**, on Beverly Boulevard. It's run by a pair of clever Japanese girls with a great sense of style. They've got wonderful handbags, Bakelite bracelets, Lucite purses ($150), and straw handbags, as well as the more typical vintage jeans and cowboy boots. Their stock changes often, so it's worth stopping in regularly. For about a week they had 20 alligator handbags in mint condition, selling for $50.

Strange and bizarre, disturbing and wonderful...

"Part of you thinks it's in poor taste. Part of you wants an XL." That's the motto of **Skeletons in the Closet**, the gift store at the L.A. County morgue on North Mission Road. Simply *dying* to have a beach towel with the chalk drawing of a body's outline? Or a baseball cap with "Los Angeles County Coroner" stitched on the brim? How about some body outline–shaped Post-its, or a garment bag labeled Body Bag? For those with subtler tastes, there's even a lapel pin of a foot with a toe tag on it. Delightful. They only accept cash and checks, however. And while you can order a lot of this stuff by mail, there's nothing like a visit to the gift store itself, located on the morgue's second floor, down a drab institutional hallway. In a similar open vein is **Necromance**, on Melrose, which is basically a gift shop for Satanists, anatomy students, and people who just dig bones. Need an alligator skull for your ex-spouse? Or maybe a rat skull for your agent? This is your boneyard of choice. The prices aren't great, but just think about the poor creature who gave its all for your sick sense of decor. They also sell vintage funeral items and lots of books about and featuring dead people. Speaking of books, certainly the strangest bookstore in L.A. is **Amok**, on N. Vermont Avenue in Los Feliz. Here you'll find a mind-wrenching collection of books, comics, 'zines, videos, music, and art. The general themes are subversion (political and moral), surrealism, decadence, cults, serial killers, self-mutilation, Nazis-with-attitude, anarchy, Satanism, and psychedelics. It draws a heavy assortment of sickos with a sense of black humor, including celebs like Janeane Garofalo, Bruce Wagner, and Paul Reubens. Why aren't you surprised? Practically next door you'll find **Y Que**, which in Spanish means "and so?" This is where the white trash culture comes to celebrate its roots by browsing through a mix of vintage cartoon lunchboxes, Menudo artifacts, shlock-pop iconography, and black-velvet art. Everything is cheap, and it's impossible to leave without buying something. Y Que was into the retro appeal of the '70s long before it became a movie high concept. This is the perfect place to buy stocking stuffers for your favorite Gen-Y slacker. Around the corner from Y Que is **Billy Shire's Soap Plant**. It's impossible to say too much about this place. This all-purpose boutique was the original anchor for the explosion of retail madness along Melrose back in the early '80s; it has the best and strangest assortment of must-have pop-culture books (embracing every culture and every aspect of pop), and their assortment of Mexican arts and crafts, both kitsch and otherwise, is astounding. Plus, there are tons of toys, earrings, dishes, and weird accessories. And there's always the soap and body unguents that were the original impetus for the store's existence. This is truly one of L.A.'s great treasures. Bonus points for La Luz de Jesus Gallery in the back, where Billy satisfies his lust for cartoonish fine art.

Living treasures of little Tokyo... Although New York is more like Tokyo in feel (i.e., concrete and skyscrapers, plus zillions of pedestrians, all out shopping wildly), L.A. is a lot closer in terms of history, culture, and a sense of kinship. The Japanese imprint on L.A. is deep and significant. Little Tokyo could easily have been Disneyfied, but in spite of misguided attempts at community redevelopment and the bully tactics of Japan-based corporations, the flavor of the area remains intact. When you shop here you get a little taste of everything relating to contemporary Japanese aesthetics, fads, trends, and obsessions—and all of it about six months late. We're talking last year's cute robots to the hot *Anime* character of the moment, skateboard fashion, and car-culture trinkets. And then there are places like the **S.K. Uyeda**

Department Store, a Little Tokyo veteran. It's a time capsule of the '50s, offering well-made and affordable futons and coverlets, *yukata* (light cotton summer kimonos), *geta*, or wooden-block sandals made in China for $14 (the Japanese ones, made from better wood, are way more expensive), *happi* coats, *tabi* socks, bolts of cloth, and Nagon hair dye (a must for Japanese women of a certain age). **Magic Cat** is essentially Elvis and cats. What's not to like? Obviously a labor of love, this quirky yet charming gift store is the sort of place that locals pass every day and never enter. It's evocative of a particular sub-species of Japanese culture, a love of innocence and an unquenchable fascination with Elvis. Then there are the cat culture items: bumper stickers, T-shirts, calendars, beckoning "lucky cat" figurines (which you see in just about every business in Little Tokyo), and loads of '80s' *namennayo* memorabilia—a nationwide fad in Japan that merged Elvis, rockabilly, biker gangs, and kittens dressed like '50s' American greasers. Magic Cat also has a very large Japanese video rental section and new samurai movie tapes (mainly Kurosawa and Zatoichi) for sale. For gardeners and carpenters, **Anzen Hardware** is the sort of secret you don't ever want your rivals to know about. It's been here since just after WWII. If you need any highly specialized and super-sharp Japanese wood-carving implements, this is the place to look. They also have stools for outdoor bathing, culinary knives, and assorted '50s-style Japanese home tools. Back on 2nd Street is **Rafu Bussan**, a Little Tokyo landmark that has managed to survive redevelopment, the era of the strong yen, and riots. They sell really affordable household Japanese ceramics, tea sets, sake sets, and instant sushi-rice mix way cheaper than the grocery stores. They also have great sale prices, and the elderly Japanese women clerks are so polite and graceful that you'll feel guilty you're not buying more.

Clothes for hipsters... The **Stussy** store on La Brea Avenue is the only one on the West Coast, and as you'd expect, everything in here has that big, messy, scrawled logo on it: shoes, hats, accessories, bags, sunglasses, swim trunks, T-shirts. The store has been on La Brea forever and draws loads of Japanese tourists, skateboarders, and hip-hop soldiers. They come here because of the great

selection (the biggest variety aside from the New York outlet), plus there are loads of sizes in every style. This store
for people who have been wearing Stussy since it first
emerged out of the skate-punk scene a decade ago. For
them Stussy is the streetwear of choice, hipper than Polo or
Tommy Hilfiger. The place is lit by super-hot halogens,
the floor is concrete, and on the wooden display racks
you'll find cargo pants, trainers, shorts, cyber-camouflage
zippered jackets with hoods, capris, short skirts, and
Hawaiian shirts. You'll get a similar vibe from **X-Large**, the
Los Feliz outlet for the Beastie Boys mini conglomerate—
where the soundtrack is straight Grand Royale, and the
skate-punk clothes have a heritage that traces back to
Sonic Youth's Kim Gordon. These are clothes for the
white-boy hip-hop nation, DJs, and wannabes. **Lucky
Brand** is another baggy fave among the goateed masses,
and now that they're in the mall department stores it's not
quite so special when you unzip your fly and the message
"Lucky you" stares out from the inner flap. It *used* to be
good for a laugh. Still, the retail outlet on La Brea is the
first in L.A. and has a bigger selection than you'd normally
find. There are the jeans, of course, but they also stock
jackets, boxers, khakis, tees, even a guayabera-style
embroidered shirt-jacket and perfumes...er...scents. This
fall they plan to start a kids' line—thus completing the
Gap-ization of Lucky. The shoppers are your standard-
issue foreign tourists, Hollywood in-crowd, and fashion
designers who turn their noses up at the bigger chains.

Unmentionables for the fairer sex... Are your undies
looking a little tattered? Float into **Lisa Norman Lingerie**
on Montana Avenue. With quiet gray carpeting, soft area
lighting, and smoky mirrors, it's just the place for the well-
to-do matron who still wants to look dishy under the
sheets. The knowing expression in the eyes of the owner,
your new, unspoken accomplice in sexual staging, reassures
you that pleasure is not just for kids, and there's still much
more to learn....On the other hand, if quick 'n' dirty shag-
ging is your aim, **Trashy Lingerie** is certain to put some
sparkle into your sex life. Saunter into this underwear-only
boutique near the Beverly Center to check out everything
from leotards to G-strings, crotchless panties to camisoles.
Remember that bustier Madonna wore on her Blonde
Ambition tour? She bought it here. The parade of

celebrity shoppers includes Gwyneth Paltrow, Winona Ryder, Liv Tyler, and Cher, just to name a few. The dainties aren't that expensive, and the store will make sure everything is altered to fit before you leave. Men are allowed in, but like everyone else, they have to pay an annual $5 entrance membership. Inside, the walls are deep red and the helpful salesclerks model their wares—a sight worth the price of admission alone. Cross-dressers alert: They *do* carry those sizes for the larger "woman."

A fedora like Frank's... Hats aren't a fashion statement here so much as they're the only way to keep that pesky sarcoma from popping up again on your forehead. The summer sun can be brutal in L.A., even on the short trip from parking garage to sidewalk. So be sensible and cover up. **Drea Kadilak** has hats handmade by Drea, a talented designer who has moved north on La Brea and expanded into toiletries and clothing. They're very one-of-a-kind chic, constructed from cotton, straw, and braided ribbon all stitched together into an adorable package. There are mad-hatter hats to be had, as well as blue pastel cowboys, line ripple hats, and '40s-gangster fedoras. A floppy "golfer hat" starts at $50, while you can spend as much as $210 for a wide-brimmed, shapeable horsehair "Brittany" hat. For the beach there are reproductions of vintage bathing caps for $18, as well as glitter headbands for just $5, or two for $9 (what a deal!). Forties music plays nonstop in the background, and the salesclerks are totally sweet. They also have books, tin toys, bags, sunglasses, and lotions, but the hats are the thing. Celebs Jennifer Aniston and Rose McGowan shop here, among others. For you B-Boys out there, the baseball caps at **X-Large** (see above) are strictly dope. And the prices are dopey. And so must you be, if you're willing to shell out $15 to wear an ad on your head!

Gewgaws, knickknacks, frou-frou... If you can't lose those last five pounds and aren't rich enough to afford a boob job or a new dress—accessorize! Isn't that what Cosmo says? Come on in to **Polkadots and Moonbeams**, on West 3rd Street, where you'll find rhinestone multicolored hair clips galore, butterfly clips, bra-strap headbands, chokers, beaded vintage sweaters, and vintage bathing suits, plus some new stuff too. P. and

M. is fairly particular about the quality of the "pre-worn" merchandise, and the prices are reasonable. Also check out the crocheted bag with pink plastic roses for $75. And by the way, do you know what time it is? If you don't, it's probably time for a new watch—or maybe an old watch that evokes what it's all about: the passage of time. If that's the case, it's time to visit **Wanna Buy A Watch?** on Melrose Avenue, a wonderful oddity in this retail rave. It is simply the best source in the country for used (er..."pre-owned") quality timepieces of yesteryear, the sort of things from which chronographer's wet dreams are made. We're talking vintage Cartier, Breitling, Omega, Movado, Girard, Tudo, Patek, Rolex—the jewelry cases are crammed full of classics. Got $22,000 burning a hole in your pocket? How about a circa 1950 Rolex Oyster Chronograph? Or, for those on a budget, an "adorable" little lapel-pin watch that plays a musical phrase—only $350. Everything is restored and guaranteed to work. Browsing for a timepiece here is the way watch-shopping should be: elegant, slow, and respectful.

Trolling for chotchkes? **Momo**, located in the old pharmacy on West Beverly Boulevard that used to be underneath Slash Records, is a very cute little store with loads of very cute stuff from Japan, part of a mixture of collectibles and new items. They have action figures, a funny room divider made out of pink paper cups, a variety of key chains, purses, knapsacks, and Japanese notebooks, and a huge line of Astro Boy paraphernalia, almost all of it new. Their biggest seller is a UFO-shaped lighter with a flame that jumps out about two inches from the top of the flying saucer ($17). And finally there's **L.A. Eyeworks**, which is absolutely the best place in L.A. to get glasses frames guaranteed to stop people in their tracks at any party, from Belgrade to the Mir space station. The frames are pricey but well made, and the selection is endlessly changing. Knowledgable locals wait for the end-of-summer sale, when people line up before dawn to get first crack at the bargains.

Classic pick-up lines... Alright, maybe we don't dress up the way they do in Manhattan or up in Frisco, but that's because we don't have to: For one thing, the weather is so much better here. But that doesn't mean we don't appreciate looking sharp. The world's smallest digital cell phone will only take you so far, after all—even at the entertainment-industry glory-hole the Ivy. One of our living treasures for affordable non-Gap wear is **Fred Segal**'s complex on Melrose. They have men's clothes, women's clothes, designers from Milan to Tokyo to West Hollywood, plus luggage, shoes, jewelry—simply too long a list to itemize here. This store is the alternative to mall shopping, with a much better and hipper selection—stuff that won't look tired after two wearings. If you can't find something to improve your self-image here, you might as well just shoot yourself. Their weeks-long September sale (like that of L.A. Eyeworks) is a major reason *not* to go out of town that month.

Noodle Stories on West 3rd Street also features men's and women's clothing, streamlined and modern. Their stuff is wonderfully wearable—modern classics that are comprised of embroidered linens, knitwear, trousers, suits. They also sell bags, shawls, sarongs, tees, jewelry, and shoes. The separates average around $180, while the sweaters (cashmere, angora) are in the $200–$300 range. It's the kind of place where you walk in and start chatting with the owners, maybe take a bite from their lunch, then segue into a conversation about the clothes and what you're looking for. **Elisabetta Rogiani,** on Beverly Boulevard, is an Italian designer whose clothes sometimes look more like costumes than what you could actually wear on the street. Her clothes include "custom made, one-of-a-kind" tube dresses, sequined and beaded miniskirts, long, sheer beaded vests, kimono-style gowns, and vintage bell-bottom jeans remade with '60s-looking Indian upholstery swirls. A two-piece Chinese silk shirt goes for $1,200, the bell-bottoms for $320 (you can also get, say, an American flag sewn onto your bottom if you choose). Rogiani has designed costumes for everyone from Gloria Estefan to Angelica Huston, and the newly small-breasted Pamela Lee now frequents the store. There's a private room in back that caters to those customers who don't care to mix with the public.

Finally, just because you're not 19 and a junkie doesn't mean you have to be stuck shopping at Barney's for something decent to wear. Check out **Weathervane Two** on Montana Avenue, where you'll find grown-up sizes for women who don't match the anorexic, preteen mannequin standard that pervades high and low fashion. The store features the consistent good taste of well-made American staples, along with modern (but not trendy) European imports. Plus, they have a really great staff who will help you without being too fussy about it—making this a nice, relaxing spot to drop a few hundred bills.

Almost–New York fashions... Bleu, on South La Brea Avenue, sells clothes by a variety of New York designers, including Rebecca Daningbar, Kos-tum, and Toke. The clothes here range from minimalist but feminine body-conscious gear to sheer evening wear dresses, sheer skirts, bustle skirts, and skirts with pleats. But what's with the organza mermaid skirt, cut like a wide tail at the bottom? Who's gonna wear *that*? There are also bustle liners, bustle skirts, gathered pleat asymmetrical dresses, baby wool merino shawls. Bleu shoppers tend to be typical Hancock Park yup-wives, career-oriented women; music, TV, and film agents who like to dress better than the people they represent, stylists making buys for photo shoots, and the gofers for stars who just want to "borrow" something special and weird for the night. (You have 24 hours to return something, as long as you pay a 30 percent restocking fee.) **NYSE** (a.k.a. New York Style Exchange) claims to be a Manhattanesque boutique, but you couldn't prove it by me. Like every other boutique in this area, it's drenched in lights, with high, exposed ceilings, minimalist racks and shelves, and pale-green-curtained, slightly uncomfortable changing rooms. (Well, *that* part's kinda East Coast.) But check out the clientele: Madonna, Lauren Hill's shopper, Courtney Love, and Heather Graham all like to stop by, and so does a regular crew of stylists and personal shoppers browsing for "their people." The selection is primarily hip-hop, but there are also wool jerseys with drawstring necks, Pauline pants, little skinny tops, backless tops, and hook-and-eye skirts. Prices range from $15 for tank tops to $500 for jackets. They have plenty of tennies, too.

Shoe fetish... **Don't you dare ask for L'egg's at **Footsie, the Montana Avenue shrine to toe jam coverings. This extensive funhouse of socks, nylons, and various other tootsie warmers is an ideal quick stop when you're searching for something very unusual that's sexually silky and doesn't reek of a mall. They also have sportswear and strawhats during the warmer months, when the naked-sandal look rules. And for you masochists, be sure to check out the selection of Chinese foot-binding torture shoes at **Golyester** (see above). They're closer to folk art than footwear, ranging in price from a four-inch-long squeezer for $300 to some amazingly intricate toe-smashers (price: nearly $5,000). Some have arches as high as the one in St. Louis and are loaded down with embroidery. There are also simpler Mongolian platforms, Spanish, Chinese, and Japanese stylings, plus a selection of Native American slippers and moccasins. Some you can wear; some are simply weird art pieces. Either way, they're totally unique.

For shoppers of both sexes with a major sense of retro style, there's only one place to go: **Remix**, owned by Paul Glynn—whose late, lamented Cowboys and Poodles store helped to ignite the current boom in high-grade vintage wear back in the '80s. Glynn has a huge selection of '20s–'70s dead stock (items that were never worn and never sold). Best of all, you sit in these elaborate Jon Bok folk-art thrones to try the footwear on. Remix has more women's shoes than men's, and the stock is constantly changing—which is why people tend to go a little crazy when they discover this place. (Susan Sarandon reportedly came in and bought 19 pairs in one visit.) The prices are also extremely reasonable, ranging from $35 to $120—less than you'd pay for a new tennis shoe. Here you'll find suede '30s dress Oxfords, pumps with lizard backs, black leather granny shoe lace-ups, gabardine-covered low-heel button-ups. The store is a major source for costumers and film stylists. Be warned, though—people 50 years ago had narrower feet than we do, probably because they were carrying less body weight.

Museum shops... Yeah, I know. You came out to L.A. for the art, the culture. It just so happens, however, that right next door to one of our city's leading art palaces is a great little shopping experience where you can bow down shamelessly to Mammon under the guise of self-improvement. I'm not your priest—make no excuses to me. Just pop into the **Museum of Contemporary Arts Gift Store**, on Grand Avenue in Downtown. It's a great resource for contemporary art books, MOMA catalogue gift items, local artists' limited editions, jewelry, weird books, magazines, dishes, and decor, and all sorts of additions to your house or body that are sure to stop (or start) conversation. *Highly* recommended. The gift store in the **George C. Page Museum** at the La Brea Tar Pits is much more scientifically oriented. You need to have a major obsession with extinct species to get your rocks off here—which makes it perfect for that *Jurassic Park* teen (or pre-teen) who's just hypnotized by the geologic past. In a similar vein is the **Dino-Shop at the Natural History Museum**, in Exposition Park. You can easily imagine Steven Spielberg–wannabes cruising the aisles in search of inspiration from items like the Camptosaurus Replica ($350), a 7-by-15-inch resin reproduction from an original skull of one of the largest animals (1,100 pounds) that ever walked the earth (and that includes Spielberg). There are also educational Dino Hunt Games (awarded the Dinosaur Society's seal of approval) for just $25. Meanwhile, at the **Japanese American National Museum** in Little Tokyo, you'll find specialized books about the Japanese immigrant experience in the U.S., along with "got rice?" T-shirts, nice but pricey pottery, and videos on Japanese cuisine. This is basically a feel-good store for Manzanar concentration-camp survivors and their kin, and I bet you a pint of sake you'll never see a genuine passport-carrying Japanese in here.

Music/records... **Vinyl Fetish** is where punk music first found a home on Melrose back when the avenue was still a hipster hangout. Now that CDs are old hat, Melrose is a joke, and punk is hatching yet a third generation, Vinyl Fetish has opened a second outlet on the East Side. They still have the best collection of new and used imports and indies, ranging from punk to goth to industrial to very, very strange and scary. Right up the street is **Phat Beats**, located inside the X-Large store. This is essentially a low-key but super-contemporary resource vinyl store for hip-hop DJs. The prices aren't cheap, but the selection is outstanding, and the guys who run it have zero attitude. **Rockaway Records**, farther east in Silver Lake, has a huge collection of collectible vinyl, '60s memorabilia, and bins and bins of used and new CDs. Being right in the heart of hipster heaven, they also have loads of Silver Lake bands on indie labels at rock-bottom prices. The selection of new CDs isn't red-hot, especially if you're looking for something other than rock, and their prices,

I'm sorry to say, kind of stink. But they're my local non-chain-store outlet, so I put up with them. Besides, they do get a hefty and constantly changing supply of used CDs (there are a lot of music-industry drones in the neighborhood, and around the first of the month a lot of people unload their collections to make rent).

Vinyl Surplus, on Pico Boulevard, is a cavernous warehouse that runs the gamut from decent collectibles on vinyl to really terrible things that the Salvation Army wouldn't even try to sell. The variety is so extensive, however, and the prices so reasonable (they also give great trade-in rates) that it's always worth a drive to the West Side to check them out. Over at the opposite end of the city is **La Casa del Músico**—a landmark East L.A. music store known by mariachi lovers all over the world. They have the largest selection of mariachi music you could ever hope for, and the posters to go with it. But it's also a famous mariachi musician's resource center, with violins and their replacement parts, classical guitar strings, accordians, and every guitar type from *bajosextos* to *guitarrones* for sale. They also have really good prices on Mexican CDs.

Bookstore landmarks... The **Bodhi Tree Bookstore**—named for the spot where Buddha finally got hip—is the prototypical L.A. outlet for all things spiritual. It's a facility made for wandering, and as you move from sections marked Buddhism to the Kabbala to Shamanism to Channeling, you can't help wondering if there are enough hours left in your life to ever turn into a fully realized soul. The place reeks of incense, and the people drifting through have blissful looks of focused determination as they search for the One True Path. Feng Shui or ESP? Astrology or angels? Whiskey or wine? The previously mentioned **Amok** on North Vermont Avenue represents the dark side of this same obsession, the yang to Bodhi's yin, if you will. But at Amok the game is all about trying to decide what's controlling you—the CIA or the Scientologists? Is Hitler really alive and leading a cult from a bunker beneath the Capitol? Should you get a tattoo or buttock implants instead? Back on planet Earth, **Book Soup** is just about the only reason I can think of for coming over to struggle with parking on the Sunset Strip. It's a full-service bookstore, blessed with one of the largest and best selections of new literature and hard-to-find but still-in-print titles anywhere in the city. Plus, the guys in the back really know publishing. It's also a great place to pick up autographed copies by local writers. They get bonus points for giving a discount at the cafe next door when you buy something.

The wonderful **Hennessey & Ingalls** is a rarity on the 3rd Street Promenade: an establishment that caters to something other than your gut or your image. They have L.A.'s largest collection of books on art, interior design, and architecture, ranging in tone from totally academic to kitsch/camp obsessiveness. If you're in town during the first week of November, be sure to drop in on their annual 20-percent-off sale—no small chunk of change for some of the items here. In Hollywood, the **Samuel French Theatre & Film Bookstore** is like a time trip back into a far, far different era from the one tripping down the Walk of Fame outside. They have a huge (and ultimately very depressing, when you think about it) collection of scripts from movies and TV shows. Many of them you won't recognize, either because they were failed pilots or because they were on the tube way, way before your time. All those former-cheerleader actress-wannabes from Indiana who've just arrived at the Greyhound station down the street head straight here to start working on their audition performances. (They'd be smarter to go directly to Frederick's for some trashy underwear.) English teacher alert: If you need some examples of terrible writing, you'll find tons of material here.

S'more words about words... Tucked in the back of the modern Edgemar complex in Santa Monica, you'll find the **Form Zero Architectural Books and Gallery**, a specialty bookstore you might easily miss at first glance. The books are very sophisticated here: They include many European editions, and cover all phases of city planning and home building. The small and ever-changing photo gallery of architect-designed homes, with attendant explanations of their place in design history, is especially welcome now that the Santa Monica Museum has moved out of the complex.

Looking for a special gift for that book-collector friend of yours? How about a tasty first edition of Lewis Carroll's classic *An Elementary Treatise on Determants with*

Their Application to Simultaneous Linear Equations and Algebraic Geometry? I mean, I doubt that Borders carries it. But step into **Michael R. Thompson Books**, where rare books are common, and there it is—the 1867 edition, with the covers just slightly bowed. But hey, what do you want for $1,750? At the other end of the rainbow is a folio containing the original transcriptions of the first trip to the moon, containing every single line of the entire trip's conversation between the Eagle and Houston. It's the original handout that NASA gave to the press at the time. There are probably only 50 of them in existence, and at $950 you'll be getting a piece of modern history cheap.

IL-Literature, in West Hollywood, is the kind of place that writers love, especially if they're suffering from writer's block. There are a lot of would-be and actual authors in the neighborhood, so of course the store stocks a large selection of inspirational books. There's a well-chosen best-sellers area, and a lot of well-written but not-necessarily-commercial novels. Don't look for a one-hour romance novel here: One-third of IL's customers come by every 10 days or so—it's that kind of bookstore, a place where you'll always enjoy browsing and probably end up buying more than you intended. There's a high celeb quotient here, because everybody just ignores them. Lots of stuff on art, photography, design, lighting, and architecture, as well as resource books for visual artists.

Finally, it may cost you more than taking the kids to a theme park by the time you get out, but a trip to **Storyopolis**, in West Hollywood, will certainly leave an impression on their burgeoning little brains. You've got to do *something* to compete with the Playstation, and you're likely to find that something here. This isn't a mass-market children's bookstore. They carry only "fine-art-quality" children's literature, including large-format lithographs and paintings from some of the most popular kids' books of all time. There's even a large collection of comic-book and editorial art. Most Saturdays, the store also hosts story hours featuring an author or illustrator.

Paper, plus... Located next door to IL-Literature is a classy little gift store called **Pulp**, which (as you might expect) has all kinds of great paper products, including desk accessories, handmade Italian leather journals, handmade paper, an extensive eclectic left-of-center card line, reproductions of vintage card cases, hand-sewn Japanese notebooks, retro clocks, and Italian spiral paper clips—in short, a smorgasbord for any writer who might like to go shopping in an effort to avoid the real drudgery. The prices are reasonable, so you'll easily find something you like without dropping a wad of money. Because they've got a hefty assortment of foreign periodicals, the shop is also a hangout for international travelers. Much less affordable but very impressive is **Claudia Laub** on West Beverly. This is definitely *not* your neighborhood Kinko's. Claudia's is a print shop with a difference: They actually use antique letterpresses to handprint your order. Virtually any image can be made into a die, then set into a block and printed onto paper. Being so labor-intensive, the result obviously costs an arm and a leg. Business cards, for example, can run $500 to $800 a set—not the sort of thing you'd toss around casually. They also sell beautiful graduation and wedding cards, "charm cards" ($6.50) which have charms pasted or sewn on them, wrapping papers and ribbons, handmade papers, and individually printed memo pads ($7.50 apiece).

Fab fabrics... If you're looking for fake leopard-print spandex or something to cover that Jetsons-style sofa you grabbed at a garage sale, the best place to go is **Michael Levine**, in Downtown, where you'll find a huge line of "discount" fabrics, from crazy-colored fake fur to fine cotton and rayon blends, wedding dress silks and satins, and beaded trims, plus an extensive accessory and pattern library. Across the street is their upholstery shop, where you can pick up heavy, wider fabrics for cushions, curtains, or chairs. Although they are a discount store, they ain't exactly cheap, but they're a terrific resource for stylists and photographers in the Downtown photo district.

Another good source of basic material is **Diamond Foam**, which (despite the name) is primarily a designer's fabrics shop. They're also the best place to come for foam, naturally, offering a highly varied selection of densities, thicknesses, and cuts. D.F. is supposedly a "discount" fabric outlet, but Michael Levine's has better prices. Finally, if you need something to sparkle up that new fabric, check out the **Berger Bead Speciality Company** right around the corner from Michael Levine's in the heart of the downtown fabric district. If you can't find a bead here you can't find it anywhere. They have wood, ceramic, and Moroccan trade beads, plus an extensive line of rhinestones, jewels, pearls, trimmings, nail-heads, jewelry findings, and appliqués.

Some dish!... The **Dish Factory** is right in the center of the downtown toy district, bordering Skid Row and Little Tokyo. While the neighborhood may not be the greatest, where else could you find matching Fiesta Ware saucers for your cups? They have loads of other dishes, too, mainly intended for sale to restaurants—but the prices are so good and the atmosphere so laid-back, you could easily spend hours here. This is the place to buy that three-gallon iced tea dispenser or meat chopper, or perhaps those hard-to-find Bakelite replacement stove knobs (a deal at $4 each). For hand-painted glasses that look just like '30s and '40s classics, check **Momo** on West Beverly Boulevard. My own favorite shop for cheap Japanese tea sets and heavy, stove-top sukiyaki ceramics is **Rafu Bussan** in Little Tokyo. Their selection is good and their sale prices are the best, especially at the end of spring and autumn.

Stinky stuff for your mouth... **Say Cheese** is a badly named, overpriced mini Dean & Deluca in the heart of Los Feliz, a gourmet store specializing in good salads, sandwiches, and coffee. But the real reason you come here is for the infused vinegars, the Nepalese teas, and Belgium chocolates, and especially those cheeses from Mars. "Is this cheese stinky?" an overweight matron in sweat pants demanded recently from the Gen-X Latina counter girl. "Because I don't like stinky." Well, if you *do* like stinky, this is the place to come. As they say south of the border, *Vaya con quesos*: "Go with the cheeses."

Dildos r us... All lit up like a supermarket and laid out like a chain bookstore, you can spot this newest addition to the Sunset Strip from several blocks away. Step over owner Larry Flynt's cement handprints, immortalized next to a tall pole where colorful fluorescent lights spiral up and down towards a giant rotating globe, and prepare to enter another realm. Welcome to **Hustler Hollywood**, where you can find Menage à Trois massage oil, sexual greeting cards, and videos detailing every possible physical penetration known to man (and woman). And if you should happen to be in the market for a shiny new, flesh-colored silicone dildo, you'll be glad to know they have a huge selection. As for you bad boys, Flynt's store also offers dominatrix outfits and homosexual jigsaw puzzles. You'll even find the Dalai Lama's book *The Art of Happiness* down in the bookstore—right next to *Monica's Story* and Larry Flynt's official biography, *Relax—It's Just Sex*.

The Index

A–1 Grocery Warehouse. Tiny aisles but the best fresh fish and Asian tropical produce at great prices anywhere. Looking for durian in season? Dill and mint and cilantro and boxes of strawberries? Or how about every packaged variety of Thai curry paste or fish sauces from Bangkok to Manila to Vietnam? I *love* this place.... *Tel 213/482-4803. 1487 Sunset Blvd., Echo Park.* **(p. 169)**

American Rag Cie. Fairly pricey vintage clothes from the outlet that started it all, from jeans to shoes to hats to bathing suits.... *Tel 323/935-3154. 150 S. La Brea Ave., Los Angeles.* **(see p. 178)**

Amok. Without a doubt this is the strangest and most disturbing bookstore in L.A., and maybe the world. The last word on cults, paranoia, fetishes, obsessions, and general craziness. A local treasure.... *Tel 323/665-0956. 1764 N. Vermont Ave., Los Feliz.* **(see pp. 178, 188)**

Anzen Hardware. This Little Tokyo landmark carries highly specialized and super-sharp Japanese wood-carving implements, stools for outdoor bathing, culinary knives, and assorted '50s-style Japanese home tools.... *Tel 213/628-7600. 309 E. 1st St., Little Tokyo.* **(see p. 180)**

Arte Design Imports. Wrought-iron furniture and Mexican crafts for not that much money.... *Tel 323/931-0678. 133 S. La Brea Ave., Los Angeles.* **(see p. 176)**

Back Door Bakery. Where just about everyone in Silver Lake comes for breakfast. Dog-friendly, and the coffee is way good. A great bulletin board if you're looking for an apartment.... *Tel 323/662-7927. 1710 Silverlake Blvd., Silver Lake.* **(see p. 173)**

Berger Bead Specialty Company. Beads, rhinestones, jewelry paraphernalia, and appliqués—wholesale and retail. If it can be strung or sewn, they've probably got it here.... *Tel 213/627-8783. 413 8th St., Downtown.* **(see p. 191)**

Bezjian's. Although a lot of the original Armenians who supported Bezjian's have fled Hollywood for Glendale and beyond, this longtime Santa Monica Blvd.-at-Vermont landmark continues to survive. If you're looking for the spices and staples of any Middle Eastern cuisine, they'll have it here. Plus cookbooks and implements.... *Tel 323/663-1503. 4715 Santa Monica Blvd., Hollywood.* **(see p. 168)**

Billy Shire's Soap Plant. Combination gift store, bookstore, and crafts store, with loads of pop culture items from all over the world. Everyone copies the Soap Plant, but nobody carries it off so well... *Tel 323/663-0122. 4633 Hollywood Blvd., Los Feliz.* **(see p. 179)**

Bleu. Power women shop here, getting just the right pleated dress to go with the Nokia.... *Tel 323/939-2228. 454 S. La Brea Ave., Los Angeles.* **(see p. 185)**

Bodhi Tree Bookstore. This major New Age resource brings seekers of truth from all over the world. Improving your spiritual life has never been easier or more confusing. Books, tapes, videos, incense, candles, etc.... *Tel 310/659-1733. 8585 Melrose Ave., West Hollywood.* **(see p. 188)**

Book Soup. Without a doubt this is one of the top five bookstores in the city, maybe the state. Like Midnight Special in Santa Monica, Book Soup concentrates on an exhaustive assortment of new and classic fiction along with very deep nonfiction genres. You'll find it here or they'll find it for you.... *Tel 310/659-3110. 8818 Sunset Blvd., West Hollywood.* **(see p. 188)**

Buffalo Exchange. Vintage clothes, for sale or trade. Recycle your youth and pick up someone else's. The stains and vibes are free.... *Tel 323/938-8604. 131 N. La Brea Ave., Los Angeles.* **(see p. 176)**

Burkes Country Pine. An outdoor furniture stand that's always open, rain or shine. High prices, unless you really like pine. Ask about their European Shipment Sales, when prices come down into a more reasonable range.... *Tel 323/655-1114. 8080 Melrose Ave., West Hollywood.* **(see p. 176)**

La Casa del Músico. This is mariachi central, and right down the street from the plaza where bands come to look for work.... *Tel 213/262-9425. 1850 E. 1st St., East L.A.* **(see p. 188)**

Chestnuts & Papaya. Very eclectic fashion and interior decor gathered from the Pacific Rim and beyond. They go there so you don't have to. Nice and unusual fabrics, weird items of clothing you'll never wear but are fun to have anyway.... *Tel 323/937-8450. 459 1/2 S. La Brea Ave., Los Angeles.* **(see p. 173)**

Claudia Laub. High-quality letterpress paper printing and paper products. Anyone who appreciates nice paper will enjoy this place immensely... *Tel 323/931-1710. 7404 W. Beverly Blvd., Los Angeles.* **(see p. 191)**

The Continental Shop. Just dying for a Malto, or last week's *Irish Times*, or that Mr. Bean episode where he gets the computer mouse clamped to his ear? Brits who just can't adjust to Hershey's or Mad TV can be found roaming the aisles of this far-flung Santa Monica outpost of the Empire. If for no other reason, come in for the tea selection.... *Tel 310/453-8655. 1619 Wilshire Blvd., Santa Monica.* **(see p. 168)**

Diamond Foam. This is actually a designers fabric shop, supposedly at discount prices—but if you really want discount, go to Michael Levine's downtown instead. They do have beautiful and sometimes one-of-a-kind fabrics, upholstery supplies, custom cushions, and foam cut to size.... *Tel 323/931-8148. 611 S. La Brea Ave., Los Angeles.* (see p. 191)

Dino-Shop at the Natural History Museum. Dinosaur-reproduction toys and dino-related games for the junior dinophile.... *Tel 213/763-3486. 900 Exposition Blvd., Los Angeles.* (see p. 187)

Dish Factory. The neighborhood is a wee bit funky, but the prices and oddball selection are primo. This is a great source for obsessed home cooks and professional chefs building a kitchen on a budget. And they've got Fiesta Ware, sold as separates. *Tel 213/687-9500. 310 S. Los Angeles St., Downtown.* (see p. 192)

Distant Lands Travel Bookstore & Outfitters. Travel books, accessories, backpacks, and maps.... *Tel 626/449-3220. 56 S. Raymond Ave., Pasadena.* (see p. 171)

Drea Kadilak. Rose McGowan comes in for hats and hat boxes, as do hoards of young, upcoming actresses.... *Tel 323/931-2051. 463 S. La Brea Ave., Los Angeles.* (see p. 182)

East Meets West. Crazily expensive quilts, horse blankets, shawls. From the collectible to the simply useful.... *Tel 323/933-8900. 160 S. La Brea Ave., Los Angeles.* (see p. 172)

Elisabetta Rogiani. You have to be a woman with a particular personality to carry off some of her more flamboyant designs, but that doesn't mean you can't try them on. Gloria Estefan likes them—maybe you will too. *Tel 323/634-7383. 7466 Beverly Blvd., Los Angeles.* (see p. 184)

Fat Chance. Very expensive mid-century original furniture, much of it quite rare and in immaculate condition.... *Tel 323/930-1960. 162 N. La Brea Ave., Los Angeles.* (see p. 175)

Footsie. Who could ever imagine a store dedicated to nothing but socks? Not shoes—socks—plus nylons, hosiery, and other foot coverings.... *Tel 310/393-2205. 1105 Montana Ave., Santa Monica.* **(see p. 185)**

Form Zero Architectural Books and Gallery. An essential architecture, design, and city planner's resource center.... *Tel 310/450-0222. 2433 Main St., Santa Monica.* **(see p. 189)**

Framm Ltd. Antique wedding dresses and all the essential frou-frou for that Special Day.... *Tel 310/392-3911. 2667 Main St., Santa Monica.* **(see p. 177)**

Fred Segal. This mini mall has designers from Milan to Tokyo to South Central—clothes, shoes, luggage for men, women, and kids. Their fall sale is legendary. *Tel 323/651-4129. 8100 Melrose Ave., Los Angeles.* **(see p. 184)**

Geographia Map and Travel Bookstore. Their travel literature section could be larger; still a favorite travel-specific store, especially for maps.... *Tel 818/848-1414. 4000 Riverside Dr., Burbank.* **(see p. 171)**

George C. Page Museum at the La Brea Tar Pits. The La Brea Tar Pits are so L.A. it's hard to imagine any other location with as much significance. The bubbling pools of goo out front are a constant reminder of where we come from and where we're headed. The gift store here is ideal for the dinosaur freak in your family.... *Tel 323/934-7243. 5801 Wilshire Blvd., Wilshire District.* **(see p. 187)**

Ginza Ya Bakery. Absolutely perfect-looking pastries and cakes made to suit the Japanese taste. Best bet is the curry-filled donut. This is a must.... *Tel 213/626-1904. Yaohan Plaza, 333 S. Alameda St., #106. Also on the West Side, 310/575-1131. 11301 W. Olympic Blvd., West L.A.* **(see p. 174)**

Golyester. High-end vintage clothing with high-end prices and a vaguely snotty attitude to match.... *Tel 323/931-1339. 136 S. La Brea Ave., Los Angeles.* **(see pp. 177, 186)**

Govinda's International Imports. An Indian outpost where the karma is great, the ghee flows freely, and you can get all kinds of Indian textiles and accessories. You won't be sari....

Tel 310/204-3263. 3764 Watseka Ave., Culver City.
(see p. 170)

Grand Central Market. You can't get closer to a Mexico City produce/fish market than this. The produce can be a little *too* ripe sometimes, but the shopping experience itself is worth it. Looking for freshly killed goat or a pig's head? They've got it here. *Tel 213/624-2378. 317 S. Broadway Ave., Downtown.* **(see p. 169)**

Great Wall Books & Art. This is a major outlet for Sinologists, where you come for your Cantonese language tapes, Chinese history, and the definitive word on the Party line. It's not camp—yet. Invest now. *Tel 213/617-2817. 970 N. Broadway Ave., Chinatown.* **(see p. 171)**

Hardware Antique. Parts and pieces for houses on their last legs, and for renovators with too much money and no sense.... *Tel 323/939-4403. 453 S. La Brea Ave., Los Angeles.* **(see p. 173)**

Hennessey & Ingalls. Art and architecture books for everyone from the professorial level on down.... *Tel 310/458-9074. 1254 3rd St. Promenade, Santa Monica.* **(see p. 189)**

Hustler Hollywood. The World According to Larry Flynt. Dildos, dykes on bikes, butt plugs, horny housewives, crotchless panties, lubricants, dirty pictures, dirty movies.... *Tel 310/860-9009. 8920 Sunset Blvd., West Hollywood.* **(see p. 192)**

IL-Literature Bookstore. This is a great local bookstore/magazine outlet right on the edge of Beverly Hills. It carries lots of writerly resources and local small-press output.... *Tel 323/937-3505. 452 S. La Brea Ave., Los Angeles.* **(see p. 190)**

In House. Extraordinarily inventive and attractive handmade furniture, built and designed by local artists.... *Tel 323/931-4420. 7370 W. Beverly Blvd., Los Angeles.* **(see p. 175)**

Japanese American National Museum. Books and videos about the *issei* experience, as well as tea sets and some clothes.... *Tel 213/625-0414. 369 E. 1st St., inside the museum, Little Tokyo.* **(see pp. 187)**

Kinokuniya. Japanese magazines, books, language tapes, kanji workbooks, culture, and history, and pure garbage—whatever you want. It's always packed with young tourists.... *Tel 213/687-4447. 123 Astronaut Ellison S. Onizuka Way, Little Tokyo.* **(see p. 170)**

L.A. Eyeworks. You've seen the ads and drooled over the specs. Well, this where you can find that frame that matches your beautiful face. But if you're cheap, wait for the fall sale. *Tel 323/653-8255. 7408 Melrose Ave., Los Angeles.* **(see p. 183)**

Lisa Norman Lingerie. Sexy without being trashy, presented and sold with a minimum of attitude. For women who are comfortable with their age, size, and sexuality.... *Tel 310/451-2026. 1134 Montana Ave., Santa Monica.* **(see p. 181)**

Long Beach Antique & Collectible Market. They claim that this is the largest regular antiques and collectibles (i.e. junk) swap meet on the coast. Third Sunday of every month.... *Tel 562/422-6987. 5000 Lew Davis St., Long Beach.* **(see p. 167)**

Lucky Brand. If you can't find your Lucky jeans in the size you want, come here to their retail outlet. It has a large stock of sizes and clothes you won't find elsewhere.... *Tel 323/933-0722. 120 S. La Brea Ave., Los Angeles.* **(see p. 181)**

Magic Cat. Japanese videos (for rent and sale), but everything else is Elvis and cats, cats and Elvis—that's it.... *Tel 213/625-8485. 336 E. 2nd St., Little Tokyo.***(see p. 180)**

Maison Midi. This is the housewares section of American Rag. Features some gorgeous Ikat fabric, cement tiles from France, Moroccan tea glasses.... *Tel 323/935-3157. 148 S. La Brea Ave., Los Angeles.* **(see p. 173)**

Michael Levine. Fabrics of every conceivable texture and weave, all at almost discount prices. Their upholstery shop is across the street.... *Tel 213/622-6259. 919-920 Maple Ave., Downtown.* **(see p. 191)**

Michael R. Thompson Books. This rare-book seller specializes in Western Philosophy, but that doesn't really describe the

SHOPPING | INDEX

variety of dusty old books you'll find.... *Tel 323/658-1901. 8312 W. 3rd St., Los Angeles.* **(see p. 190)**

MOCA Giftstore. It ain't cheap, but the gift store at the Museum of Contemporary Art has things you won't find anywhere else: art books, 'zines, one-of-a-kind objets d'art, catalogues of past shows, and disturbing decor. *Tel 213/621-2766. 250 S. Grand Ave., Downtown.* **(see p. 186)**

Modernica. Mid-century furniture madness writ large. Tons and tons of pieces from the '50s on.... *Tel 323/0933-0383. 7366 Beverly Blvd., Los Angeles.* **(see p. 174)**

Momo. Cute collectibles and gifts with a Japanese eye, lots of it imported direct from Tokyo.... *Tel 323/938-1018. 7385 W. Beverly Blvd., Los Angeles.* **(see pp. 183, 192)**

Necromance. It's Halloween year-round at this creepy little boneyard on Melrose Ave. They have skulls and all sorts of toys and artifacts to put you in touch with your dark side.... *Tel 323/-934-8684. 7220 Melrose Ave., Los Angeles.* **(see p. 178)**

Noodle Stories. Wonderfully wearable men's and women's clothing, streamlined and modern, but at prices that won't knock your socks off. It's the kind of place where you can hang as long as you like... *Tel 323/651-1782. 8323 W. 3rd St., Los Angeles.* **(see p. 184)**

Not So Far East Trading. If you're a fan of tropical woods, then check out this furniture store, where they recycle home building materials from Southeast Asia. You can rest your fat fanny on pieces of some Indonesian family's former wall.... *Tel 323/933-8900. 160 S. La Brea Ave., Los Angeles.* **(see p. 172)**

NYSE. New York fashions at L.A. prices—which isn't that great a deal, necessarily. A healthy selection of women's clothes, from working girls to starlets.... *Tel 323/733-1958. 7385 Beverly Blvd., Los Angeles.* **(see p. 185)**

OK. For mid-century glassware and a huge selection of books on same, this is the place. Plus, the store has refurbished Enico phones, for $250. It's Austin Powers heaven.... *Tel 323/653-3501. 8303 West 3rd St., Los Angeles.* **(see p. 174)**

Outside. A tasteful selection of patio and garden furniture of a certain age, pots and ceramics, and "transitional" furniture for those in-between spaces.... *Tel 323/934-1254. 442 N. La Brea Ave., Los Angeles.* **(see p. 176)**

Pasadena City College Flea Market. This is considered by many to be one of the best swap meets in the city because it's not too huge, the prices are reasonable, and it's free. First Sunday of the month, starting at 8 a.m.... *Tel 626/585-7123. 1570 E. Colorado Blvd., Pasadena.* **(see p. 167)**

Polkadots And Moonbeams. Zillions of hair accessories, bags, some vintage and new clothes at really reasonable prices.... *Tel 323/651-1746. 8367 West 3rd St., Los Angeles.* **(see p. 182)**

Pulp. A paper store but also much more, including handmade paper, leather journals, desk accessories, and tasty little gadgets for your downtime.... *Tel 323/937-3506. 456 S. La Brea Ave., Los Angeles.* **(see p. 190)**

Rafu Bussan. Really affordable household Japanese ceramics, tea sets, sake sets, and instant sushi-rice mix—way cheaper than the grocery stores. Good sales, too.... *Tel 213/614-1181. 326 E. 2nd St., Little Tokyo.* **(see pp. 180, 192)**

Remix. Absolutely stunning new/old '20s–'70s shoes you'll want to frame, not wear.... *Tel 323/936-6210. 7605 W. Beverly Blvd., Los Angeles.* **(see p. 186)**

Rockaway Records. Used CDs and rare vinyl, new alternative and L.A.-based product, '60s memorabilia, and videos. Plus they sell tickets for Spaceland shows.... *Tel 323/664-3232. 2395 Glendale Blvd., Silver Lake.* **(see p. 187)**

Rose Bowl Flea Market. This is the original thing, a magnet for junk-store junkies from around the world. Used clothes sold by the truckload, a landfill's worth of bad amateur art, toys, knickknacks, crap, and thousands of vendors. Second Sunday of every month, starting at 6 a.m.... *Tel. 626/560-7469. 1001 Rose Bowl Dr., Pasadena.* **(see p. 167)**

Rubbish. Didn't you always want your apartment to look like the Nelsons' rec room? This is where to find your old, your tired, your scratched and waiting-to-be-refurbished furniture, priced much more reasonably than on the West Side.... *Tel 323/661-5575. 1627 Silverlake Blvd., Silver Lake.*

(see p. 175)

Samuel French Theatre & Film Book Store. Used scripts, used dreams, posters, celebrity iconography. This is a *major* Hollywood landmark and should not be missed if you're slumming.... *Tel 323/876-0570. 7623 Sunset Blvd., Hollywood.* **(see p. 189)**

Santa Monica Antique & Collectible Market. Will you find a better class of junk in Santa Monica? Maybe, but it'll still cost too much. Held on the fourth Sunday of every month, starting at 6 a.m. *Tel 310/933-2511. Santa Monica Airport, Airport Ave., off Bundy Dr., Santa Monica.* **(see p. 168)**

Santa Monica Farmer's Markets. For chefs and home cooks who fancy the freshest and cheapest produce in season: Wed. 9–2 and Sat. 8:30–1.... *Tel 310/458-8712. Arizona & 2nd Sts, Santa Monica. Also a* **Latin-accented farmer's market***: Sat. 8–1. Tel 310/458-8712. Pico Blvd. and Cloverfield Ave., Santa Monica.* **(see p. 171)**

Say Cheese. Wonderfully expensive cheeses and gourmet oils and flavorings from everywhere, for people with too much money.... *Tel 323/665-0545. 2800 Hyperion Ave., Los Feliz.* **(see p. 192)**

Shabon. A vintage store featuring an always-varying inventory that shows off its owners' great sense of style. Smart handbags, Java cloth skirts, purses, accessories, and more.... *Tel 323/692-0061. 7617 1/2 W. Beverly Blvd., Los Angeles.* **(see p. 178)**

Shelter. Mid-century style reproduced by local craftsmen.... *Tel 323/937-3222. 7920 W. Beverly Blvd., Los Angeles.* **(see p. 175)**

Skeletons in the Closet. A gift shop at the County Morgue? You need a well-established sense of black humor to get some of the macabre merchandise here. A beach towel with a body outline on it is typical fare.... *Tel 323/343-0760. 1140 N. Mission Rd., Los Angeles County*

Department of the Coroner, 2nd Floor, Downtown.
(see p. 178)

S.K. Uyeda Department Store. Really good prices on kimonos, futons and accessories, and Japanese footwear.... *Tel 213/624-4790. 230 E. 1st St., Little Tokyo.* **(see p. 179)**

Storyopolis. A children's bookstore with very high-quality, "fine art" kids' books. Kind of a waste when you consider that they'll be scribbling with crayons and smearing peanut butter all over them inside of 10 minutes... *Tel 310/358-2500. 116 N. Robertson Blvd. West Hollywood.* **(see p. 190)**

Stussy. The local outlet for the skate-surf sportswear fashion line, with a much wider selection than that found at your local mall.... *Tel 323/937-6077. 1122 1/2 S. La Brea Ave., Los Angeles.* **(see p. 180)**

Thailand Plaza. You come here to fulfill that panang curry urge. Fish sauces, curry pastes, fresh and dried noodles, absolutely anything you need to make a perfect Thai meal. And if asked they'll even fillet and fry fresh fish for you. *Tel 323/993-9000. 5321 Hollywood Blvd., Hollywood.* **(see p. 169)**

Trader Joe's. This is an essential inner-city lifestyle resource for the young, hip, and alcoholic of L.A., with tons of boutique wines, vitamins, knock-off trend foodie stuff, and reasonably priced frozen fish. Half of my grocery bill is dumped here— and I don't resent it in the least. *Tel 323/665-6774. 2730 Hyperion Ave., Los Feliz.* **(see p. 170)**

Trashy Lingerie. Ohhh...really nasty undies, and I mean *really* nasty, where the sales clerks model their wares. The $5 membership card is well worth the price of shopping here.... *Tel 310/652-4543. 402 N. La Cienega Blvd., West Hollywood.* **(see p. 181)**

Traveler's Bookcase. Maps, travel guides, and a very good remaindered selection out on the sidewalk for just pennies on the dollar.... *Tel 323/655-0575. 8375 W. 3rd St., West Hollywood.* **(see p. 171)**

Vintage Vintage. Undoubtedly the best vintage clothing store

SHOPPING | INDEX

on Montana for impeccable '40s-era couture. A fave among the ladies who lunch.... *Tel 310/393-5588. 1611 Montana Ave., Santa Monica.* **(see p. 177)**

Vinyl Fetish. One of the best vinyl outlets in L.A. for imports and indies. Indulge your taste in punk, goth, industrial, strange.... *Tel 323/660-4500. 1750 N. Vermont Ave., Los Feliz. Also Tel 323/935-1300. 7305 Melrose Ave., Hollywood.* **(see p. 187)**

Vinyl Surplus. For fans of petroleum-based recording tools, this is the place. They have a huge selection of vinyl, mostly used, as well as CDs (new and used). Good trade-in rates also. *Tel 310/478-4217. 11609 Pico Blvd., West Los Angeles.* **(see p. 188)**

Wanna Buy A Watch? Totally refurbished Swingers-era Timex, Rolex, you name it. Not cheap, but you'll never find a better or longer-lasting accessory.... *Tel 323/653-0467. 7366 Melrose Ave., Los Angeles.* **(see p. 183)**

Waste Land. Cleaning out the closet? Or want to fill it up for cheap? Come to this trade-in "pre-worn" emporium. Prices aren't Salvation Army, but neither is the style or quality. Or so they'd have you believe. *Tel 323/653-3028. 7428 Melrose Ave., Los Angeles.* **(see p. 176)**

Weathervane Two. The prices aren't outrageous, and they understand that all women aren't anorexic, junkies, or size-4 4 models who want to dress like Russian washerwomen. Major West Side resource for real women... *Tel 310/393-5344. 1209 Montana Ave., Santa Monica.* **(see p. 184)**

X-Large. This is the Beastie Boys in-house fashion line, a place for everything baggy, urban, and skate-rat. Overpriced baseball caps, reasonable knapsacks, pants, and more. It's almost-lifestyle shopping, thanks to Phat Beats, in the back. *Tel 323/666-3483. 1766 N. Vermont Ave., Los Feliz.* **(see pp. 181, 182)**

Y Que. George Jones cat food, World War II underwear, 7-day prayer candles, Mexican kitsch. Way cheap prices and a wonderful vibe.... *Tel 323/664-0021. 1770 N. Vermont Ave. Los Feliz.* **(see p. 179)**

Yaohan. This two-story mall in Little Tokyo is a one-stop shopping source for anything Japanese, from magazines to take-out sushi to those air fresheners that give Tokyo cabs that very distinctive smell to just about anything you'd need for any homemade meal, from sukiyaki cuts to pickled daikon and prepared hijiki salad.... *Tel 213/687-6699. 333 S. Alameda St., Little Tokyo.* **(see p. 169)**

Zipper. Furniture, crocheted bean-bag chairs, stools filled with polyurethane foam, paper star lights, cute weird knickknacks, pricey watches, travel clocks, plastic nuns.... *Tel 323/951-9190. 8316 W. 3rd. St., Los Angeles.* **(see p. 176)**

nigh

6

tlife

Angelenos don't
have to take their
nightlife seriously,
for the simple
reason that clubs,
bars, and hang-
outs are merely

an alternative to inviting a few friends over to have a Q on the deck while you watch the sun dropping behind the Santa Monicas. Going out in L.A. should be *fun*—not simply a way to see friends without bringing them back to your squalid sixth-floor walk-up. The velvet-rope snobbery that fuels hype in other places doesn't really work here. Once a nightspot starts to show attitude, that's when the true night crawlers know it's time to move on to the next undiscovered dive. Attitude is the province of the audience, not the doormen. The *Swingers* phenomena could only have happened here, where there are scores of fading, weathered piano bars and lounges, welcoming of any new patron, no matter how dripping with piercings and irony. The regulars don't mind newcomers—it's just more company in the quicksand.

And because we live in a city where everything eventually winds up in a movie or on TV, compressed, homogenized, and somehow neutered in the process, we savor our pockets of reality all the more. The mosh pit was invented here: Slamdancing is the product of overstimulated South Coast teenage boys working out a mixture of anger, fear, boredom—basically too many monkeys cavorting in too small a cage. That's not to say that Angelenos don't drift into pretentiousness and unintentional self-parody from time to time. The nature of nightlife is ephemeral, and scenes ebb and flow along with the mass culture, pushed and pulled by capitalism and the Hollywood sausage grinder. After all, perfection means there are no surprises. When you're roaming the streets at night, hoping you won't get pulled over for a DUI, you *want* the unexpected. Sweaty, stinking of stale beer and cigarettes, with just enough cash for a couple more drinks, you just *know* that the next club is where you'll get lucky and lose all sense of self. And that's what it's all about, isn't it?

The Lowdown

The A list... It has to begin with **Al's Bar,** the grandfather to all good things born of the gutter. Al's has been here for 20 years, playing host to punks, poets, and performance geeks who take the foot-high stage with nothing in mind other than to shake the audience up while working out their private demons. The walls are covered with disturbing messages—scrawled, barely legible Bukowski-esque mutterings that amuse and threaten at the same time. The drinks are cheap, and the loyal regulars include Artist District veterans, an ever-changing new generation of art-damaged punks, and fringe musicians who realize that they'll never make a dime playing music. The place is A&R-free, since nobody with a decent car would dare to leave it on the streets down here at night—which is great because it keeps the riff-raff out. Sample bill: Jazz From Hell with Satan's Cheerleaders and the Immortals, Spastic Colon, and Ape Has Killed Ape With Toothpick Elbow. For some reason Wednesdays have been decreed No Talent Night. If you're not yet persuaded, check out the shows they put out on the Internet. Over in Silver Lake, **Spaceland** has managed to survive the Next Big Thing curse and soldiers on. The booking here remains consistent, like the decor, unchanged from the days when Beck would play with his back to the audience. The big addition—and this shows where its sensibilities lie—has been to enclose the upper level behind glass, so that smokers can puff away legally and still enjoy the show. Other than that touch, the place still feels like the failed disco it once was. Like Al's, Spaceland reflects the immediate community's attitude, a place dedicated to building bridges by blowing them up. It's still cheap as hell and books everyone from the total unknowns to bands with an almost cult following. And the sound is way better than it once was. This is alt.rock without any attitude. God help us if Brent Bolthouse ever buys it.

Mr. T's Bowl is a hybrid mutation, a ragged Highland Park bowling alley that was forever altered when the late Jac Zinder started bringing in his club Fuzzyland for occasional shows. Fuzzyland is long gone, but its spirit remains. This is still a dive, a place where you get drunk quickly and listen to music played loudly over an uneven sound system. Hey, there's always the bowling. You know that **The Smell** is doing something right because 1) there's no alcohol served here, 2) it's in the Valley, and 3) it gets very ripe, very quickly—hence the name. Located in a storefront next to a coffeehouse, the "club" is reminiscent of the best underground-punk venues of decades past, and is home to indie acts, art-damaged bands, and touring acts from the Northwest who heard about it on the DIY grapevine. A typical night here is half crazy art opening and half party, with way scratchy loud noises blaring from within. Industrial, ambient, punk. Like a butterfly, it won't be around long—yet defying all logic, Hollywood's **Bar Deluxe** manages to continue year after year. It is relentlessly unpretentious, scuzzy, and filthy in the corners, with a decor that demands visions. Suspended from the ceiling is a 125-gallon aquarium that contains fish floating over a bed of skulls. This is bare-bones Hollywood, a throwback to a simpler, more biker-friendly time. Rockabilly and blues are staples here, but punks and weirdos are always welcome too. When this place closes they should give it a star on Hollywood Boulevard. (Instead, they'll probably burn the place down to kill any lingering pestilence.) **The Garage,** a tiny hole-in-the-wall in East Hollywood, has turned into one of the most happening places imaginable, thanks largely to Dr. Vaginal Davis, the tall queen who books groups for Sucker on Sunday afternoons. The room is small, the crowd ambi-sexual, and you never know what will happen next. It's a playpen for the fringe hipsters of Silver Lake, with two bars and a back lounge that is the perfect place to do some serious groping. This is where Silver Lake's name bands come, either to perform or to party. The cover is only $5, and for that you get four to five bands. What a deal!

In the wings... Okay, so **The Joint** is in West L.A., but at least it's on Pico. They frequently have four bands a night throughout the week, so no matter when you drop in you're sure to hear a variety of acts—and with the groovy new sound system, you can at least hear what the singer is trying to say. The interior itself is worth the trip—gilded elephant tusks, mirrors and mirror balls everywhere, plus a thick carpet that feels as if you're walking through the harem of some dissolute sultan who has built himself his own little disco. This place is for up-and-comers, bands that have exhausted the East Side circuit and are trying to build a fan base. **Gabah** is the new kid on the rock block on the East Side. It's run by the same people who handled the late-great Raji's for years. The nightspot is now located at the former home of the punk/new wave landmark, the Anti-Club. The place has been redone with fake leopard, and there's a smoking patio—besides which it's freeway-close. Come here for a look at what's bubbling up from the playing-for-beers-and-not-much-more circuit.

Blue notes... The Mint, on Pico, has what some say is the best sound for any club of its size in the city. Harry Dean Stanton apparently loves the place. It has expanded and now has a 24-track soundboard for live recordings, which brings out the best in the visiting musicians. It has one of the most solid booking policies around—an always reliable selection of name blues and jazz bands. The ceiling covered in 45s says it all. It's a little pricey, but you can eat here, too, and probably for half as much as you'd spend at the Baked Potato. **Babe's and Ricky's Inn** is one of the oldest blues clubs in the city, and though it's no longer on Central Ave, it's kept the feel of the original venue. Every young blues musician in L.A. has played here at one time or another. It's got live music six nights a week, and there's no bullshit. Even in new digs, this is the roadhouse of your dreams—come any night and you'll hear great music, guaranteed. Miles away by car and even further in atmospheric distance is **B.B. King's Blues Club,** part of the legend's chain. It would be great if this place were on Central or even in Downtown, but instead it's smack-dab in the middle of Universal City, a juicy bit of pork set in between two slices of tasteless white bread. It's a high-class place that keeps busy making the blues safe for tourists just back from the Universal Studios Tour. The club books big-name acts, and the 500-seat room can't be faulted for either viewing or sound, boasting three levels and great acoustics. It gets bonus points for having a decent Cajun/soul-food menu, although the prices are a tad high. When you throw in the cover charge and the outrageous parking fees, you'll be lucky to get out of here for less than $80 for two. On the other hand, the acts you can catch here play nowhere else in town.

So last year/clubs... The Derby is one of those places that has let success go to its head: The doormen are boors, the drinks are way too expensive, and the cover charge is insane—but they're still roping 'em in, teaching swing to the yokels who've just caught *Swingers* (which was partly filmed here) on video, or read about the new dance craze in *USA Today*. The room is outstanding, particularly the oval bar with its mountain of bottles. If you're out on an expense account or trying to impress that special date, come here for dinner, grab one of the curtained booths, and order a couple of martinis. Don't even think about dancing unless you've really got your moves down—the dancers who take to the small dance floor in front of the low stage are like something out of a '40s musical (actually better, because their spanking new "vintage" outfits fit them so well). **LunaPark,** the oh-so-eclectic and snooty cabaret in West Hollywood, could have been a contender once, with its decent food and well-decked-out surroundings. There's a small downstairs stage for acoustic acts and private parties, plus a nice stage on the main floor, and occasionally they get the odd name you might recognize—but should you shell out $15 for some deejay you never heard of? Up to you. For a couple of years this was the darling of local clubgoers, but high covers and an overdose of Eurotrash attitude has worn away its support among the younger club set. Now the place is strictly amateur's night out, preferably someone carrying a Platinum card. Too bad—for a while there you could ignore its drawbacks because of the club's great booking policy.

So *last year*/bars... Reluctantly, I have to put the **Dresden Room** in this category—another bar spoiled by its *Swingers* association. The bright 'n' beautiful alkies who made this spot wonderful have moved on, and the sense of scene is now vanished. The prices haven't gone up, the people who run the place are the same—maybe they don't notice what's happened—and it still has that heavy Bavarian feel of brick, dark wood, and leather (with booths around the piano). It even gets the same geriatrics stumbling in on walkers for their afternoon shots. But you're now getting West Side yups stopping by later in the evening on their way to the Derby a few blocks away. Don't fret, though—the Dresden Room and its lounge ambience will survive: it's been here too long to let a little trendoid stink kill it. The place just needs some time out of the public eye. Right around the corner, the **Good Luck Club** continues to pack in a similar clientele. When it finally goes out of business, sacrificed to the next trend, no one will care. The place is beautiful and cozy inside, all done up like a Hong Kong whore with red lanterns hanging over the red roll-and-tuck booths. But it has no sense of where it is—perched on a busy Sunset intersection, in limbo between East Hollywood, Los Feliz, and Silver Lake. This bar feels more like a movie set than a place to drown your sorrows, and the people who do drink here spend way too much time checking themselves out in the mirror. Good drinks, though. Say sayonara as well to the **Circle Bar** in Santa Monica. For years this was the perfect beach dive, a place where everybody knew your name but were so drunk they couldn't remember it. A pool table dominated the room, and when an unfamiliar face walked in people stopped their game to look you over. Now the bar has been discovered by West Siders looking for a slummy experience in their own backyard. All the locals who supported it for so many years have departed for gutters unknown—which is just as well, since it's gotten so crowded now they could never fight their way up to the bar. The place is being renovated, the bartenders are now all pretty young girls (like the new clientele), and they're painting the black walls white. *White.* What *were* they thinking?

Tiki ti... There is no need to say another word. Bars may come and bars may go, but the **Tiki Ti** will outlive us all. Small as a closet, with only a handful of tables and stools, this is one of L.A.'s best-known oddities. The bar serves nothing but tropical drinks, the sort of thing you'd find at a Trader Vic's—only then it would cost a lot more money and be nowhere near as tasty. It's been on this grimy section of Sunset for nearly 40 years, open just four nights a week, cash only. The interior is a hallucination of neon, skulls, sparkling waterfalls, and other eye candy that fascinates at first, but then after your second drink makes you a bit nauseous. It fills up early, with the crowd often spilling out on the sidewalk. The drinks are cheap, potent, and endlessly varied. You can choose from among more than 40 recipes, all formulated with one purpose in mind: to knock you on your butt while concealing the taste of the alcohol. It's one of the few well-known nighttime icons where the tourists and locals blend easily, and makes for a great first date spot, as evidenced by the high ratio of couples here. The **Lava Lounge** was one of the first establishments to take a page out of the Tiki Ti's book, re-creating a so-with-it, post–*Pulp Fiction* hang for people who want a little peace and quiet but also a little style, and maybe an umbrella in their drink. They have a stage...sort of...for the occasional lonely troubadour wailing tunes of urban angst.

NIGHTLIFE | THE LOWDOWN

Hotel bars... When you get sick of looking for the next in-crowd dive currently being rediscovered by a new generation of hipsters, maybe it's time to check out the watering holes within the tastier hotels in the city. In case you haven't heard, hotel bars are not just for hotel guests anymore. If you're trolling for some uncomplicated romance, this is where you're most likely to meet someone of like mind. Be warned, however—you'll be paying through the nose for the opportunity. The cheapest domestic beer at any of the spots listed below is $4.50. The Queen of all hotel bars has to be the **Polo Lounge** at the Beverly Hills Hotel. The decor is classic pink and green, and the landscaping is fabulous. During the week its clientele is mainly 90210 fat cats who come here after work to schmooze 'n' booze. There's always a piano player tinkling standards, and even on weekends the place is jammed. This is one of the entertainment industry's major deal-making venues, and the possibility of seeing a famous face is always good here. A similar Industry odor emanates from the bar at **The Peninsula Hotel,** also in Beverly Hills. CAA is headquartered just across the street, so a lot of agents come here to sharpen their knives. The interior is dark wood and marble, including leather seats around a fireplace—perfect for hatching Machiavellian schemes. The end result is the feeling of being in an exclusive men's club where whispered conversations are not rude, but just part of doing business. At the **Beverly Wilshire** you'll also encounter the feel of a private club, all wood paneling and leather chairs, but it's the place's proximity to ICM and William Morris that brings in the packs of agents for after-work drinks. Mixed with the Industry crowd are older hotel guests and shoppers lugging armfuls of packages from their trip down Rodeo Drive. If you can't get into the butterfly-encrusted **Bar Marmont,** amble next door to the **Chateau Marmont** itself and sit outside on the patio. The feeling here is far more relaxed and pleasant than at most hotel bars. Despite all the hype, the atmosphere is charmingly old Hollywood, slightly down-at-the-heels but comfortable enough not to take itself too seriously. The only agents you'll find are those haranguing their writer-clients to get the goddamn rewrite finished already. The money-making machinery of Hollywood seems a million miles away from this place.

If you see any celebs, leave them alone—that's why they come here. The most happening hotel bar of the moment is the **Skybar** at the Mondrian. Its faux-Balinese decor aside, the reason people come here is for the hipster factor, plus one of the most glorious views of the city out by the pool. If you're staying at the hotel, you can get in easily. Due to its recent popularity, however, only locals with juice can usually make it in the door during peak hours. My advice is to go early in the evening, or dress in a sarong and pretend you're one of the waiters.

Where the real swingers have moved on to... The **Roost** in Atwater still believes you should have your cocktails with cancer if that's your choice, so nobody complains here about cigarette smoke. This is a bar from the old school: There's a terrible jukebox, two TVs running with the sound off, free popcorn, and red-leather tuck-and-roll booths. It has a kitchen, but most people come for the bar. It's like a scaled-down version of the Dresden Room with a more Valley suburban feel. The drinks are kickass and cheap ($2 for a beer), and the mood is nice and mellow. It's a place for locals, mainly production people and retirees, that's been here 50 years, right next to the L.A. River. When the aerospace industry used to have factories in the Valley, the engineers on the graveyard shift would come in at 6 in the morning. You'll find a similar good vibe at the **Club Tee Gee** on Glendale Boulevard, also in Atwater (notice how the Silver Lake scene is gradually inching eastward?), but this is more of an alkies bar. There's lots of country music on the jukebox, and on a Tuesday night everyone looks up when you walk in. Strangers in town...which is okay: They chill out again after a few minutes. The drinks are cheapo-deluxe, and if you ignore the jukebox it's a nice, divey sort of place to hang for an hour or so. Beers are still just $2 (be prepared to pay $4 and up at the trendoid bars), and the decor is, well, real. Over on the West Side, **Liquid Kitty** is the latest hang for Fox production people and middle-management company assholes smoking cigars and imagining themselves as Swingers. The place is the latest spinoff from the people who made the Burgundy Room and the 3 of Clubs into two of Hollywood's best hideaway bars. Like the 3 of Clubs there's no sign out front, just a flashing neon martini. The specialty drinks are ultra-strong—just one could put you under the table. It gets packed late at night when a deejay comes in, and-between the '50s-style wavy bar and multicolored tables lining the other side of the room—the floor becomes rather difficult to negotiate.

Living L.A. rock roots... The Sunset Strip keeps on ticking somehow. An endless supply of air-guitar heroes and their girlfriends is its blood supply; there's still something magical about playing a club on the Strip. The **Roxy** retains a cachet for touring name acts, thanks partly to its history, its A&R-friendly atmosphere and the fact that it has one of the best sound systems in the city. It's also a gathering place for all ages, which has an appeal. This is the Strip's class act. Right down the block is the **Whiskey A Go Go,** which, like the Roxy, has instant name value for touring acts. It's a big, boxy room with decent sound and a bar. Every young band that came out of L.A. played here...and so should you. Coconut Teaszer and its downstairs acoustic room, the **Crooked Bar,** are where Hollywood Trash was nurtured and first flourished. The basement bar still pushes local acts, and remains a faithful home for the side projects of name musicians. The **Key Club** is where Gazzarri's used to be, but the heavy-metal memory is only rekindled in the Thursday-night "metal meltdown" shows. The rest of the week the live music is anything from jazz to loungecore. Not on the Strip but *of* it nonetheless is Doug Weston's **Troubadour,** which for 40 years pushed everything that L.A. produced, from folk-rock to punk to metal. The place has a lot of room, good sound, no age limit and three bars. Even though Weston is no longer with us, the Troubadour's booking policy is surging once again—proving that sometimes the veterans do know how to do it best.

Bars for locals... Akbar is a wonderful new addition to East Hollywood. It was a former alkies bar that got taken over by new owners who didn't mess with the mood. Located in a bunkerlike box on Sunset right next to a McDonald's, with no windows and little indication of what goes on inside, it's full of little Moorish touches, with a nice long bar, comfortable seats, healthy-sized drinks, and a smoke-if-you-want-to flexibility. Although gentrified, it has none of the glitter or Disneyland feel of the Good Luck Club, just up the street. This is a bar for locals, production people from ABC or KCET, spillover from the backdrop rental place down the street, and Silver Lake artists. It's got a great vibe and a wonderful jukebox. The same could be said about the **Smog Cutter,** the archetypal East Hollywood/Silver Lake alkie dive that advanced to the forefront of punk karaoke and suddenly found itself jammed with a whole new crop of kids with buzz cuts. The trend has since spread elsewhere, and now the Smog Cutter has settled back into its former dingy self. It's one small room, funky and spartan, run by a very charming Vietnamese woman. They still do the punk karaoke stuff, but it's not as jammed as it once was, for which the locals are thankful.

Toujours gay... Oh, where to begin? There's just so much to cover... Let's be civilized and start with **360 Beige House,** at the top of a Hollywood office building. This place is a throwback to the old faggot-chic days of the '50s when get-togethers were held in private houses. The view is stunning, and the lights are bright enough to let you see just how pretty your date really is (or isn't). It's for the Chatty Cathy set, and the clientele tends to be very mon-eyed people. We're talking sweater-core, not hard-core. If you want hard-core, go to **Cuffs** for an evening of dark, sweaty cruising in leather and a denouement that could possibly include arrest or at the very least protein stains on your best shirt. You'll encounter much the same ambience at **The Gauntlet,** which is filled with leathery, steroid-pumped up bruisers waltzing through a dark, smoky room. **The Study** is popular with slightly older Latin and black cruisers. It's very casual, but there's a three-drink minimum if the bartender doesn't like you. At the **Faultline** we're back to a very blue-collar, Silver Lake sensibility—lots of leather, tattoos, piercings, shaved heads, exposed buns. **The Spike** is dark, butch, and strictly for after-hours tweakers. **Numbers,** above the Normandy Room, is a favorite spot for the older man–young protégé thing executives who are still in the closet, but working on it. **The Spotlight** is just plain scary. It's like some medium-range bar just off Revolucion in Tijuana, where ex-con lovers dance together while hookers work around them. Mature and with nothing to prove, **The Detour** is a Silver Lake landmark, old school in feel, with the cheapest drinks around. **Axis** has the largest dance floor of any gay club, with great sound and lights. The big night here for the ladies is Friday, when Girl Bar takes over (supposedly the largest dance club for women in the country). **Catch One** is a huge place with two dance floors, loads of drag queens, and a mixed crowd that just has to keep going until dawn. The club has live music as well, but it's the dancing and the drag shows that keep it hot. Located on a seedy block of Pico, it draws gays and straights from all over the city. **Rudolpho's** is where Dragstrip 66 takes place on the second Saturday of each month. This is a major monthly mardi gras for all East Side queers. For a drag show you can take your parents to, there's the **Queen Mary** in Studio City. Finally, just down Ventura (and rapidly turning into The Next Big Thing on gay radar) is **Oil Can Harry's,** featuring country-western gay line dancing.

Beer, Beer, Beer... The rusted sign above **My Father's Office** announces "BEER" next to a lit-up arrow that points down toward the one and only male stronghold on Santa Monica's Montana Avenue. By 5 p.m. the motley, after-work crowd begins to straggle in, and by eight the joint is hopping, fortified by postgraduates of both sexes. The wooden tables have been heavily carved with the names of girlfriends past and present. Only Pacific Coast draft beers are served here, and closing time is twelvish. Incongruous, delicate hanging vases along the walls have sprigs of fresh flowers sticking out of them, and the photo of a popular female bartender killed in a car accident a few years ago triggers authentically maudlin memories among the gents on the bar stools. Over on the Promenade there's **The Brew House,** which looks like a funky bar but actually has good beers and even better Hungarian sausages. The best move is to sit out on the Promenade itself so you can watch the parade go by as you sip on your ale. In Pasadena you'll find **Crown City Brewing,** a British-style pub bar with 25 bars on tap and bottled beers from all over. It's the perfect place for white-collar beer-heads to de-stress in after work. A recommendation: Try the Lord Stanley Bitter.

Sobering up... Okay—it's late, you've had too much to drink, and you can barely read this. O_2. Got that?

Otherwise known as the **Oxygen Bar,** this tucked-away temple, located across the street from Tower Records on the Sunset Strip, was founded by a Hollywood doctor and herbalist as a healthful alternative to Angelenos' perennial quest for mind-altering substances. It's based on the theory that normal air is made up of 21 percent oxygen, but in L.A. that figure is only 12 percent, resulting in asthma, cancer, and you name it. You come here to have tiny tubes put up your nose so that you can breathe 95 percent pure oxygen for about 20 minutes at $15 per hit, plus another $2 for optional flavoring. While you're sitting there with the tubes in your nose, you can also order organic snacks and fruit elixirs with names like "Love Laced," "Fast Screw," and "Don Juan Colada," reinforcing the bar's motto displayed on the help's T-shirts: "Eat...drink...breathe...love." All this is fine. The problem for me was that the oxygen made me feel queasy, necessitating a long walk on Sunset to suck up the good old L.A. air, such as it is. The establishment's desired love-vibes are also undercut by the hard edge of the predominantly cement room and the cold windows overlooking, well, the Strip. There's music in the evenings, and after-hours dancing with a $5 cover. Open from 11 a.m. till 4 a.m. on weekends. Now be careful out there.

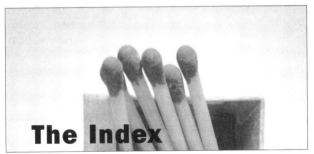

Akbar. This charming little bar on Sunset where Hollywood, Silver Lake, and Los Feliz meet is a good example of how to make an alkie's hang into something cozy, friendly, and feeling ungentrified—even though it is. Dark, close to the East Hollywood studios.... *Tel 323/665-6810. 4356 Sunset Blvd., West Hollywood/Los Feliz.* **(see p. 216)**

Al's Bar. Twenty-year-old club that has hosted the city's greatest

NIGHTLIFE | THE INDEX

punk and rock acts. It offers a self-described "loud sound system," big dance space, and cheap drinks.... *Tel 213/626-7213. 305 S. Hewitt St., Los Angeles.* **(see p. 208)**

Axis. A major gay dance club in West Hollywood, it draws men and women of all sexes. The dance floor is huge.... *Tel 310/659-0471. 652 N. La Peer, West Hollywood.* **(see p. 218)**

B.B. King's Blues Club. Topflight blues from major touring acts, with great sound plus good soul food. Priced for the tourists.... *Tel 818/6-BBKING. 1000 Universal Center Dr., Universal City.* **(see p. 211)**

Babe's and Ricky's Inn. This is one of the best local blues roadhouses, a reliably great place to see all sorts of blues acts, young and old, established or just getting out of the garage. The jukebox is legendary.... *Tel 323/295-9112. 4339 Leimert Blvd., Leimert Park.* **(see p. 211)**

Bar Deluxe. The interior is a little bizarre, as are the patrons, but the music is down-home and honest as a rusty screwdriver. It's a nasty neighborhood, though.... *Tel 323/469-1991. 1710 N. Las Palmas Ave., Hollywood.* **(see p. 210)**

Beverly Wilshire Hotel bar. Clubby hotel bar that pulls in area ICM and William Morris agents.... *Tel 310/275-5200. In the Beverly Wilshire Hotel, 9500 Wilshire Blvd., Beverly Hills.* **(see p. 214)**

The Brew House. Boutique beers on tap, Hungarian-style meats, and a great view of the Promenade.... *Tel 310/393-2629. 1246 3rd St. Promenade, Santa Monica.* **(see p. 218)**

Catch One. Drag shows, lesbian lip-synching, and assorted after-hours madness on a funky part of Pico. Very friendly, and it draws all types of people.... *Tel 323/734-8849. 4067 W. Pico Blvd., West Los Angeles.* **(see p. 218)**

Chateau Marmont. Try the cozy patio next door to the Bar Marmont for an old-Hollywood drinking experience.... *Tel 323/656-1010. 8221 Sunset Blvd., West Hollywood.* **(see p. 214)**

Circle Bar. Once the perfect beach dive, now discovered by West Side slummers who have crowded out the locals.... *Tel 310/ 392-4898. 2926 Main St., Santa Monica.* **(see p. 213)**

Club Tee Gee. Forties-era neighborhood bar in interesting area that has been rediscovered by the youngsters.... *Tel 323/669-9631. 3210 Glendale Blvd., Atwater Village.* **(see p. 215)**

Crooked Bar. Probably the most soothing place to hear acoustic music on the Strip (though it is a little claustrophobic). Located in the basement of the Coconut Teaszer.... *Tel 818/353-6241. 8121 Sunset Blvd., West Hollywood.* **(see p. 216)**

Crown City Brewing. It's full of lawyerly-looking types, but the deli food is decent and the boutique beers are choice.... *Tel 818/ 577-5548. 300 S. Raymond Ave., Pasadena.* **(see p. 218)**

Cuffs. The place to do some gay cruising for that leather man of your dreams and/or nightmares.... *Tel 323/660-2649. Hyperion Ave., Silver Lake.* **(see p. 217)**

The Derby. Outstanding room that reeks of Hollywood's golden age. Swing rules here, but the swingers had better have some real dough to pay for drinks and cover charge.... *Tel 323/663-8979. 4500 Los Feliz Blvd., Los Feliz.* **(see p. 211)**

The Detour. If you want to experience the original Silver Lake gay scene, check out this low-key legend. Cheap drinks, nice people.... *Tel 323/664-1188. 4100 Sunset Blvd., Silver Lake.* **(see p. 217)**

Dresden Room. Swingers' lounge that should survive its tren-doid overexposure.... *Tel 323/665-4294. 1760 N. Vermont Ave., Los Angeles.* **(see p. 212)**

Faultline. The dress code is carefully observed at this gay leather bar. Includes jeans, piercings, butt plugs, whatever.... *Tel 323/660-0889. 4216 Melrose Ave., East Hollywood.* **(see p. 217)**

Gabah. Come to this nightspot to check out up-and-coming rock band.... *Tel 323/664-8913. 4658 Melrose Avenue, East Hollywood.* **(see p. 210)**

NIGHTLIFE | THE INDEX

The Garage. Happening little hole-in-the-wall where the fringe hipsters come to hear Silver Lake's name bands.... *Tel 323/662-6166. 4519 Santa Monica Blvd., East Hollywood.*
(see p. 210)

The Gauntlet. Stinky and all puffed up with testosterone and steroids, this is gay hard-core heaven-slash-hell—your choice.... *Tel 323/669-9472. 4219 Santa Monica Blvd., East Hollywood.* (see p. 217)

Good Luck Club. A homage to Hong Kong that feels more like a movie set than a place to get cozy over drinks.... *Tel 323/666-3524. 1514 Hillhurst Ave., Hollywood.*
(see p. 212)

The Joint. A new place in West L.A. showcasing the always-struggling, gonna-make-it-next-year local bands. A great interior that suggests some sort of bad opium dream, with elephant tusks, thick carpets, etc.... *Tel. 310/275-2619. 8771 W. Pico Blvd., West Los Angeles.* (see p. 210)

Key Club. Music club with heavy-metal roots.... *Tel 310/786-1712. 9039 Sunset Blvd., West Hollywood.* (see p. 216)

Lava Lounge. This place came into existence long after the Tiki Ti, but it gets high marks for taking inspiration from the master, tropical drinks and all.... *Tel 323/876-6612. 1533 N. La Brea Ave., Hollywood.* (see p. 213)

Liquid Kitty. With Señor Amor deejaying every Thursday, this is one dance club to check out mid-weekish.... *Tel 310/473-3707. 11780 W. Pico Blvd., West Los Angeles.*
(see p. 215)

LunaPark. Snooty cabaret that was once the place to be before high covers and a heavy dose of Eurotrash attitude drove supporters away.... *Tel 310/652-0611. 665 N. Robertson Blvd., West Hollywood.* (see p. 212)

The Mint. This is one of the best intimate blues rooms in town. The 45s all over the roof are a lesson in pop-music history all by themselves. Good sound system.... *Tel 310/764-0763. 6010 W. Pico Blvd., Culver City.* (see p. 211)

Mr. T's Bowl. That's right, a bowling alley that also hosts live music and deejays while the bowling balls roll in the background. Got a problem with that?... *Tel 323/256-7561. 5621 1/2 Figueroa Ave., Highland Park.* **(see p. 209)**

My Father's Office. Boutique beers served up on the oh-so-precious Montana Avenue—in this neighborhood, it's a rare island of testosterone and stale urine.... *Tel 310/393-2337. 1018 Montana Ave., Santa Monica.* **(see p. 218)**

O₂. Woody Harrelson's oxygen bar, where you come after you've bonged yourself into outer space or drunk yourself into a whirlpool of nausea. Also features organic snack food and juices.... *Tel 310/360-9002. 8788 Sunset Blvd., West Hollywood.* **(see p. 218)**

Oil Can Harry's. Gay country-western line dancing. Do you need to know anything more?... *Tel 818/760-9749. 11502 Ventura Blvd., Studio City.* **(see p. 218)**

The Peninsula Hotel. This bar is just across the street from CAA, for all you Lana Turner wannabes. All leather and wood and marble.... *Tel 310/551-2888. 9882 S. Santa Monica Blvd., Beverly Hills.* **(see p. 214)**

Polo Lounge. A top-notch hotel bar and a major entertainment-industry hang.... *Tel 310/276-2251. In the Beverly Hills Hotel, 9641 Sunset Blvd., Beverly Hills.* **(see p. 214)**

Queen Mary. Female impersonators strut their stuff in a very safe mom 'n' pop environment.... *Tel 818/506-5619. 12449 Ventura Blvd., Studio City.* **(see p. 218)**

The Roost. This is one of those classic forgotten lounge bars that has remained unchanged since the days of the Beaver, when some of Pop's pals worked for the Lockheed factory nearby. Clean, friendly, perfect for the swinger in you.... *Tel 323/664-7272. 3100 Los Feliz Blvd., Los Feliz/Atwater.* **(see p. 215)**

The Roxy Theatre. Historic rock club on the Strip, with big-name acts and a great sound system.... *Tel 310/278-9467. 9009 Sunset Blvd., West Hollywood.* **(see p. 216)**

Rudolpho's. Cross-dressers take note: This is primarily a salsa club/restaurant, but on the second Saturday of every month it metamorphoses into the notorious DRAGSTRIP 66!.... *Tel 818/576-0720. 2500 Riverside Dr., Silver Lake.*
(see p. 218)

Skybar. This open-air bar feels like a beach bungalow for millionaires. It's a hotspot, so getting in may be tricky; try coming early.... *Tel 323/650-8999. In the Mondrian Hotel, 8440 Sunset Blvd., West Hollywood.* **(see p. 215)**

The Smell. A storefront art gallery and nightclub, covering the full range of acts from punk rock to experimental, ambient, avant-garde performances. No alcohol served, and all ages are welcome.... *Tel 818/761-7241. 5229 Lankershim Blvd., North Hollywood.* **(see p. 209)**

Smog Cutter. This tiny Virgil Avenue bar has the seedy ambience of an East Hollywood local's hangout, right on the border between three gangs. No windows, and a bathroom for the weak of bladder only. But it was the leader in punk karaoke, which gives you an idea of why this place clicks.... *Tel 323/667-9832. 864 N. Virgil Ave., Hollywood.* **(see p. 217)**

The Spike. It really picks up after hours at this gay hang in WeHo—and you know what *that* means.... *Tel 323/656-9343. 7746 Santa Monica Blvd., West Hollywood.*
(see p. 217)

The Spotlight. This is Chicken Hawk Delight, very quiet and soothing, where you bring your young man (or are brought) to be instructed in the ways of the world.... *Tel 323/467-2425. 1601 N. Cahuenga Ave., Hollywood.* **(see p. 217)**

The Study. An interracial gay cruising scene—very low-key and mature, but not geezer-ville.... *Tel 323/464-9551. 1723 N. Western Ave., Hollywood.* **(see p. 217)**

360 Beige House. Very toney, reserved yet tasteful. Understated yet successful. Like a closeted gay party from the '50s. Sweaters rule.... *Tel 323/871-2995. 6290 Sunset Blvd., Hollywood.* **(see p. 217)**

Tiki Ti. It's all crazed bar decor, shimmering, spinning, super-strong tropical drinks, no place to sit, all situated on a stinky section of Sunset. It's only open Thurs.–Sat. and is jammed all the time. Like Hollywood Boulevard, you must come here at least once.... *Tel 323/669-9381. 4427 Sunset Blvd., Hollywood/Los Feliz.* **(see p. 213)**

Troubadour. The late, great Doug Weston's roadhouse is still going strong. It's been documenting the local music scene, from the Eagles to Ratt to Slaves on Dope. Good sound system, entertaining crowd.... *Tel 310/276-6168. 9081 Santa Monica Blvd., Hollywood.* **(see p. 216)**

Whiskey A Go Go. Another historic rock club that still packs 'em in with big-name acts.... *Tel 310/652-4202. 8901 Sunset Blvd., West Hollywood.* **(see p. 216)**

enterta

7

inment

Los Angelenos
are shallow, okay?
I admit it. The
typical local's
interest in high
culture runs just
about as deep

as his tan. What's that Woody Allen line about how culture in L.A. means being able to turn right on a red light? He had it 100 percent correct. The fact that he was expressing this view in an art form that was *developed* in L.A. has nothing to do with it, I suppose. Film is pretty thin, too, Woody. Welcome to the kiddie pool.

Los Angeles has a ballet, an opera, and a symphony—all those grown-up institutions that signify some sense of adulthood. Who cares if no one takes them very seriously?

There are world-class jazz artists residing here, but they all make their livings playing as studio musicians: backing up the next Flavor of the Month or providing auditory tension for an animated Tarzan. That's okay—at least they can go home to Neutra split-levels in the Hollywood Hills, instead of some cold-water flat where they survive on crackers and heroin. The lounge life is a subject strictly for screenplays and Gen-Xers dripping in irony. And while there are 99-seat non-Equity theaters are all over Hollywood, nobody makes any money from them. They only continue to exist because there are so many actors hanging around with nothing to do once they're through with their day jobs. The same might be said for L.A. comedy: Live stand-up does exist out here, but who wouldn't prefer a job writing for *The Simpsons* or Jay Leno, and pulling down that nice, fat weekly check?

It's a bitch in L.A., trying to be serious and suffer for your art in the manner you've been taught is respectable. The temptation to sell out is all around you, nosing his or her Lexus into the last parking spot, while making a deal for overseas rights over the cell phone. Meanwhile, your 1982 Olds is starting to overheat and making that weird choking-grinding sound in the transmission—again.

Getting Tickets

There's always Ticketmaster (tel 213/480-3232; www. ticket-master.com) or their outlets in music stores around town, like Tower Records, the Wherehouse, or Ritmo Latino. You can also find outlets at Robinson's-May Stores at the malls. If you've got a liberal conscience, consider Golden Circle Tickets (tel 888/777-3044; 10 Universal City Plaza, #2000, Universal City), which claims that a percentage of its sales goes to the "Wheels For Humanity Foundation." To get tix delivered right to your front door, try Tyson Ticket Services (tel 310/289-3000; 9601 Wilshire Blvd., Beverly Hills). And finally, if you really have to be in the front row and don't care *what* it costs, consider Eddie's Tickets (tel 323/255-7841; 1937 Ventura Blvd., Tarzana). They claim they can always get the first 10 rows for all concerts.

Sources

Figure it out yourself—don't even bother checking out those telephone poles. Your best source for what's happening, right here, right now, are the weekly Thursday freebies, *The L.A. Weekly* and *New Times*. Here you'll find the most extensive listings for everything that's happening locally. *The L.A. Times'* laughable Thursday Calendar "Supplement" section, intended to rival the weeklies, comes in a poor third. On-line, however, the calendarlive.com web site from the *Times,* is a killer, with loads of info and maps and "Editor's Reviews" (which actually can be quite useful). It's stiff and *Times*-ish, but at least it's accurate. You can also check out laweekly.com, newtimesla.com, or caprica.com/~aot/links.htm, which has everything from freeway conditions to club listings to maps of LAX. It's even got the home page for Glendale. What could be more nerdish but oddly welcome?

The Lowdown

Class acts... The epicenter of high culture in L.A. is obviously the Music Center, a three-stage complex on Bunker Hill that's home to the Tony Award-winning **Mark Taper Forum**, nestled in the middle of the Music Center Plaza. The Mark Taper has nearly 800 seats, and every one is a winner. The stage is thrust into the room, giving viewers the sensation of sitting in an enclosed amphitheater. Presentations run the gamut from drama to comedy, and a number of their premieres (*Children of a Lesser God*, Part Two of *Angels in America*, *Burn This*) have gone on to Broadway. That's in New York, I think. Then there's the **Ahmanson Theater,** the Taper's bigger, more responsible brother, where only true live-for-the-centuries drama and music perform. The big sister of the Music Center trio, however, is the **Dorothy Chandler Pavilion**. It's got over 3,000 seats on four levels, complete with chandeliers, curving stairways, and bathrooms I'd move into tomorrow if I could afford the rent. The L.A. Philharmonic plays here now, but once the Walt Disney Concert Hall is finished— if it's ever begun—they'll be moving. The Pavilion was built in the early '60s, and feels like it. The decor is horribly overdone, but the seats are way comfortable—it's just the right place to see an opera. In Hollywood, there's the **Pantages Theater**, a great old Art Deco house with a lobby that has to be seen to be believed. The mid-orchestra and front low balcony are the best seats in terms of acoustics. It generally hosts touring shows that can't get into the Mark Taper, as well as more lively events like Outfest and rock groups such as Morphine and Soul Coughing.

Outdoor venues... Summertime means picnics, fireworks, and a trip to the **Greek Theatre**. There are just over 6,000 seats here, and the parking setup is wretched, but you're in Griffith Park, so the walk from your car to the theater is actually pleasant. Even if you're stuck sitting in the cheap seats, at least you have a great view of the park. Who cares if the performers look like tiny little stick figures? The booking policy is just a little too mainstream for my tastes—too John Tesh, not enough Fatboy Slim—but it's still a wonderful facility, the kind of place parents think it's okay for Junior to go to on his own. Mom and Dad, meanwhile, have a picnic packed and a bottle of wine chilling for their evening out at the **Hollywood Bowl**. This is truly one of the special life experiences in Los Angeles. I can't say the acoustics are all that great, but the Bowl sure is pretty. It's also huge, however, and parking can be a major bitch. Use the Bowl's shuttle service if at all possible.

The best mosh pit in the world... At one time the **Hollywood Palladium** was a classy Art Deco venue, one of the premiere Hollywood halls. But that was before punk came to town. Today the Palladium is one of the biggest playpens in town for crowd surfers, with its huge dance floor where the moshing churns and rages nightly like an angry sea. If you're primed and ready to bounce off thousands of sweaty chests, this is the place for it. On the other hand, the view from the balcony is great if you're not quite ready for the insanity down on the floor. Drinks are expensive, and security is very uptight, with good reason. The sound isn't that great, but the stage isn't all that high either, and besides, you're not here for the acoustics.

Moving-picture palaces... The classy little **Music Hall** theater, in Beverly Hills, used to be Liberace's stage set for his TV show, and now his ghost gets blamed whenever the projectionist screws up. Once a vaudeville hall, it's been chopped up into a three-screen movie house, like so many other classic theaters in L.A. Happily, however, the Music Hall has carved out a niche as a place where you can see the sort of international films that never make it into wide distribution. When was the last time you attended a Hungarian film series? The **Orpheum Theater** is one of L.A's classic movie palaces, constructed with the over-the-top European-style flourishes and attention to detail that defined mid-'20s splendor. With more than 2,000 seats, five gold chandeliers, and a working pipe organ, the Orpheum was once Downtown's premiere stage for vaudeville performers like Bob Hope, Bing Crosby, and Gypsy Rose Lee, and it's also played host to musical giants like Duke Ellington, Stevie Wonder, and Aretha Franklin. It was the L.A. Philharmonic's home base for many years, as well. Today the place stands fully restored, and still has only one giant screen inside. The interior alone is worth the price of admission.

Another restored theater from the Golden Age of cinema is the **Egyptian**, in Hollywood. Built in 1922, it was designed to resemble an Egyptian temple, complete with statues, hieroglyphics, and an entrance framed by palms. The film society American Cinematheque oversaw its restoration and reopened the theater in 1998 with a screening of Cecil B. DeMille's *The Ten Commandments*, which had premiered there 75 years before. It is now the organization's showpiece, where they screen everything from the latest first-run hits to silents, classics, independent films, and retrospectives. This is the way movies were meant to be seen.

One movie house that could use a little restoration is the **Nuart Theatre** in Venice, one of the few theaters in L.A. that is not run by a huge national chain and has not been spliced up into a multiplex. It survives on a policy of running all kinds of weird things: independents, animation festivals, documentaries, foreign films—stuff you won't find in the "Cult" section at Blockbuster. The Nuart is a holdover from the '60s, when there were scores of houses that showed movies you'd never see anywhere else.

The seats are lumpy as hell, parking is a bitch, and there are no cheap matinee specials, but coming here is like buying your books at an independent: It's a vision of film that deserves your support. Besides, where else can you see a Betty Boop marathon? They don't sell tickets in advance, so if you plan on attending a popular event—which many are—then get here early. Cult Alert: *Rocky Horror* still screens here every Saturday at midnight.

Like the Egyptian, the **El Capitan** was built in the mid-'20s. "Hollywood's First Home of Spoken Drama" is a glorious faux–Spanish Colonial building, and a certified historic site. It closed down during World War II after premiering *Citizen Kane*, then changed names and underwent its first renovation, reopening as the Hollywood Paramount. Nearly 50 years later, Disney teamed up with Pacific Theaters and restored the theater again, this time back to its original glory. In the '90s it was renovated one last time, bringing the stage back to its 1926 size and installing the latest special-effects gadgets. El Capitan then reopened with another world premiere—not quite of *Citizen Kane*–quality, unless you're six—entitled *A Bug's Life*.

Special stages... For a town whose main entertainment industry relies on endless repetitions of the exact same performance, it's a surprise that there is such support for live theater in L.A., including many big and small houses. What's even more surprising is that one of the most respected companies is in Glendale. **A Noise Within** is an Equity theater that focuses on the classics, from Shakespeare to Molière, Ibsen to Albee. They're based in a former Masonic Temple on Brand Boulevard, with church pews for seats. The production values are very high, with great costumes and sets. The result is a quality live theater experience in an intimate setting (about 150 seats)—a fairly rare experience here. The **Wolfskill Theater**, in the Downtown Artists District, is the new kid among the mid-range houses. It's in a large space (actually a converted welder's studio), although it still has the typical black-box feel. The oversized setting is perfect for both the productions and the surrounding community—and community is what the Wolfskill is all about. They actively promote local writers and artists who are doing quality (or quirky) work. Beck and Sukia are among those who have performed here. In the four years since their 1995 opening, the group has put on 41 plays, many of them world premieres. Another good reason to live Downtown!

The **Theatricum Botanicum** is a theater with a totally different feel and background than anything else in L.A. It's in Topanga Canyon, in what was once the backyard of Grandpa Walton—a.k.a the late actor Will Geer. He built the stage as a place for blacklisted actors to exercise their craft while the Red Scare was sweeping Hollywood. Famous lefty artists like Woody Guthrie hung out here for months at a time, sitting on the tiered railway-tie seats and supporting each other while Hollywood moguls squirmed under the bleary gaze of Senator Joe McCarthy. The railway ties are gone now, as is Will Geer, but the Theatricum lives on with his guiding spirit intact. In the '80s it became a true professional summer repertory theater, overseen by Ellen Geer, Will's daughter. The theater focuses on the classics, primarily Shakespeare, but they've also done more modern thematic productions, such as Arthur Miller's *The Crucible* (which, appropriately enough, was based on the blacklisting period). Watching a performance here is a family-friendly experience—you're encouraged to bring your own picnic—in a bucolic setting that is wonderfully soothing, especially on a warm summer afternoon. It's the perfect place to see Shakespeare.

The Asian-American theater company **East West Players** has finally found itself a home worthy of its quality in the David Henry Hwang Theater, located Downtown in Little Tokyo. In their 35 years of existence, this group has put on more than 100 plays, many of them premieres, and all of them concerned with what it means to grow up in a cross-cultural world. With their strong community involvement, East West offers a unique outlet for young playwrights to develop work into a professional material, making the transition from dialogue into drama. Production values are also much higher now than they were at the group's old space in East Hollywood.

Big dreams, small spaces... Meanwhile, the beat goes on in the 99-seat theaters, so-named because anything over that number means the house must pay union scale. These black-box spaces are concentrated mainly in Hollywood, but they can also be found in Pasadena, Santa Monica, and Culver City. The gay experience is the focus at the award-winning **Celebration Theater**, a 65-seater that is the country's best-known proponent of queer stagecraft. The shows run from manic and experimental to more standard fare, and, as you might expect, AIDS is a theme that gets explored in depth. Their AIDS-educational shows, aimed at gay teens, are particularly effective. The **Tamarind Theater**, on Franklin Avenue just below the Hollywood sign, is right in the middle of a little mini scene that developed here in the '80s. Located well away from the frenzy of Theater Row on Santa Monica, the Tamarind hosts traveling shows with funky production values inside a not-terribly-comfortable facility with a small stage. Why do they bother? Maybe it's because they also stage some quirky late-night shows—and besides, the Bourgeoisie Pig coffeehouse is right next door.

If you like the aesthetics of actor/director Tim Robbins, you'll probably enjoy anything you see at the **Actors' Gang**, a highly respected 99-seater in Hollywood with great sight lines and a versatile stage setup. It was started in the early '80s by a group of UCLA grads, and was led for years by Robbins as its artistic director. They've received the *L.A. Times* Drama Critic Circle Award for excellence in theater, as much for their production values as for the arty projects they launch. Plus the seats are comfortable, the politics are impeccable, and there's free parking. The **Coast Playhouse** is smack in the middle of West Hollywood, and thus draws on a huge supply of visiting New York actors, as well as some famous big-screen faces (like Samuel L. Jackson) who feel the need to perform live without a huge amount of stress or hype. At one time it was *the* 99-seat theater in town, but increased competition in recent years and an uneven choice of material has brought their consistency down a bit. Still, you can be sure that whatever you see here will be staged with highly professional talent—the writing just may be a little weak at times. The **West Coast Ensemble Theater** is much the same: it's a quality house with 67 seats, great sight lines, and a handful of hit productions under its belt. Audiences rave about the space, and now that they've moved from an old mortuary (their base for 13 years), the production values have increased greatly—although the new place doesn't have quite the same underground ambience. Before it was a live-theater venue, the **Tiffany Theater** was a movie house on the Sunset Strip. It has two stages, each of them a 99-seater with good sight lines. Productions here have varied widely over the years, ranging from light and fluffy stuff to one-woman shows by comedian Emily Levine, to serious work by new writers. Bonus points for devoting about 30 percent of their work to in-house original projects.

Hollywood's **Hudson Avenue Theatre** is the closest thing to a multiplex you'll ever find in live theater. Located on its namesake avenue, the place has four 99-seat theaters, each with its own distinctive character. The productions run from Ibsen classics to mainstream Neil Simon. They can be a bit too PC sometimes, but get bonus points for taking chances on outside producers with something new to offer. The **Odyssey Theater**, in West L.A., is considered to be one of the city's best small houses. The theater contains three 99-seat halls, and the productions, which range from Ionesco to Odets to Mamet, are well-subscribed and enthusiastically supported by the live audiences. Sight lines are good, parking is easy, and the production values are high, even when a minimalist stage is used.

Making it up... Improvisational theater is one local arena where talented performers can make a quick jump from the 99-seaters to the tube, either as performers or as writers. Pee Wee Herman, Jon Lovitz, Phil Hartman, and Julia Sweeney all came out of the best-known improv group in town, the Groundlings. The ever-popular ensemble performs in the **Groundlings Theatre**, a comfortable but small theater with tiered seats and a live band to punctuate the skits. The audience is youngish, pop-culture savvy, and boisterous—just the right mix for riffing. **Acme Comedy Theater**, on North La Brea Avenue, is another famous sketch-training ground. They've sent alumni on to "Mad TV" as performers, and have also produced Emmy Award–winning writers. The group is based in a renovated 99-seat theater that features great viewing from every seat, state-of-the-art production values, even AC. (Some folks claim they can't hear very well when the band is playing.) **Bang Improv Studio**, over on Fairfax Avenue, is a different story. It's a small, black-box joint—only 40 seats and bare-bones staging, with no band and no cushy chairs, but the price is right—just $6! *And* they give you free coffee. They also work things with a unique angle—taking skit ideas from men-only on a given night, for example. Sometimes it works, sometimes it doesn't, but it's always fun watching them struggle. Some of Bang's performers are grads of Second City TV, so they've got the chops to dig themselves out of any hole.

The new kid on the block is the **HBO Workspace**, which has gotten a reputation for pushing the comedic envelope into realms rarely encountered. It's known for its one-person shows and works-in-progress. The limited seating is on a first-come, first-served basis, so get here early. The **Improvisation**, on Melrose Avenue in West Hollywood, is the best-known club for old-school-style stand-up comedy, and it's hosted more name acts than any other stage in town. The Improv has gone through long slack periods but never seems to lose the crowds. You'll see famous faces here, on the stage and off, but unless you're one of them, your seat could well be lousy. And they really push that two-drink minimum.

Jazz-a-ma-tazz... From swing to be-bop, fusion to mainstream, L.A. has just about every type of jazz you can think of. The scene simply doesn't get the press that rock does, except during the Playboy Jazz Festival at the Hollywood Bowl, held every June. An evening of jazz is an adult experience here, high-priced and usually accompanied by decent-to-excellent food. The **Baked Potato** is where many jazz novices encountered 5/4 for the first time. After decades of working out of a tiny space in the Cahuenga Pass, the Potato has sprouted and now boasts an additional upscale room in Hollywood. The place actually has windows, and is the kind of establishment you feel you should wear nice clothes to. The Baked Potato has mined the studio musician population for years, while also bringing in name acts from all over. Prices are steep at the new locale, but the sound is always great, and the spuds on the menu are a bonus. The **Atlas Bar & Grill**, in Miracle Mile, is a rarity among the good jazz rooms in the city, in that as many people come here for the food and drinks at the classy bar as to hear the swing bands. The room is a stunner, with over-the-top decor that includes huge metal renditions of gods and goddesses. The food isn't quite what it was when founder Mario Tamayo was alive, but the place still has a wonderful sensibility, a choice dance floor, and good sound.

The **Catalina Bar & Grill**, on North Cahuenga Boulevard, is the premiere jazz room in the city, bringing in top-name acts for weeklong stays—mostly mainstream stuff like Art Blakey, McCoy Tyner, Chick Corea, Ron Carter, and Joe Henderson. Its top-drawer talent also tends to attract a celebrity audience, including such notables as Clint Eastwood, Joe Pesci, and Iman and David Bowie. And the food is good, too. Don't head for Culver City's **The Jazz Bakery** expecting to be fed. Located in the old Helms Bakery factory, this is a bare-bones facility in a warehouse-like setting. The seats can be uncomfortable, but the loyal fans don't care. This is a place where the audience takes the music as seriously as the musicians, and nothing distracts from the listening. It serves beer, wine, and coffee, but that's about it. There aren't even any tables to rest your arms on, so pay attention. Finally, the **Cinegrill**, inside the Hollywood Roosevelt Hotel, is fun for several reasons, not the least of which is the sophisticated location. Mirrors abound, and you'll find yourself surrounded by images of Hollywood in its glory days. So it makes total sense that Steve Allen is playing the piano for some velvet-throated thrush. This is cabaret jazz, stuff you can talk over softly without having to take notes.

Salsa picante... Latino music in Los Angeles has usually been relegated to second-class status, heard only in the barrios or at Hispanic nightclubs. Mexican *ranchero* and *banda* were (and are) the biggest sellers in the genre—but recently the general public, Anglos to Asians, has discovered salsa in a big way, and it's having a huge impact. Fueled by a steady immigration of New York refugees, salsa music is blossoming here in a way never seen before. Any New Yorker would feel right at home with the quality of the bands and the variety of rooms where you can dance. Some of the major touring acts that sell out around the country, like Conjunto Amistad and Rudy Regalado, are actually L.A. house bands. The **Conga Room**, a tropicalismo venue started by a crew of big-name Latino celebrities, has become the city's premiere place for salsa dancing. It's a beautiful space, and the owners bring in national names like Tito Puente. The cover charge can run as high as $100 a pop (!). **El Floridita** is smack in the middle of a strip mall in Hollywood, but it's well-known as one of the best Cuban restaurants in town, and its bands are among the city's best. The place is always jammed, and the dancing goes on until way late. Unless you have your moves down, however, you might prefer to just sit and watch. **Grand Avenue**, in Downtown, is a

ENTERTAINMENT | THE LOWDOWN

cavernous space, popular among Latinos from all over. The house band, Costenos, has become a big name outside L.A. The dance floor is large, and it's probably the most forgiving location for novices who can't quite get the beat. My favorite salsa joint, though, is **Rudolpho's**, in Silver Lake—a slightly beaten-up roadhouse next to the I-5 freeway. People here dress to the hilt and simply have a hell of a good time, swirling under the disco ball in wild abandon as they check out their moves in the mirrors. There's none of the snooty pretension you run into at the big-ticket venues. Even if you suck, you'll enjoy yourself here. Plus the drinks are pure rocket fuel.

For those who don't want to suck, there are lessons at the following clubs, all starting at 8 p.m., followed by live music: **Conga Room**, Thursdays; **El Floridita**, Wednesdays; **St. Mark's**, Tuesdays; **Mayan**, **Grand Avenue,** Fridays and Saturdays; **Rudolpho's**, Mondays and Wednesdays.

The Index

Acme Comedy Theater. One of the hottest improv companies in town. If you think "Mad TV" is funny, you'll love these guys.... *Tel 213/525-0202. 135 N. La Brea Ave., Hollywood.* **(see p. 235)**

Actors' Gang. Started by a group of UCLA graduates, and led by Tim Robbins for years, this small theater group always puts on interesting productions, many of them developed in-house. Good politics, excellent delivery.... *Tel 213/465-0566. 6209 Santa Monica Blvd., Hollywood.***(see p. 234)**

Ahmanson Theater. This is where the class Broadway acts come to provide a complete theatrical experience for the local moneyed classes. If it plays the Ahmanson, you know it's culture with a capital C. Best production values for live theater in town.... *Tel 213/628-2772. 135 N. Grand Ave., inside the Music Center, Downtown.* **(see p. 229)**

Atlas Bar & Grill. A supper club with hallucinogenic decor in a classy room. Good food, salsa, jazz, and martinis that will lay you flat.... *Tel 213/380-8400. 3760 Wilshire Blvd., Miracle Mile.* **(see p. 236)**

Baked Potato. This is one of the longest-lived jazz rooms in the city, the place that gave birth to fusion. If you're a history buff, check out the Caheunga location first. For a fancy date, try the one on Sunset.... *Tel 818/980-1615. 3787 Cahuenga Blvd. W, North Hollywood. Also Tel 323/461-6400. 6266 1/2 Sunset Blvd., Hollywood.* **(see p. 236)**

Bang Improv Studio. Improvisational sketch comedy with a pronounced experimental tone and approach. Cheap and never boring.... *Tel 323/653-6886. 457 N. Fairfax Ave. Hollywood.* **(see p. 235)**

El Capitan Theater. Built in the mid-'20s and recently renovated, this is one of the classic movie palaces in Hollywood. Even if you don't want to see a movie, come by to check out the cast-concrete facade.... *Tel 323/467-7674. 6836 Hollywood Blvd., Hollywood.* **(see p. 232)**

Catalina Bar & Grill. This is the premiere jazz venue in town, popular with celebrities and national talent alike. Not cheap, but the intimacy of the room and the quality of the music is worth it.... *Tel 323/466-2210. 1640 N. Cahuenga Blvd., Hollywood.* **(see p. 236)**

Celebration Theater. Nothing but gay and lesbian themes. The theater has won numerous awards for acting, directing, and writing.... *Tel 323/957-1884. 7051B Santa Monica Blvd., West Hollywood.* **(see p. 233)**

Cinegrill. The best thing about this tasty little jazz room is that it's inside the Hotel Roosevelt. It sometimes gets major name acts that shine memorably in such an intimate setting.... *Tel 323/466-7000. 7000 Hollywood Blvd., Hollywood.* **(see p. 237)**

Coast Playhouse. This 99-seat theater has a reputation that people back on Broadway know about. It's had its hits and misses, but never disappoints in presentation.... *Tel 213/962-9092. 8325 Santa Monica Blvd., West Hollywood.* **(see p. 234)**

Conga Room. This is where Latino entertainment-industry culture surfaces big time. Prices are stupid, the acts top-drawer, and the decor tropicalismo.... *Tel 323/938-1696. 5364 Wilshire Blvd., Miracle Mile.* **(see pp. 237, 238)**

Dorothy Chandler Pavilion. This was the anchor for the Music Center back when it was being built in the '60s—and the over-the-top opulence reflects the mood of the era. With more than 3,000 seats, all with good sight lines and sound, the Pavilion is the home for the big-city culture we need: Eas-Pekka Solonen's L.A. Philharmonic, the Opera, and the Master Chorale.... *Tel 213/972-7211. 135 N. Grand Ave., inside the Music Center, Downtown.* **(see p. 229)**

East West Players. For a dramatic insight into the fears and dreams of Asian/Pacific-Americans, the East West Players are just the ticket, especially in their fancy new Downtown digs.... *Tel 213/625-7000. David Henry Hwang Theater, 120 N. Judge John Aiso St., Little Tokyo.* **(see p. 233)**

Egyptian Theater. This is one of the classic movie palaces of Hollywood, built in the '20s and decked out in elaborate Egyptian-style decor. Has a nice big screen and an entranceway fit for Cleopatra.... *Tel 323/466-FILM. 6712 Hollywood Blvd., Hollywood.* **(see p. 231)**

El Floridita. Cuban restaurant featuring great salsa bands.... *Tel 323/871-8612. 1253 Vine, corner of Fountain, Hollywood.* **(see pp. 237, 238)**

Grand Avenue. Nightclub featuring plenty of music, from salsa to house to disco, with plenty of room to shake it.... *Tel 213/747-0999. Corner of Olympic and Grand, Downtown.* **(see pp. 237, 238)**

Groundlings Theatre. The best-known improvisational troupe in L.A. has produced scads of Ready For Prime Time comedians. The productions are always inventive, always entertaining. If you have no idea what to do some evening, this is an easy, safe choice.... *Tel 323/934-4747. 7307 Melrose Ave., Hollywood.* **(see p. 235)**

HBO Workspace. Experimental sketch comedy with one of the newest improvisational groups in town.... *Tel 323/993-6099. 733 N. Seward St., at the Melrose Theater, Hollywood.* **(see p. 236)**

Hollywood Bowl. This landmark facility needs no introduction. The setting is beautiful (despite the roar of traffic on the nearby 101), and the Bowl plays host to orchestras, jazz, and pop performers. Best of the bunch is the Mariachi Festival in June.... *Tel 323/850-2000. 2301 N. Highland Ave., Hollywood.* **(see p. 230)**

Hollywood Palladium. This big sweaty barn of a place has been the site of more squashed toes, damaged eardrums, and ecstatic epiphanies than any other big hall in the city.... *Tel 323/962-7600. 6215 Sunset Blvd., Hollywood.* **(see p. 230)**

Hudson Avenue Theatre. Four different stages, four different theatrical approaches, one cohesive direction. This is the multiplex of 99-seat venues.... *Tel 323/769-5858. 1110 Hudson Ave., Hollywood.* **(see p. 235)**

The Improvisation. This is the oldest and most Industry-connected of L.A.'s improv houses. The audience sucks, the performers know they're being judged. Or ripped off.... *Tel 323/651-2583. 8162 Melrose Ave., West Hollywood.* **(see p. 236)**

The Jazz Bakery. Serious jazz fans head to this jazz performance space (an old bakery factory) for attentive listening to the real stuff.... *Tel 310/271-9039. 3233 Helms Ave., Culver City.* **(see p. 237)**

Mark Taper Forum. The "experimental" section of the Music Center, the would-be gritty edge of theater and music that the Ahmanson and the Chandler Pavilion wouldn't touch. But it ain't Al's Bar, either. Good sound and sight and no vomit in the restrooms.... *Tel 213/972-0700. 135 N. Grand Ave., inside the Music Center, Downtown.* **(see p. 229)**

Mayan Theater. The exterior is wonderful, all plaster Mayan motifs, but inside is pretty cool, too. This is a rare confluence of great Art Deco architecture, contemporary Latino culture, and top-class production values, all presented in a convenient Downtown location. Music, performances, dance, ballet, rap. You want it, they got it.... *Tel 213/746-4674. 1038 S. Hill St., Downtown.* **(see p. 238)**

Music Hall. Although this old theater has been divided into four mini screens, it is still one of the very few places in L.A. that consistently shows unknown foreign films.... *Tel 310/274-6869. 9036 Wilshire Blvd., Beverly Hills.* **(see p. 231)**

A Noise Within. This well-established theater group in Glendale is conservative in their choice of material but inventive in its delivery, always respectful of the classics and never gimmicky. They deliver top-quality work consistently, from sets to acting to direction.... *Tel 818/546-1924. Glendale Masonic Temple, 234 S. Brand Blvd., Glendale.* **(see p. 232)**

Nuart Theatre. Funky and showing its age, this Venice-adjacent landmark always brings crowds in, despite the broken seats and uneven sound. Don't be surprised if you see Sony and Fox executives here. It has a totally unique booking policy, sort of a throwback to the '60s, that still works well.... *Tel 310/478-6379. 11272 Santa Monica Blvd., West Los Angeles.* **(see p. 231)**

Odyssey Theater. Three stages, only 99 seats apiece, but all are well-supported. The company covers everything from ancient classics to modern classics. One of the most popular small theater houses in the city.... *Tel 310/477-2055. 2055 S. Sepulveda Blvd., West Los Angeles.* **(see p. 235)**

Orpheum Theater. A beautifully renovated classic movie palace in the heart of Downtown. Now it is as likely to be showing a movie as hosting a revival meeting.... *Tel 213/896-9114. 842 S. Broadway, Downtown.* **(see p. 231)**

Pantages Theater. This Hollywood matron of grand theaters continues to chug along, bringing in decent road shows and the occasional music act. The lobby is stunning, but the sight lines and sound are only so-so.... *Tel 323/468-1770. 6233 Hollywood Blvd., Hollywood.* **(see p. 230)**

Rudolpho's. This great little Silver Lake restaurant has some of the best salsa dancing in town, plus zero attitude and a great (if tiny) dance floor.... *Tel 323/669-1226. 2500 Riverside Dr., Silver Lake.* **(see p. 238)**

243

St. Mark's. There's still the feeling of Old Venice here, somewhere between the hippies and the bums and slumming Westsiders. The space is sparse, the dance floor very adequate, the music mainly jazz-based or salsa—on Tues. If you feel adventurous, take a walk on the beach, only a block away.... *Tel 310/452-2222. 23 Windward Ave., Venice.* **(see p. 238)**

Tamarind Theater. The theater is pretty funky and minimalist, but the neighborhood is charming; it's about the only lively spot on Franklin until you hit Vermont. Its late-night shows are the best.... *Tel 818/557-6693. 5927 Franklin Ave., Hollywood.* **(see p. 234)**

Theatricum Botanicum. Actor Will Geer started this outdoor facility for blacklisted actors. Its Shakespearean shows in the summer are well-received and expertly performed. The Canyon location alone is worth a visit.... *Tel 310/455-2322. 1419 N. Topanga Canyon Blvd., Topanga.* **(see p. 233)**

Tiffany Theater. Two stages, and a strong commitment to local writers and their projects. They have a good reputation for taking the work seriously and selecting quality material.... *Tel 310/289-2999. 8532 Sunset Blvd., West Hollywood.* **(see p. 234)**

West Coast Ensemble Theater. This two-stage facility gets lots of new works and L.A. premieres. They've produced lots of name stars and have received an armful of major drama awards.... *Tel 323/871-8673. 6240 Hollywood Blvd., Hollywood.* **(see p. 234)**

Wolfskill Theater. This Downtown theater has established itself as the voice of Downtown drama. It's a serious place that manages to produce good stuff week after week, despite the gritty surroundings.... *Tel 213/620-9229. 806 E. 3rd. St., Downtown.* **(see p. 232)**

ENTERTAINMENT | THE INDEX

hotlines & other basics

Airports... **LAX International** (tel 310/646-5252). This is pretty much your only choice if you're flying in from most parts of the world. You'll land here, wait 20 minutes for your bag, then spend another half hour trying to find your way out of the airport. The airport is laid out in a horseshoe shape, with the Tom Bradley International Terminal at the bottom. You depart from the upper level and arrive on the lower level. If you're leaving from terminals 5 through 8, cut through the midpoint access road so you don't have to make a full circuit. And if you're dropping someone off, do *not* leave your car at the white zone—it will be ticketed immediately. **Burbank Airport** (tel 818/840-8830), which serves the San Fernando Valley, is a much more pleasant traveling experience. If at all possible, fly in here. There are two terminals in one building and one baggage carousel. This is 1950s *Brady Bunch*–Land: there's not even a guard matching claim checks to bags.

Airport transportation... The subway was supposed to come to LAX but somehow that never happened. You can, however, catch a free shuttle from the airport to the Green Line Airport station. Most visitors—who don't have friends coming to pick them up—take either a shuttle, taxi, or bus. The cheapest way to get into the city is the MTA's **Bus.** Catch a free shuttle bus to Parking Lot C where the MTA station is. From there you can get buses to Downtown, Santa Monica, Torrance, or Culver City for $1.35. Shuttle vans for hire also troll around the airport (they're limited to three circuits), and taxis with official seals can be found hanging out at special taxi zones spaced irregularly around the airport (the most reliable is the one near the Bradley terminal). You should get a card from the taxi driver giving you an approximate cost to various locations. Taxi fares are standardized, but the cost of a shuttle can vary depending on the company. Hollywood by shuttle is $16-24, while by taxi it's $28; Downtown by shuttle is $10-17, $24 by taxi; Santa Monica by shuttle is $14-19, $20 by taxi; Venice is $10-13 by shuttle or taxi. **Super Shuttle** (tel 310/775-6600) is the biggest of the shuttle lines, but you can also ride in **Prime Time** (tel 800/733-8267) or take the **Apollo Express** (tel 213/480-1112). If you're living large, by all means call for a limo. **L.A. Runners** (tel 323/465-6366, 800/640-0700) will take you to Hollywood for $50, Downtown for $55, and to Santa Monica for $45, but you'll need to call at least a couple of hours ahead. They can carry up to 10 people in a stretch, and the cars come with a fully stocked bar, cell phone, and color TV. Finally there's **Black & White** car service (tel 800/924-1624), roughly $35 for a ride anywhere in the city.

Buses... A one-way trip on the **MTA** buses costs $1.35; if you plan to change buses, buy a transfer for an extra 25 cents (good only for that day). You'll need exact change, although they do have machines on the buses that will take dollar bills. The driver handles no money. Supermarkets sell tokens (a bag of ten for $9) and you can also buy a monthly pass for $49. **Santa Monica City** buses (tel 310/451-5444) serve Venice, Santa Monica, and Malibu, at only 50 cents per ride. In WeHo there's a shuttle service from **West Hollywood Cityline** (tel 800/447-2189) that covers most of West Hollywood for 50 cents, as well. There are also **Commuter Express** (tel 800/266-6883) freeway buses that go from Downtown to points all over the city and into the San Fernando Valley for fares ranging from $1.10 to $2.70. Buses supposedly run every 10 minutes during peak times. After 11 p.m., however, they'll be coming only every hour, provided they're on a route that goes all night. Check the bus schedule at the stop for running times.

Bus-bike combination... The MTA has installed new front-mounted bike racks on its **Metro** buses, enabling bicycle enthusiasts to use public transportation, then bike on to complete their destination. More than 700 MTA Metro buses now have these racks, with another 700 due to be installed by the end of July 1999. The racks hold two bicycles each, and have easy latches for loading and unloading. MTA bus lines with the new bike racks serve the areas of Burbank, Glendale, Pasadena, Central Los Angeles, the South Bay, the Eastside, and the San Gabriel Valley. The next wave of racks being installed will include routes serving Southeast L.A. County and the Westside. No permit is required to use the Metro Bus bike racks, but you will need a permit to take your bike onto the **Metro Rail** system.

Dash... This acronym stands for **Downtown Area Short Hop** (tel 808-2273, no area code) and it's the best deal in town. A one-way trip costs a mere quarter, which includes a transfer, and if you're coming via Union Station or have a Metrolink pass you can ride it for nothing. The shuttles are fast, cleaner than buses, and come more frequently. You can get them from Downtown to Wilmington, Studio City to Crenshaw and Watts, Pacific palisades to Echo Park. On the weekends there are special DASH routes: the Downtown Discovery Route (Bunker Hill, Civic Center, Chinatown, Olvera St., Little Tokyo Financial district); Route E for shopping (fashion district, Broadway, jewelry district, Seventh St. Market Place, Cooper Building; and Route F (Exposition Park, Sports Arena, Central Library). The buses only run from 10 a.m. to 5 p.m. on the weekend, though. The weekday routes A-F, run from 5:30 a.m. up until 7 p.m. (depending on the route) and come every five minutes.

Car rentals... Everyone knows this is a car town. In Los Angeles you are what you drive, and if an econobox is who you are, then be my guest: **Avis** (tel 800/831-2847), **Alamo** (tel 800/327-9633), **Budget** (tel 800/221-1203), **Dollar** (tel 800/800-4000), **Hertz** (tel 800/704-4473), and **National** (tel 800-227-7368) are all at the airport, and all have locations in Hollywood, Downtown, and Santa Monica as well. For something a little different, however, consider **Beverly Hills Rent-A-Car** (tel 800/479-5996,

9220 S. Sepulveda Blvd.) where you can get a Viper or a Corvette convertible, perhaps even a BMW 740 iL. What about a Jaguar? A Porsche? Or, for that *Swingers* feel, a classic convertible like a '57 T-Bird, a '65 Mustang, or a '69 Cadillac? Hell, why not a Hummer? Nobody'll mess with you then. The company will pick you up at your hotel or the airport and even toss in a cellular phone for you to use while you're cruising Hollywood. (Gotta have the phone, dude.) These exotics will run you about $150 a day—a cool $1050 per week—but people *will* notice. Too over the top, you say? Well, nothing is as subtle and ostentatious at the same time as an electric car. And besides being quiet, they're not that expensive. At **EV Car Rentals** (tel 877-EV RENTAL, 9775 Airport Blvd.) you can get a Toyota RAV4 for only $60 a day—and buy *no* gas the entire time you're here. Finding a charging station is up to you. EV Car Rentals has a list of the locations around town.

Child care... Best bet: **Babysitters Agency of Santa Monica** (tel 310/306-5437). You pay $9 an hour (with a four-hour minimum) plus transportion. In return, you get an adult sitter who will take your kids to the beach, on a bike ride, or anywhere else you choose. Or try the **Babysitter Guild.** (tel 323/658-8792), which handles requests from hotels all over the city. Rates start at $8-11 per hour (four-hour minimum) plus transportation. All their babysitters speak English, drive, and have CPR training, and (did I mention?) drive. They've been in business for over 50 years.

Dentists... Call the **Dental Referral Service** (tel 800/428-8775) or the **L.A. Dental Society** (tel 213/380-7668) for a list of dentists in your area.

Disability services... The **Disabled Riders Information Hotline** (tel 800/621-7828) has information on public transportation for disabled passengers. MTA has reduced fares for disabled riders, and some of their buses have kneeling lifts. Los Angeles has had strict codes since 1982 requiring equal access to buildings, so the newer structures usually have better ramps and other facilities than the older ones. In addition, **Dial-A-Ride** (tel 800/431-7882) provides transportation for senior citizens or others with mobility disabilities. If you want to talk to City Hall, the **Mayor's Office for the Handicapped** (tel 213/485-6334) has information about community resources and employment referrals. Finally there's the

Society for the Advancement of Travel for the Handicapped (tel 212/447-7284) which offers excellent advice for travel anywhere in the U.S.

Doctors... It is a state law that every emergency room must accept any emergency patient, regardless of his or her insurance status. Of course, you may bleed to death while they're trying to get you to pay up front. Fortunately, they do take credit cards. If you're planning a trip here, it would be smart to get some traveler's insurance. If you're *really* broke, consider the **L.A. Free Clinic** (tel 323/653-1990. 8405 Beverly Blvd., West Hollywood). They provide all sorts of non-emergency medical care, from mental health to dentistry to birth control. You may wait a while to see someone, but it's clean, it's free, and the doctors are good.

Driving around... For starters, **learn the names and the numbers of the freeways and notice that they change.** The 101 can be the Santa Ana (south of Downtown), the Hollywood (north of Downtown), or the Ventura (north of Studio City). The 11 is the Harbor Freeway going south towards Long Beach and the Pasadena when it heads towards Pasadena. Happily, the 10 is always the Santa Monica Freeway, and the 405 is always the San Diego. The 5, on the other hand, turns into the 101 below the Pomona split. Confused? Get yourself a **Thomas Brothers Guide**—it's essential if you're going to be doing much driving. I have three copies, and I've lived here most of my life. We who live here measure distances by the time it takes to get from one place to another, rather than by miles. The West Side? Twenty-five minutes, taking Melrose and then jumping down to Beverly just before you hit La Brea. The Sunset Strip? Give yourself at least a half hour, especially if you're driving on Sunset itself. Going Downtown? Since I live in Echo Park, I prefer to take Sunset and avoid the 101 completely. See what I mean? *Traffic congestion in SoCal is growing by 3 percent a year*—there are 19 million vehicles here now, and over the next 20 years that figure will rise by another 7 mil. That's a lot of cars. Rush-hour driving speeds now average 35 mph—and are expected to drop to 15 mph by 2010. L.A. has the four busiest freeways in the state. The worst of all is the San Diego, with 331,000 cars per day inching down it. For every minute a car is stalled in a lane, there are four minutes of slowed traffic behind it. How to get around the mess? **Avoid the freeways during rush hour:** Use

Washington or Adams Boulevard instead of the Santa Monica; Broadway, Figueroa, or Main instead of Harbor; Riverside Drive instead of Ventura. Remember, **between 6–9 a.m. and 3–7 p.m.** you're driving with about 3 million other motorists in Metro L.A.—roughly the entire population of Dallas. Check the **CalTrans website** (www.dot.ca.gov/hq/roadinfo) for reports on current problems, or call (tel 800/427-7623); for distances and incidents/weather, go to www.dot.ca.gov/onroad.htm. And while you're on-line, also pay a visit to speedtrap.com/losangeles.html to see where the cops are waiting with speed guns. Finally, if you're in Beverly Hills be extra cautious when going through Wilshire at Santa Monica: it's the fourth-most dangerous intersection in the country in terms of crashes.

Earthquakes... Did you feel that? If you have to ask, then you don't need to worry. It's when it sounds like the earth is screaming and the room is shaking up and down that you have to start being concerned. **If you can get on the floor and under a table, do it**—and hold on until the shaking stops. **Keep away from all windows.** If you're in bed, stay there. Don't go outside immediately, because glass and wires may be falling. If you're already outside, **get into an open area away from buildings and power lines.** If you're driving when a tremor strikes, **stop anywhere out of the traffic flow as long as you're not under a bridge or overpass,** then stay inside your car. If you're in a crowded area, don't rush for the exits. Try to stay calm. After a quake, **check your house for gas or electrical damage.** Don't light any matches until you're absolutely sure there are no gas leaks. Don't use your phone except for emergency aid. Outside, watch for downed power lines and broken glass. Open all doors carefully following a quake, always take the stairs, never an elevator—and be aware that there will be aftershocks. Call the **American Red Cross** (tel 213/739-5200) for more disaster-oriented information.

Emergencies... When the rental car suddenly poops out on the freeway and you just barely make it to the shoulder, don't panic: There are call boxes located about every quarter mile. NEVER attempt to cross the freeway on foot. For **police, fire, and ambulance,** call 911. Other useful emergency numbers: the **Suicide Prevention Hotline** (Tel 213/381-5111), **Dept. of Mental Health**

(tel 800/854-7771), **Poison Information Center** (tel 800/876-4766), **Southern California HIV/AIDS Hotline** (tel 800/590-2437), Traveler's Aid (tel 310/646-5252), **California Relay Service** (TDD tel 800/735-2929, voice 800/735-2922), the **Rape Crisis Center/Hotline** (tel 310/392-8381), and the **Child Abuse Hotline** (tel 800/540-4000).

Foreign currency exchange... American Express Travel Agency has offices in Downtown (tel 213/627-4800), Beverly Hills (310/274-8277), Santa Monica (tel 310/395-9588), Pasadena (tel 626/449-2281), and West Hollywood (tel 310/659-1682). **Thomas Cook Currency Services** (tel 800/287-7362) has outlets in Beverly Hills, West Hollywood, and Santa Monica, as well as in AAA offices in Downtown, by the airport, and in Venice. In Hollywood, try **Foreign Exchange Limited** (tel 323/467-9764). For "the best rate in town" there's **Foreign Currency Express** (213/624-3693) in Downtown. At the airport, **L.A. Currency Exchange** (tel 310/417-9735) has five counters that stay open until 11:30 p.m. every night. In Beverly Hills you'll find **Associated Foreign Exchange** (tel 310/274-7610), open until 3 p.m. on Saturday. Finally, most large banks have exchange windows as well—although you may not like the rates you get.

Gay and lesbian resources... The Los Angeles Gay & Lesbian Center (tel 323/993-7400. 1625 N. Schrader Blvd., West Hollywood) is the largest gay and lesbian community full-service facility in the world. It provides legal and medical referrals and advice, has a great outreach program, and runs the fabulous **Village at Ed Gould Plaza** (323/461-2633) which contains a performance space, a coffee shop, an Internet cafe, and art galleries. Finally, we don't have a gay ghetto here but rather a largely gay city—our newest one, West Hollywood. Check with the **West Hollywood Convention and Visitors Bureau** (tel 310/289-2525) for free booklets on the town's nightlife and cultural activities.

HIV/AIDS... It's not just a gay disease anymore, but an equal opportunity killer. The **AIDS Clinic for Women** (tel 323/295-6571) and the **AIDS Healthcare Foundation Clinic** (tel 310/657-9353. West Hollywood Cedars-Sinai Medical Office Towers, 8631 W. Third St., Ste. 740E) will both give you help and advice regardless of your insurance situation. For outreach programs there's **AIDS**

Project Los Angeles (323/993-1600). And to get a free, anonymous /HIV/AIDS test, come by the **Jeffrey Goodman Special Care Clinic** (tel 323/993-7500, 1625 Schrader Blvd., Hollywood).

Limousines... Simply can't bother to talk on the cell phone while drinking vodka and watching Jerry Springer? You need a limo, bro. Check out the **A-1 West Coast Limousine Service** (tel 310/671-8720), **Gold Coach Limo** (tel 800-546-6232), or **The Ultimate Limousine** (tel 800/710-1498).

Newspapers... If you want hard news, there's really only the *Los Angeles Times.* Sorry about that. If you don't mind getting newsprint all over your fingers, however, there are also the various Thursday weeklies to peruse. First there's the *L.A. Weekly,* which has a left bias, an insanely dense layout that's nearly impossible to read, and the most reliable and comprehensive listings in town. Coming up behind it is the much more tabloid-style *New Times.* It's brash, somewhere between Howard Stern and Rush Limbaugh, but at least you won't go blind trying to scan a story. For classifieds of every variety, from autos to apartments to guns to real estate to jobs, pick up the *Recycler.* There are also a slew of gay and lesbian throwaways like *Frontiers* and *Fab* as well as regional journals such as *Venice* and the *Argonaut,* all of which can be found at coffee shops, record stores, clubs, and restaurants. For a real take on your neighborhood look for the *L.A. Independent,* a free weekly with a "Crime Blotter" list of the week's weirdest police reports, delivered in a deadpan Joe Friday–style. Finally, the *Big Issue* is an excellent homeless-related publication that was started in England and has taken root here.

Parking... Depending on where you're going, the eternal quest for a parking spot can make your trip heaven or hell. ALWAYS check the parking signs, because some meters are active on Saturdays until 8 p.m. Conversely, there are many areas where there is only meter parking at nonrush-hour times, usually prior to 3 p.m. Some of the meters Downtown cost 25 cents for seven minutes, so get a roll of quarters if you plan to be going there a lot. Also check the costs in underground parking lots—the **ABC Entertainment Center** can cost you as much as $22 if you're there all day. (It's the same amount if you lose your ticket.) On the West Side, permit parking is the deal—

which means you have to be a resident to park there during certain hours. There are also **street cleaning days** almost everywhere which require you to shift your car to the other side of the street. And be careful: you will get zero grace time when there are time limitations. The meter cops here are very busy, and very ruthless. If the sign says you can't park on Sanborn between 10 a.m. and noon, you'll get a ticket at 10:05—guaranteed. Ditto if you park in a handicapped space. (That fine is $350.) If you're driving a rental car the tickets are your responsibility—and all fines double in cost if they aren't paid within 30 days. Overall, West Hollywood is the worst area in the city for nonresidents to find parking. **Use valet parking** if you're in a heavily restricted area. When you're in Beverly Hills, Glendale, or Santa Monica, **the city-run parking lots** are your best option (most stores will validate). Downtown the lots are all private, and the further you are from City Hall the cheaper they are. Little Tokyo and below Alameda are the best. Large mall parking structures often have three-hour grace periods. If you get towed instead, don't call me—contact the nearest police station to find where your car went. It'll cost you about $150 in cash, plus the ticket, to get your wheels back, depending on where you were illegally parked.

Pharmacies... Most **Savon Drug** stores (tel 800/627-2866) are open 24 hours, as is the **Rite-Aid Drug Store** (tel 310/273-3561) in Beverly Hills.

Phone facts... Once upon a time, the whole city used to be area code 213. Nowadays that covers just a tiny area of Downtown. Silver Lake, West Hollywood, and Hollywood are all 323; Beverly Hills is 310 or 323, and West L.A., Santa Monica, and Venice are also 310. This is all in a state of flux now, however, since an overlay system was put in place and then rescinded after huge caller complaints. Pasadena and the east Valley is 626, while the Valley itself is 818. Basic calls are 35 cents; after that it depends on who owns the phone you're using. If you're in the market for cloned cell phone numbers, try MacArthur Park.

Post offices... The **Worldway Postal Center** (tel 310/337-8845, 5800 W. Century Blvd., Inglewood), located near LAX, stays open until midnight. You can also send express mail 24 hours a day from here.

Radio stations... On the commercial side of the FM dial the only recommended listening is **KROQ (106.7),** the alternative/new rock king. Everything else worth tuning into is commercial free: **KPFK(90.7),** the best alternative left-leaning station in the city, featuring a huge selection of music, news, and commentary; **KCRW (89.9),** the yuppies' choice, smug and pretentious but also the home of "Le Show," "Which Way L.A.," and "Metropolis;" **KPCC (89.3),** the alternative to listening to NPR programs on KCRW; **KUSC (91.5),** mostly classical; and— if you can get their signal—**KXLU (88.9),** the youngest station and the one with the most street cred, playing all types of noncommercial music. On the AM dial, it's talk, talk, talk: **KMX (1070)** traffic and news; **KABC (790)** more traffic and news; **KFWB (980)** still more traffic and news; and **KFI (640),** offering basic right-wing rant radio.

Restrooms... Oh, just hold it, can't you? If you really have no control, there are zillions of gas stations and fast-food outlets to duck into. (At gas stations in the funkier parts of town you may have to ask for the key.)

Smoking... Is bad for you. Plus it'll stunt your growth, make you impotent, rot your teeth, and earn you nasty stares from all sorts of normally nice people. In the state of California, you cannot smoke in any public building, bar, restaurant, or office. Even Dodger Stadium has a smoking-only area. Aside from the airport, which has little smoking patios in every terminal, you basically can't smoke inside anywhere. That said, some bars will let you smoke as long as other people don't complain. Check with the bartender.

Subways... The newly opened **Metro Rail's** Red Line can make the trip from Union Station in Downtown to Hollywood in just under 20 minutes—about as long as it would take you to find a parking space. There are now nearly 60 miles of Metro Rail (including two light-rail systems). The inter-connected line also links Long Beach to Downtown (Blue Line, change at Seventh & Figueroa) and El Segundo to Norwalk (Green Line, change at Leimart Park). A one-way ticket is $1.35, same as the bus. **Metrolink** is the commuter-rail system that serves the counties around L.A.—Orange, San Bernardino, Riverside, and Ventura—with everything coming together in the center of the web at Union Station (tel 213/683-6987. 800 N. Alameda Ave., Downtown). Even if you don't need to travel by subway, the art at the various stops is worth the price of a ticket.

I especially like the musical handrails at the Hollywood/Vine station that play "Hooray For Hollywood" as you descend into the bowels of the earth.

Taxis... It's notoriously difficult to get a cab in L.A. Either you have a car of your own or you take the bus. There are virtually no trolling cabs looking for fares. The only way to get a taxi is to call one. On the West Side there's **Beverly Hills Cab** (tel 310/273-6611), while Downtown is served by **Checker Cab** (tel 213/481-1234). **L.A. Taxi** (tel 877/203-8294) covers the entire city and has 24-hour airport service. **Independent Taxi** (tel 800/521-8294), driver-owned and operated, is the oldest cab company in the city; they'll quote prices over the phone and "no trip is too short." All cabs take credit cards, and they'll usually be at your door in 15 minutes or less. The basic fare is $1.90 plus $1.60 for each additional mile.

Tipping... Like New Yorkers, we double the tax for the tip, maybe adding a little bit on top to put it in the 17-18% range. Doormen get $1 for hailing a cab, porters $1 a bag, bartenders 15-20% of the bill, coffee shop drones all of your returned change, and panhandlers 50 cents per handout.

TV tapings... For shows at **CBS Television City** (tel 323/852-2624. 7800 Beverly Blvd., West Hollywood) it's easiest just go to the walk-up window between 9 a.m. and 5 p.m. Tickets are free and given out on a first-come, first-served basis. For tickets by mail write to: CBS Tickets, 7800 Beverly Blvd., Los Angeles, CA 90036. Specify the show, date, number in your party, and include a stamped, self-addressed envelope. You can also check on local TV tapings, regardless of the network or production company, by contacting **Audiences Unlimited** (tel 323/467-4697). They can reserve you seats for TV shows, or hire you to be a faceless member of a crowd scene for TV show, movies, and commercials. Lotsa laughs....